Mergers & Acquisitions

Crushing It
as a
Corporate Buyer
in the
Middle Market

"The Corporate Buyer's Guide
to Successful M&A Deals"

By Kevin Tomossonie

Rock Center Financial Partners, LLC

Published by Rock Center Financial Partners, LLC
Rockville Centre, New York

ISBN 978-1-7350522-1-2 (Hardcover)
ISBN 978-1-7350522-0-5 (Paperback)
ISBN 978-1-7350522-2-9 (eBook)

Cataloging-in-Publication Data
Names: Tomossonie, Kevin, 1974- author.
Title: Mergers & acquisitions : crushing it as a corporate buyer in the middle market / by Kevin Tomossonie.
Description: Rockville Centre, New York : Rock Center Financial Partners, LLC, [2020] | "The corporate buyers guide to successful M&A deals." | Includes index.
Identifiers: ISBN: 978-1-7350522-1-2 (Hardcover) | 978-1-7350522-0-5 (Paperback) | 978-1-7350522-2-9 (eBook) | LCCN: 2020908613
Subjects: LCSH: Consolidation and merger of corporations--Handbooks, manuals, etc. | Business enterprises--Valuation. | Corporations--Valuation. | Private companies--Mergers. | Sale of business enterprises. | Negotiation in business.
Classification: LCC: HG4028.M4 T66 2020 | DDC: 658.1/62--dc23

About the Author

Kevin Tomossonie is a co-founder and partner at Rock Center Financial Partners, LLC where he provides management consulting and advisory services to both buyers and sellers involved in mergers and acquisitions. He holds an MBA from the University of Southern California and is a licensed CPA in New York State.

Kevin has spent the majority of his professional career specializing in mergers and acquisitions. He has designed and implemented best practices for executing deals, built financial and valuation models, led financial due diligence projects, and has been involved in well over 150 transactions domestically and internationally as both an executive and a consultant.

To learn more about Kevin, Rock Center Financial Partners, or to find contact information, you can visit rockcenterfinancial.com

Table of Contents

Introduction

This book is intended to be an educational guide for executives, consultants, advisors, students, or anyone else that's either responsible for, involved in, or interested in learning more about mergers and acquisitions (or "M&A").

As you can probably tell from the title, this book was mostly written with corporate buyers in mind. Why? Because there seem to be a lot of studies out there that say corporate buyers don't have a good success rate when it comes to doing M&A deals. If you don't believe it, do an online search for 'M&A failure rates' and you'll see the statistics for yourself. There are many studies that say corporate M&A deals fail to achieve their expected results, fail to create value, or that they even destroy value a majority of the time. But why is this? And even more importantly, how can corporate buyers avoid from being one of these statistics?

With this being said, the main purpose of this book is to educate corporate buyers. In fact, it's been written specifically for U.S. corporate buyers that do deals both domestically and internationally. In it, we explain how these buyers can have the strategic mindset, best practices, and technical skills that are so important for achieving success in M&A. The truth is that there's no one thing to getting an M&A deal right. No one person that does it all, and no magic formula. There's a mindset and a process to it. Corporate buyers that have the right mindset to approaching their deals, and a good process that involves the right people with the right skills, are much more likely to have success in M&A.

While M&A can be a very complicated topic, this book tries to keep things as clear and as straight forward as possible. The intent is so that readers from different backgrounds, with different skillsets, and different levels of experience can all benefit from it. It contains practical, real-world knowledge that has been applied in actual deals. And while some of the concepts do become quite advanced at times, the book tries to build each reader's base of knowledge from the ground-up, so that whether you're a novice or an experienced practitioner, this book can help you better understand some of the most important M&A concepts, and how to apply them.

Part one of the book begins with a basic overview of the M&A market. It explains who the buyers are, who the sellers are, and what motivates each of them when doing a deal. It then turns its attention to the corporate buyer. It explains some of the more common reasons why deals tend to fail for corporate buyers and how to avoid from making those mistakes. It goes into detail on how corporate buyers can develop their own playbooks for approaching and executing deals in a consistent, reliable, and repeatable way.

Part two of the book begins to cover some of the more technical details that a buyer should know when doing a deal. It takes a deep dive into how M&A deals are structured and negotiated. It explains some of the most commonly used deal structures and terms. Describing what they are, what they do, and the mechanics of how they work. It also points out where buyers in particular need to be careful as they negotiate deals so that they're choosing the right structures, keeping the economics of a deal fair, and aren't taking on any unnecessary risks. This part of the book does begin to get somewhat technical at times. And while it's not necessary, it is helpful if readers have an understanding of what the basic financial statements of a business are, like an income statement and a balance sheet. This way, as these technical concepts are discussed, they can be more fully appreciated.

Part three of the book explains how businesses are valued with a focus on the middle market where many of the businesses that are bought and sold each year are privately owned. It explains in detail some of the most common methods that buyers use to value the businesses they buy, including purchase price multiples, discounted cash flow analysis, and how to measure returns. It also explains how accretion and dilution are created from a deal and why that's so important to a corporate buyer. After the different valuation methods and concepts are explained, the book provides a framework so that buyers can use all of this information together in order to objectively decide for themselves what a business should be worth when negotiating a deal.

While part three of the book does cover some very technical topics, it tries to keep the conversation at a practical level. So that again, readers from different backgrounds with different levels of experience can all appreciate the concepts that are explained, and the types of questions that should be asked when making valuation decisions. This is done by focusing the text of the book on the concepts and pushing the detailed calculations behind those concepts into the appendix of the book. This way, readers who are less interested in seeing the detailed calculations can focus on what's discussed, and readers who are more interested in seeing the calculations and applying them in their own deals, can go to the appendix to see exactly how they're done. Readers can also visit rockcenterfinancial.com/resources for free downloadable word and excel versions of this book's appendix.

Part four of the book covers some of the more advanced topics that buyers should be aware of when doing deals, so that they don't run into unexpected surprises after a deal has closed. This includes explaining what a quality of earnings is, why it's important, and how it can affect a buyer's view on the future projections and valuation of a business. It also discusses how to navigate the complexities of carve-out and cross-border transactions. Earn-outs and intangible asset valuations are also discussed in part four of the book.

From having an appreciation for the mindset and process that goes into executing deals, to understanding how they're structured, negotiated, and valued, this book is intended to be the most useful, practical, and hands-on guide ever written for corporate buyers doing M&A deals in the middle market. We hope that you enjoy it.

Part One:
Building an M&A Playbook

'If you're thinking of buying a business, any business, you're not going to do it alone. There's too much to do, too much to look at, too many questions to ask.
You're going to need a team.'

Chapter 1: Defining the Middle Market

Mergers & acquisitions (or "M&A") is a term that refers to the act of buying and selling businesses. It provides sellers with liquidity (meaning access to cash when they want to sell), and it provides buyers with opportunities to either expand their own existing businesses or invest for financial purposes. It's a global activity that happens between buyers and sellers every day both domestically and internationally.

Sometimes, you'll hear about the largest of M&A deals in the news. The amounts can be enormous with values in the tens of billions of dollars. And when the companies are well known, it can give analysts and reporters plenty to talk about. But for all of the press and publicity that the big deals get, they only represent a small percentage of the actual number of deals that take place every year.

To put it in perspective, in a typical year there are somewhere around 13,000 M&A transactions announced in the U.S. alone. But out of all these deals, only around 300 to 400 of them (or around two to three percent of them), are valued at over $1 billion. In fact, the majority of deals that take place every year fall well below that amount, in a space known as the middle market.

Deal Sizes

It probably goes without saying, but the sizes of businesses that are bought and sold each year can range from very small to very large. When a small business is in play, it can be fairly easy for a buyer to evaluate it and negotiate a deal to buy it. But as a business gets bigger, it can become much more difficult for a buyer to evaluate. And negotiating a deal to buy it, can become much more complicated. Bigger businesses also tend to command higher prices. Harder to evaluate, more complicated to negotiate, and higher prices, tend to mean more risk for buyers as the size of a deal increases.

The M&A market is more or less segmented along these lines and defined based on the sizes of businesses that are bought and sold. These segments are basically referred to as small deals, middle market deals, and large deals.

Small deals are usually thought of as involving businesses with less than $10 million a year in revenue. Startups fall into this category, but for the most part, when it comes to M&A, these are usually thought of as your main street types of businesses like convenience stores, delis, hairdressers, and other local establishments.

Middle market deals are the next level up. These are usually thought of as involving businesses from as low as $10 million a year in revenue, all the way up to $1 billion a year in revenue. It's a very wide range of values that includes businesses of all different types. Manufacturers, distributors, service providers, technology companies, you name it. And as you can imagine, because of the wide range of values that are involved, businesses at the lower end of the middle market will often look very different than businesses at the higher end of the middle market. Which is why many professionals who work in the space tend to use the terms lower-middle market when referring to businesses below $50 million and upper-middle market when referring to businesses above $500 million.

At the highest ends of the M&A market are the large and mega deals. The large deals are usually thought of as involving businesses from $1 billion to $10 billion a year in revenue and the mega deals are those that have revenues over $10 billion.

Too Small, Not Interested

When it comes to the small deals, which for the most part are thought of as being the main street types of businesses, these are often not seen as being scalable, or in other words growable enough, so that an investor would be interested. You see, investors want returns on their investments, and their returns need to be big enough that it makes the risk of investing worthwhile. If they don't see a business as something that has 'legs' which can grow, or something that they'll be able to pull their money out of when they want to at some point, then they won't want to invest. While these types of businesses are still bought and sold each year, they're usually done between individuals (like moms and pops) for personal reasons. For example, when a seller wants to retire, and a buyer is looking for a source of income. While it can be, it's usually not something that a corporate or financial buyer would be interested in.

Too Big, Too Expensive

When it comes to the large deals, and the mega deals, north of $1 billion, it's really only the big players with a lot of capital that can afford to do these. And with the big deals, there are no guarantees. Things can still go wrong. So, with a lot of money at play, and the risk that things can still go wrong, the big deals are not for everyone. They're for buyers with deep pockets who can afford to fix things if they have problems. In fact, when it comes to acquisitions in general, most buyers don't want to bite off more than they can chew. They'll have a range of deal sizes that they're willing to play in based on how much capital they have to invest and the amount of risk they're willing to take on.

The Middle Market, A Sweet Spot for M&A

If small deals aren't really that interesting, and large deals are too expensive, then where do buyers look? For buyers with money to invest that are looking for businesses with good growth opportunities and at reasonable valuations, the middle market just might be the place. It's a big space that includes businesses from as small as $10 million a year in revenue all the way up to $1 billion, and it represents about one-third of the U.S. economy. In it, there's a wide range of opportunities, which is why it's been a long-time sweet spot for many investors.

A few examples of the types of businesses that you'll find at the lower end of the middle market include small businesses that are competing in fragmented industries, which can sometimes provide opportunities for investors that are looking to consolidate. Or, relatively young businesses with proven concepts that are experiencing growth and can provide opportunities for investors looking to participate in that growth. Or, niche products and services that can make nice add-on acquisitions to existing (more established) business.

As you work your way up the food chain from the lower-end of the middle market to the upper-end of the middle market, the businesses obviously get bigger. As they do, it's not uncommon to find businesses that are so well established that they're considered leaders in their spaces. Either geographically, or in terms of the products and services they provide. Acquisitions like these will usually bring with them a nice stream of earnings and can either provide an instant leadership position in a space or act as a platform for future acquisitions. These are just a few examples of what you'll find in the middle market, which is why it's considered such a sweet spot for investors.

Buyers and Why They Buy

In the middle market, there are basically two types of buyers. Strategic buyers and financial buyers. Both are likely to follow a similar process when they do deals, but they'll usually have different reasons for wanting to buy a target business, and different ideas for how long they plan on staying in that business. And by the way, the term 'target' refers to a target business that's about to be acquired.

A strategic buyer (which is also referred to as a corporate buyer), is usually, although not always, a company that's already operating in the same industry as the target. Usually, corporate buyers will want to acquire targets for strategic purposes. It could be that the target is a competitor that the buyer wants to take out of the picture. It could be a supplier or a customer that the buyer doesn't want someone else to acquire. It could be for geographical expansion, access to new products, or to diversify its portfolio. Whatever the reason, a corporate buyer is usually already operating in the same space as a target, where it already has an experienced management team, and it's interested in owning and operating that target for a long time, which could be forever.

A financial buyer on the other hand (which is sometimes referred to as a financial sponsor), is an investor or a group of investors that acquire businesses, hold them for some period of time, and then eventually sell (or exit) them with the goal of generating a financial return on their investment. A financial buyer could be a wealthy individual, but in the middle market it's usually a private equity group.

Private equity groups raise capital from wealthy individuals and institutions for the purpose of investing that capital and providing returns to its investors. This means that private equity groups won't hold investments forever. Instead, a private equity group will usually have a target hold time (anywhere from 3-5 years), and they'll only hold their position until it's a good time to exit, either through a sale of the company, or sometimes through an initial public offering (called an "IPO").

Usually, while a private equity group owns a business, they'll make improvements to it and do some add-on acquisitions in order to grow it and try to make it more attractive to another buyer for when they're ready to exit. The typical private equity play is to buy a business at a good price, try to grow it and improve it while they own it, and then sell it for a profit.

Sellers and Why They Sell

There can be many different reasons why the owner (or owners) of a business are interested in selling. For example, it could be a small business where the owner wants to retire. It could be a growing business where the owner wants help from a professional management team and access to capital. It could be a private equity owned business where the private equity group wants to exit. Or, it could be a corporate owned business where the corporate owners want to sell and reinvest that money somewhere else.

Whoever the seller is, and whatever the seller's reasons are for selling, it's usually financially driven in some way. After all, why else would anyone sell? From a buyer's perspective, it's important to know a seller's motivations. On the extreme end of things, the reason a seller wants out, could be a reason to not buy the business. It could be that the business is in trouble and that the seller wants to get out while they can. But on the other hand, a seller may have a completely legitimate reason for selling and it's just a good opportunity for the right buyer.

Sometimes, a seller will have other objectives in mind when doing a deal. Not just financial. In a competitive process, meaning where there are several potential buyers that are competing to buy a business, the buyer that can best help the seller achieve those objectives could have an advantage over the other buyers in that process.

For example, let's say that an entrepreneur was looking to sell a piece of her fast-growing business. She wants a good price, but at the same time, it's a growing business and she doesn't want to exit completely. She wants to stay in, continue to run it, and keep a nice piece of equity so she can continue to benefit from its future growth. She wants a partner that will not only pay a good price for a part of the business today but will also be a good partner to work with and help grow the business.

In a situation like this, price is not the only deciding factor for the seller. Which is why, understanding the motivations and intentions of a seller is important in a deal. Not only so that the buyer and seller can structure a deal that works for both sides, but also to make sure that there is a successful transition and operation of the business going forward. We'll expand more on this later in the book.

Chapter 2: Why Deals Fail and What to Do About It

Did you ever do an online search for the failure rate of M&A deals? Apparently, it's pretty high, like somewhere around 70% high, depending on the studies you read. In fact, there are many studies that say acquisitions fail to achieve their expected results, fail to create value, or that they even destroy value a majority of the time. But is this really true? Are the biggest failures of all time skewing the statistics? Are these studies actually capturing the reality of what's happening in M&A? Because if the majority of deals fail, then why would anyone keep doing them?

A skeptic might take the view that many of the studies out there are misleading. That they're mostly based on deals between public companies where one publicly traded company acquired or merged with another. You see, with deals like these, there's usually a lot of publicly available information. Information that lets academics and analysts see exactly what two businesses looked like before a deal and then critique and comment on what happened after the deal. The problem with any study that would only use public deals though, is that it would fail to capture the success rate of private deals, when buyers acquire privately held businesses. In a private deal, there's hardly ever much publicly available information on a target before a deal happens, let alone how successful it was after the deal. But setting this aside for a minute, let's say that we accept the statistics, and the premise, that most deals fail.

If most deals fail, then how can it be that private equity groups are able to generate returns for their investors, and why would so many corporate buyers keep doing deals year after year? Someone out there must be doing it right, no? Well guess what, there's actually a lot of people doing it right. But if you believe the statistics, there seem to be a lot more people doing it wrong. The question is, what can we learn from those who do it right so that we don't become another statistic?

The number one goal of this book is to explain exactly that. How to do deals the right way. You see, there's no one thing to getting a deal right. No one person that does it all, and no magic formula. There's a mindset and a process to doing deals. Corporate buyers that have the right mindset to approaching their deals and a good process for doing their deals will stand a much better chance of having successful deals and avoiding the failures.

And by the way, this doesn't just mean doing the actual deal itself. Sure, that's important. But you also need to be able to transition and operate a business after it's been acquired, so that it can be a success. In order to demonstrate how important this point is, next, we'll use a hypothetical situation to illustrate what can and sometimes does go wrong when acquisitions aren't done right. Then, throughout the rest of this book, we'll provide the framework, best practices, and technical skills that are so important for doing deals the right way.

What Could Possibly Go Wrong?

You've probably heard the story before. The story of a large publicly traded company that acquired another. The buyer wanted to do something transformational and paid a high price to acquire a target. The price was supposedly justified on the basis that together the two companies would have synergies. Synergies that would otherwise not exist. Revenues would increase, thanks to the ability to now bundle and cross-sell each other's products, and costs would go down, thanks to the ability to eliminate redundant costs and consolidate operations. A win-win. Skeptical? Why would you be?

The synergies were carefully crafted by very smart, highly paid consultants. Those consultants analyzed the two businesses in great detail. They looked at market data, compared benchmarks, and calculated all sorts of ratios and metrics. They were convinced that those synergies could all be achieved. And the high price? The buyer had an investment banker advising him and helping negotiate the deal. The buyer was told very convincingly by his advisor that the value of those synergies more than justified the price that was being paid.

The deal was top-secret. It was negotiated behind closed doors. Only the highest-level executives and advisors from the buyer and seller's teams were involved. Why was it kept to such a small group? Because, neither the buyer nor the seller wanted a leak before they knew for sure that they had a deal. The consequences could have been disastrous if word got out. Or so they thought.

The business teams that would ultimately be responsible for managing the transition, integrating the two businesses, and realizing the synergies? It turns out, they weren't involved in the deal. Why? Because, they weren't deal people and nobody thought they needed to be involved. The executives that were involved weren't worried though. Because they were convinced, that once their business teams knew about the deal, they would be excited for the opportunities. Those executives had no doubt that their business teams would be able to execute on the plans that their consultants had so carefully thought out. More than that, the consultants gave the buyer's CEO a great idea. Tie the business teams' bonuses to achieving the synergies. That would motivate them, wouldn't it? What could possibly go wrong?

On the day that the deal was announced, the buyer's stockholders immediately became concerned that the buyer was overpaying. They didn't like the amount of debt the buyer was taking on to finance the deal, and the synergies sounded aggressive. The buyer's stock price dropped 3% on the very day it was announced. When the deal was communicated to the business teams at both companies, it was received with mixed emotions. Some people were excited, but it seemed like a lot more people were concerned about their futures. The word synergies to them sounded like job cuts.

Some of the more senior business team leaders who would now be responsible for operating the combined businesses and realizing the synergies, they felt a little uneasy about not being 'in the know' sooner. And there was concern, deep concern, that those synergies were not realistic or achievable. Why weren't they consulted sooner? Didn't anyone at the top value their opinions? Maybe those business team leaders weren't as valuable as they thought? There was also some resentment that their bonuses would now be tied to achieving the synergies that they didn't think were achievable.

In the months that followed, the buyer found it harder than they thought to sell their vision for the newly combined businesses. There was turnover of some pretty important people at the target who said that they didn't like the new culture and were already frustrated with all the new rules they had to follow to get things done. They left for other opportunities.

As time went on, the revenue synergies that were so carefully thought out by those consultants, they never really happened. It turned out that bundling and cross-selling each other's products didn't really have an impact on the top-line because there was already a lot of existing customer overlap at the two companies, and those same customers were already buying products from both businesses. Now they'd just be buying their products from the same business. Guess nobody looked at that when the synergies were developed. And when the buyer's biggest competitor heard the news of the merger, they aggressively cut their own prices in order to remain competitive in the market. Some customers actually left to go to the competition, which hurt the buyer's sales.

Some of the more achievable cost cutting synergies, those were still pushed down. Mostly headcount reductions though. Duplicate job roles that were eliminated. Those took a toll on employee morale and it seemed like people were less productive after the cuts than they were before. And in the process, the buyer actually realized that not all of the expected cuts were achievable without also disrupting some of the operations at the two businesses. In fact, after combining the two operations, they realized that there were actually some additional costs that weren't planned for.

After a while, frustrated with the fact that it couldn't realize the synergies it promised, the buyer ultimately conceded and had to take a write-down on the acquisition. They recorded a big loss and the stock price dropped again on the news.

Does any of this sound familiar? Because, while this was just a hypothetical situation that we used to illustrate what can go wrong, the pattern of events and consequences are very real. The buyer overpaid, overcommitted, and ultimately couldn't execute on why they thought the deal made sense in the first place.

Maybe they misread the market? Fell in love with the deal too early? Were overconfident? Didn't do enough due diligence? Didn't involve the right people in the process? Or, maybe they underestimated the execution risks and relied a little too much on their outside consultants? Whatever the reason, this one was a fail. The question is, could any of it have been avoided?

Why Deals Fail

The basic question for whether or not an M&A deal should be considered a success or a failure, is the ability to say whether or not it produced its intended results. If it did, it was probably a success. If it did not, then it's likely that one or more of the following three things happened. One, the buyer overpaid. Two, the buyer over committed. Or three, there was poor execution.

You may be noticing that we're not directly calling out strategy right now. And while it absolutely is the case that a bad strategy, or no strategy at all, can lead to an M&A failure, in this book, we won't be telling buyers how they should be setting their own strategies. Instead, that should be up to each buyer to decide for themselves. But what we will do in this book, is explain how buyers can use M&A as a tool to support their strategies, and how to negotiate good deals.

With this being said, let's put strategy aside for a minute to explain how buyers can avoid some of the more common M&A failures, at least from an execution standpoint. And then, in the next chapter, we'll revisit the role that strategy plays in a buyer's M&A process.

Rule Number One, Don't Overpay

When a buyer overpays, it means that the returns, profits, or other financial benefits that are expected to come from a deal, don't justify the price. In other words, they're paying too much and aren't getting the value that they should. Now, to be honest, at times, a buyer may knowingly overpay, up to a limit. Why? Because, they really want the business. It could have a unique technology, or there could be a very specific strategic reason as to why they want the business so badly. And of course, when a sophisticated seller knows this, they'll tend to negotiate pretty hard and hold out for a high price. So, on the occasion when this does happen, if the buyer really wants the business that badly, then they usually have to pay up, which sometimes means accepting a lower level of returns than they normally would. We'll explain more about what this means when we cover returns later in the book.

So, while situations like this do occasionally happen, and it would be foolish to think that they don't, they shouldn't be happening very often. In fact, these should be the exceptions to the general rule which is that a buyer should always have a financial model that can justify the price they're paying.

In every M&A deal a buyer should have a financial model that captures the current and the expected future financial performance of the business that's being acquired. One that includes projected income statements, balance sheets, cash flows, and takes into consideration all of the changes that are expected to happen in that business going forward. When a model like this is done well, it can actually become much more than just numbers on paper. It can become a living tool that can help a buyer think about a business both operationally and financially. With it, that buyer can develop a deep understanding of the business they're buying, and where they think it's going.

The outputs from a buyer's model should also be providing the metrics that are used to decide what a fair price should be for a business. Things like purchase price multiples, rates of return on investment, the enterprise value of the business based on its expected future cash flows, and how accretive or dilutive the deal will be. We'll explain what these are later in the book, but for now, it's just important to know, that if a buyer's model can't justify the price, then they're probably overpaying.

Rule Number Two, Don't Overcommit

When a buyer overcommits, it means that they committed to achieving some future results that they ultimately could not deliver. They thought they could do it, but they couldn't. In the example of the failed deal we discussed earlier, the buyer overcommitted to achieving both revenue and cost synergies that ultimately could not be achieved.

What happens with commitments at the time of a deal, is that the performance of a business, and any improvements that a buyer thinks they can make to that business, like synergies, these get reflected in the buyer's model. They'll grow sales by some amount over some period of time because of, whatever. They'll cut costs by some other amount over some other period of time because of, whatever else. All these performance measures and expected changes to the business get reflected in the expected future operating results that are part of a buyer's model. Which usually means, higher expected future profits, and as a result, a higher valuation because of those profits.

If a buyer agrees to pay a price based on achieving some future results, then the universe is counting on that buyer to follow through and deliver. But if the buyer overcommitted, and can't achieve those results, then the universe is going to be disappointed because the buyer won't be able to deliver. This is why a buyer needs to involve the right people in a deal. People that have the best insight and knowledge to know what's realistically achievable and what's not. It's why including the operators of a business (in other words, the team that's going to be responsible for running that business), is a must. No exceptions.

Regardless of what executives at the top, or outsiders looking in, think is achievable, it's the people with their feet on the ground, who know the business, that are best suited to say whether the commitments being made are realistic or not. And if they are realistic, what's a practical timeframe for getting there.

We'll explain more on how commitments like revenue growth and synergies are factored into a buyer's model later in the book. But for now, it's just important to know that when a buyer makes commitments about the future performance of an acquisition, there's usually a lot depending on it.

Rule Number Three, Make Sure You Can Execute

In order for an acquisition to be successful, two key things need to happen. First, you need to close on a deal that makes economic sense. Then after you own it, you need to manage it and operate it so that it can achieve its intended purpose. Did you negotiate a good deal? And, did you realize the value you expected to realize when all was said and done? If you can answer yes to these two questions, then it was probably a success. If you can't answer yes to these two questions, then something probably went wrong.

Successfully executing on the actual deal itself and then seamlessly transitioning into operating the business, requires coordination across multiple teams throughout an M&A process. This means not only having a skilled deal team working on the deal, but also involving the business teams that will be responsible for onboarding, integrating, and operating the business going forward.

You see, the technical skills that you need to negotiate a deal to buy a business, are very different than the operational skills that you need to run a business. As a buyer, it's important that these two skillsets work together throughout a deal process. Not only to make sure that you're getting a good deal, but also to make sure that the transition from closing, to onboarding, and integrating is as seamless as possible. The right deal teams and the right business teams, asking the right questions and making the right decisions.

In the example of the failed deal we discussed earlier, one of the fatal flaws of the buyer was that the business teams that would be responsible for running the businesses and executing the plans, weren't involved in the deal. We'll cover more on this and how important it is to have a solid cross-functional team later in the book.

Where Do We Go from Here?

You're probably thinking right about now that all this seems pretty obvious, right? Don't overpay, don't overcommit, make sure you can execute. Blah, blah, blah. Anyone can point out what not to do. But how do you build a team and create a process that can do these things better? Not only that, but can you do it in a reliable and repeatable way? Even if you can, what are all the issues and challenges that you need to be aware of, so that you're only doing good deals that can be successful? How do you do it? All good questions. So, let's find out...

Chapter 3: The Strategic M&A Mindset

Talk to any number of experienced M&A professionals who work with highly acquisitive corporate buyers. In other words, corporate buyers that are always finding, acquiring, and integrating new businesses into their portfolios. And ask them, 'what are the key ingredients for success in M&A as a corporate buyer?' Chances are, you'll consistently hear the following six characteristics:

- A well-articulated strategy,
- A vision for how M&A supports that strategy,
- An organizational culture that embraces M&A,
- A disciplined approach to doing deals,
- A structured process for executing deals, and
- The involvement and alignment of the teams that will be responsible for operating the business going forward.

The Importance of Strategy

Every successful organization needs to have clearly defined goals and a well-articulated strategy (in other words, a plan) for how it's going to achieve those goals. It's these goals and strategies that help drive an organization in a common direction and make important decisions on how it should be allocating its resources.

At the most basic level, all organizations have limited resources. The most precious of which are time and money. When an organization defines its goals and plans its strategies, it should also be thinking about how it wants to use its resources. In other words, where it wants its people spending their time, and where it wants to be investing its capital, so that it can execute on its strategies and achieve its goals. Without having clearly defined goals and strategies, an organization can tend to lack focus, be unclear as to what it's trying to accomplish, and ultimately fail to use its resources wisely.

The best strategies are simple, straight forward, and can be clearly communicated so that the entire organization knows the plan and the direction in which the company is going. Of course, this isn't always easy. Especially as organizations get larger and more complicated where there can be many different business units, each having their own individual goals and objectives. But generally speaking, if a strategy is well articulated, clearly communicated, and coordinated in an organized way, then the individual goals and objectives of each business unit should still be aligned and contribute in some way to the company's overall strategy.

Now, there have been many books, courses and even professional careers build around defining goals and planning strategies. So, this book won't even begin to go down that path. But what this book will do, is tell you that going out and doing deals for the sake of doing deals is not a goal or a strategy. M&A is more like a tool. It's a tool that can help companies execute on their strategies to achieve their goals. First, a company needs to define its goals, whatever they may be, and plan its strategies. Only then does it make sense to see where M&A can help support and accelerate that company's strategy in order to achieve its goals.

How M&A Can Support and Accelerate Strategy

At the core of any strategy, there's a desire to grow and expand. Gain market share, grow revenues, expand margins, enter into new markets, new products, new services. Blah, blah, blah. Your strategy provides the roadmap for how you're going to accomplish these things.

Practically though, building a business is hard. It takes a lot of time and costs a lot of money. And in the end, after a lot of time and money have been spent, it may not work out. This is where M&A can help. To put it simply, it's sometimes better to buy a business that already exists, rather than build one from scratch. The classic buy vs. build decision. Many successful organizations throughout the world embrace this mindset when developing their strategies. They strive for a combination of both organic (meaning internally generated) growth, as well as inorganic (meaning acquisition driven) growth.

Organic growth is generated by internal initiatives, without any acquisitions. It's what you build on your own. Think for a minute, of growing sales. A purpose driven, customer focused business that offers its customers a better price, and a better buying experience, can over time increase its market share and grow its sales from its own efforts. This is organic growth. Growth from within.

Inorganic growth is growth from acquisitions. There are many situations in which it makes more sense to buy a business rather than build one. Think for a minute of expanding into a new country. Let's say, that as part of your company's strategic plan, you wanted to establish a presence in a new country so that you could have a platform to offer your products and services on a wider (more global) scale.

In this case, it could make more sense to acquire a business that already exists in that country rather than build one. Because if you did, it would already have a sales force, customers, and a management team with local knowledge of the rules, regulations, and customary ways that business is done in that country. Building this from scratch could take a lot of time and cost a lot of money. And it would almost certainly provide unexpected challenges along the way, costing you more time and more money than you initially thought. Not only that, but you'll face competition every step of the way.

When you buy a business, this work has already been done. It's already operational. It's not to say that you won't buy a business with challenges, or that you won't have to make changes to the business once you own it. But by acquiring it, you're starting with something that's already built, and you'll instantly have a presence and a platform to operate from.

Another example of where acquisitions can help accelerate a company's growth is when it wants to add a new product, a new service, or a new capability to its portfolio. Something it doesn't already have and would otherwise need to build. Let's say for example, that as part of your company's strategic planning process, you've identified a segment of the market that's gaining traction and experiencing a significant amount of growth. It's a class of products that your customer base is beginning to buy from someone else, and you don't currently offer it.

You've done some homework and you've come to learn that it's a highly specialized class of product and you think it's generating high margins. You believe it's a category that will continue to grow in years to come and the market is already shifting in that direction. You can't just ignore it and risk losing out. And building it from scratch, would take a lot of time and money.

Finding people with the right expertise, designing a product, going through R&D, getting regulatory approvals, developing a sales pipeline. In all the time it would take for you to catchup and launch your own product, someone else may have already crushed it and completely taken over that segment of the market. Maybe they've even improved their own products, making yours obsolete. But by acquiring a business that already has the expertise, the products, a sales pipeline, and a management team that has a vision for where they want to take the business next, you'll instantly be a player in that space.

Going back to the main point, it all starts with strategy. What is it that the business wants to achieve and what's the strategic plan to getting there? Only then does it make sense to see if M&A can support and accelerate that strategy. If a deal comes along that doesn't fit the strategy, then it won't help the business achieve its goals and it won't be a good use of a buyer's resources. But if a deal comes along that does fit the strategy, and can help accelerate it, then a buyer can react quickly and with purpose.

A Culture that Embraces M&A

Highly acquisitive corporate buyers who have successful track records of finding, acquiring, and integrating new businesses into their portfolios, tend to have cultures that embrace M&A as part of their daily activities. It's just part of what they do. But getting to where they are didn't happen overnight. Because building a team that embraces M&A, who can source deals and execute, all takes time to develop.

Sourcing is a term that refers to finding leads and building a pipeline for acquisitions. It is an important part of being a successful corporate buyer. When a buyer sources their own deals, it means that they are actively seeking opportunities to advance their own strategies through M&A, independently. In doing this, they can find, negotiate, and close on acquisitions through their own efforts without having to go through a competitive sales process. In a competitive sales process, a business is actively shopped by a seller who tries to attract multiple bidders in order to get the best price. But when a buyer is able to source a deal on their own, and it's exclusive, it's just that buyer and seller. No other buyers to compete with. Not only that, but when you're actively seeking opportunities, it reduces the chances that you'll hear after the fact about a business that you might have liked to own being sold to someone else.

Successful corporate buyers know how important it is to source their own deals. Accomplishing this within an organization though, isn't always easy. Especially as an organization gets larger. You see, in a small organization it may just be one person who can effectively play this role. But as an organization gets bigger and more diverse, it becomes much more important that it's not just one person playing this role, but that the entire organization is leveraging its resources.

This means that business leaders throughout an organization should be encouraged and empowered to find potential deals. Deals that can help advance the company's strategy. After all, it's the business teams in an organization that know the market, they know the customers, they know the competitors, they know the suppliers. They know about changes taking place in the market. They know where the risks are, and they know where the opportunities are. But for business leaders to effectively find deals that will drive the strategy, they need to know the strategy and see the vision for how M&A can help support and advance it. How else would they be able to find the most attractive deals? It's not to say that something the team identifies won't be ruled out at some point as something the organization doesn't really want to do, but you always want the team to be aligned and, on the lookout, so that opportunities aren't being missed.

A Disciplined Approach to Pursuing Deals

Deals can originate in a number of ways. They can be sourced internally from relationships that have developed over time. They can be brought in by CEOs, heads of strategy, or other executives. Or, they can be brought in from external sources like investment bankers or business brokers who are trying to find a home for a business. But regardless of how a deal originates, once it's on the radar, there needs to be a process and criteria for how an organization will decide if it's something they want to do, or if they should take a pass.

The fact is, doing deals takes a lot of time and costs a lot of money. And in a world of limited resources, buyers need to be selective where they spend their time, and their money. They need to be choosy. And while every organization may look at deals differently, there are some basic questions that buyers should ask themselves early on, before investing too much time and effort, just to make sure they're selecting the right deals to do. Questions like, is it a good strategic fit? Is there good cultural alignment? Will the deal have a significant enough impact that it's worth the time and effort of doing a deal? And, what's the likelihood of actually getting a deal done?

If a potential deal is missing any one of these four things, you might be better off taking a pass, at least for the time being, and focusing your time and effort on something else.

Strategic Fit

Is it a good business? Is it something you want to own? Does it fit into and support your strategy? Before a buyer even starts thinking about numbers, or spending time on something, they should be asking themselves these questions. Because if a deal isn't consistent with a buyer's strategy, then it's not going to help them achieve their goals. These are called 'off strategy' deals.

If something's off strategy, it begs the question as to why you're even looking at it. It's not to say that you won't stumble across an interesting off strategy opportunity now and then. Maybe something that's adjacent to your own business or where you have certain skills that can add value. But, off strategy deals tend to represent things that weren't previously envisioned. These types of deals should have to go through a much more cautious decision-making process when it comes to deciding if it's an opportunity you want pursue.

Understanding the business, the market it plays in, the risks, and the opportunities. These are all things that would need to be carefully thought through in a much different way than something you already envisioned as part of a previously thought out strategy in a business that you're already familiar with.

When a deal comes along that is consistent with your strategy, and can help accelerate that strategy, it's called an 'on-strategy' deal. If something is on-strategy, then it's much more likely that there will be a clear vision and a purpose, right from the beginning, as to why you want to own that business.

Cultural Alignment

Clearly, strategic fit and purpose is an important criteria to consider when deciding which M&A deals to do. But, it's not the only criteria. There are other factors. For example, who's the management team that's running the business? Are they cool? Do you get along? Are you going to need them to stick around and run the business after you buy it? If so, do you like them? Do you trust them? Are you culturally aligned in the sense that you both have a common vision for how the two businesses will come together and be successful in the future?

Having a common vision with the management team that will operate a business going forward is important for buyers to consider when thinking about their abilities to execute on the intended purpose of an acquisition. Without it, a buyer could have issues. Issues that could affect their ability to execute and realize the vision that they had when they bought the business.

If you start with the view that businesses are nothing more than groups of people that come together to get stuff done, and that you can't force people to do anything they don't want to do, then you can appreciate why cultural alignment is so important. People tend to do what they want to do. If they don't want the same things you want, it can be a problem. The things that you want to happen, won't get done. This is why having a common vision and a desire to work together toward that vision is so important. It can't be forced. You have to want the same things, or it just won't work.

Deals with Impact

There's only a certain amount of time in every day, and most buyers only have a certain amount of capital to invest. This means, buyers need to allocate their team's time appropriately, and invest their capital where it will have the biggest impact toward achieving their own goals. It may sound harsh, but organizations shouldn't waste time on small things that don't move the needle.

The fact of the matter is that small deals can take just as much time to do as large deals, which can be disproportionate in terms of the cost of doing a small deal versus the benefits you may get out of it. Organizations need to prioritize which deals they're going to do and focus their efforts where they're going to get the best growth, the best returns, the best accretion, and the best overall bang for their buck.

Is the business big enough, is it growing, is it strategically important, will it have a significant enough impact? These are the questions that decision makers need to be asking themselves to make sure that the time and effort of going through an M&A process is worth it. The truth is that some deals simply aren't worth the time and cost of doing a deal.

If it's not going to add much to the top-line, and it's not going to add much to the bottom-line, then what are you going to get out of it? If it's not going to have a significant enough impact, it may be wasting precious energy, time, and money that could be spent on bigger, more impactful things. We'll discuss more on this later in the book.

The Likelihood of Getting a Deal Done

Let's say that you've checked all the boxes so far. You found a business that fits your strategy. You like the management team and believe in their vision for where they want to take the business next. The business is big enough to make things interesting, and while they didn't share financials with you yet, they told you 'about' how much money they make, and it sounds like it would add nicely to your bottom-line. So far, it's a great fit. Just one problem. The owner isn't selling yet. Or, if they are, maybe the price they're asking is so high that there's no way you could justify it.

If a seller isn't ready to do a deal, or if they just aren't in the same place you are about what a deal would look like, then there's no deal to be had yet. It doesn't mean the opportunity should fall off your radar. Maybe it ought to stay high on your list of really nice to own businesses. But if there's no deal to be had yet, it's probably not a good use of time or other resources to be chasing it. Stay in touch, meet up for dinner or drinks every once in a while, keep your finger on the pulse, but don't put a lot of resources into chasing a deal until it's real.

A Structured Process for Executing Deals

Corporate buyers that are consistently finding, acquiring, and integrating new businesses into their portfolios, for the most part, have designated teams that follow a structured process when doing deals. They don't just wing it. You're probably thinking. Structure? Process? Isn't structure and process the reason why corporations are so slow and why it takes them so long to get anything done? Well, pretty much, yes. Nobody's going to argue that. Unfortunately though, in an M&A process, there are a lot of moving parts and there's a real need to involve people who have different skillsets. This means having a cross-functional team, and it's why a structured process becomes necessary. To organize the team, so that things do get done. What needs to be balanced though, at least in an M&A environment, is a need for speed. So that things can get done quickly. If you move too slow, you could frustrate sellers, or end-up losing a deal all together.

You Don't Know What You Don't Know

Let's think about some of the issues you might come across when buying a business, so that we can appreciate why buyers need cross-functional teams. Let's say that you were looking at a $50 million manufacturing business located somewhere in the Southeast United States. It's a direct competitor, that makes a very similar product to yours. You believe that if you buy them, you'll not only be taking a competitor out of the market, but you'll be able to shut down their manufacturing operations and produce their products in your facilities where you currently have excess capacity. You think, that when all is said and done, you'll be able to keep all the sales, and by consolidating the operations, reduce costs. By keeping all the sales and reducing costs, you'll add some nice profits to your bottom-line. At least, that's the plan.

So, what are all the things you need to start thinking about to make this happen? You're going to be moving their manufacturing operations into your facilities, right? How long will that take? How much will it cost? Should a businessperson be looking at this? When you consolidate their operations, some of the target's people will probably come over to you and some unfortunately will have to be let go. Will you need someone from HR to get involved? You plan on keeping their sales, but is that realistic? Come to think of it, are their products properly licensed and approved for sale in all the states that they do business? Should a regulatory person be involved? The target has contracts with suppliers, customers, and who knows who else. Should someone be looking at those? Who's going to do that, a lawyer? Do they have any lawsuits against them? Yup, sounds like you'll need a lawyer. It has computer systems. Will you need those? Should you have someone from IT chime in? They have financial statements, but who knows if those are right. Are they paying their taxes? Should you get accountants involved? You get the idea.

You Need A Cross-Functional Team

If you're thinking of buying a business, any business, you're not going to do it alone. There's too much to do, too much to look at, too many questions to ask. You're going to need a team, a cross-functional team. This is where the different skillsets we touched on earlier come into play. Remember when we said that the skillsets you need to buy a business are very different than the skillsets you need to run a business? As a buyer, it's important that these two skillsets work together.

You see, when it comes to buying a business, doing the actual deal itself, M&A is a very specialized field. The ability to navigate a deal, know where to look for skeletons in the closets, knowing the right questions to ask, valuing a business, and structuring a deal to buy it, all comes with knowledge and experience from years of working on deals. Finance & accounting experts, lawyers, HR specialists, regulatory advisors, and others, all with functional expertise and M&A experience. These functional experts know what to look for, what questions to ask, and can help protect you from overpaying and taking on unnecessary risks in a deal.

When it comes to the business itself, understanding the market that the business operates in, its products, how it interacts with customers, its systems, and its processes, that's the business team. They have the operational experience and the business knowledge that's needed to plan these things out. And when all is said and done, it's the business team that's going to own it. So, they need to feel sense of ownership right from the beginning.

You Need a Playbook

In reality, the only way you can coordinate all of the functional experts, businesspeople, and decision makers that need to be involved in an M&A deal, is with a structured process. But not just any process. It needs to be a process that brings the right people in, at the right times, and supports good communication. And by the way, it needs to be done fast, because M&A deals don't wait around, especially if it's an attractive business that others might also want to buy. For this, you need a playbook.

Chapter 4: Building an M&A Playbook

Every organization is different. Each one has different teams, made up of different people, with different skillsets, and different levels of experience. Some have done a lot of deals, some may only have done a few, and some may have not done any. But whatever an organization's experience has been, there's no reason that it can't be doing successful M&A deals.

As we mentioned earlier, one of the goals of this book, is to level the playing field and help with just that. To be successful though, we need to have the right people asking the right questions, to make sure that nothing important has been overlooked. We also need the right people making plans for how to onboard, integrate, and operate the business going forward. So, what should the process be to accomplish these things?

Because all buyers are different, it may not be the same answer for each one. But, if we take a look at the best practices of some of the more highly acquisitive buyers that have successful track records, we can say what things should probably look like. We can also say where outside advisors can help support and enhance a team's capabilities. That's because, outside advisors can bring years of experience and expertise, as well as instant manpower to a deal, where a buyer may not already have these things.

It's important to remember though, that while outside advisors can and often do add great value, at the end of the day it's still the buyer that needs to take responsibility for the deal, and it's the buyer's management team that needs to own it. We'll discuss more on this point in a few minutes.

The M&A Playbook and What It Should Include

A playbook is nothing more than a company's approach for getting things done. Its processes and its procedures. Some companies call it their 'standard operating procedures.' But whatever you call it, a playbook provides written instructions for how tasks should be carried out. This way, no matter who is performing the task, or how complicated it is, it can be performed in a consistent way, each and every time.

An organization's 'M&A playbook' is nothing more than its processes and procedures for doing deals. What's the process that a deal needs to follow in order to be properly evaluated? Who are the decision makers? And who's responsible for doing what? This is what the playbook explains and it's the guiding roadmap that allows for a consistent and repeatable process to be followed on each and every deal that you do.

Not sure if a playbook is necessary? Then just think about what happens, when there is no defined process, no rules to follow, and no clear sense of roles and responsibilities on a project that has more than a few people involved, like an M&A deal. What happens, is that confusion tends to set in. Confusion as to what needs to happen, who's leading, and who's supposed to be doing what. And when there's confusion, and person A thinks person B is doing something that person A is supposed to be doing, stuff just doesn't get done. 'Oh, I thought so and so was doing that, should I be doing that?' Precious time can be lost, and things can get missed.

But when there is a well-defined process, organization, and a clear sense of roles and responsibilities for the things that need to get done, there shouldn't be any confusion. More importantly, when people know what their roles are, and why their roles are an important part of a bigger team effort, and that other people are counting on them, they tend not to want to disappoint. And things get done. Especially if person A and person B both know they're being held accountable for each of their parts.

So, what should a playbook include, and how detailed should it be, or not? Starting from the top, it needs to identify who the decision makers are. What it is that the decision makers should be deciding, and what's the process that the decision makers are expecting their teams to follow so that they can make well-informed decisions with a sense of confidence that nothing important has been overlooked. It starts with the investment committee.

The Investment Committee

Someone (or a group of some ones) need to be responsible for overseeing the company's entire M&A process. Making sure that a disciplined approach has been followed on every deal, that the company is making good decisions, and that not just anyone is out there signing up deals on the company's behalf without any oversight. M&A transactions are too risky for that. Bring in, the investment committee.

The investment committee plays an important role in a company's M&A process. It provides structure and discipline. It acts as a centralized decision-making group, deciding which deals the company should and should not be doing. It decides the prices and terms of deals. It defines the process that its teams should follow, and it holds team members accountable for their individual areas of responsibility.

You might be thinking, why a committee and not just one person? Don't committees just slow things down? Coordinating calendars for meetings, catering to requests from different members. And, what if the committee can't agree on something? At least when you're dealing with just one person you can get a clear yes or no, but a committee?

To some extent, all of these things are true. But in the context of M&A, particularly on the buy-side, deals can be very complicated and risky. Too complicated and risky for just one person to be making all the decisions. Legal issues, regulatory issues, accounting issues, tax issues, strategic decisions, the list goes on. So, while things do need move quickly, it doesn't mean that things should be rushed, or that quality should be sacrificed.

There's an old saying. 'If you want to go fast, go alone. If you want to go far, go together.' It means that the decisions made by a group, are in the long-run, better than the decisions made by just one person. This is because a group can together make decisions from a broader base of knowledge and experiences than only one person can. This is especially true in the complicated environment of M&A where there can be many different issues to deal with. So, who should be on an investment committee, and just how big or small should it be?

Investment Committee Members

Ideally, an investment committee is made up of just a few key executives who are technically savvy and experienced in M&A. If a committee is too big, it will be too difficult to coordinate and manage. If it's too small, it may not have the right combination of technical skills and collective experiences. It's finding this balance of size, technical skills, and experience that can make the difference between having a committee that is effective, and one that is not.

In some organizations, it might be the CEO, the CFO, the general counsel, and the head of strategy (if there is one) that makes up the committee. In other organizations, the CEO might not want to be involved, and instead leave the committee's decisions up to a handful of carefully selected executives, while reserving the right to approve deals before they happen of course. In some cases, it may make sense for an outside advisor, or two, to play a role on the committee. But whatever the specifics, the committee needs to have executives with experience, complementary skillsets, and enough clout in an organization that they can not only make important decisions on the organization's behalf, but they can also influence others in the organization to get things done.

When it comes to some of the more technical skillsets that investment committee members should have, clearly a strategic mindset is important, so that the committee can effectively debate and decide which deals can best support and accelerate the company's strategy. But also important, are financial and legal skills. Specifically, as it relates to M&A. Remember, M&A is a highly specialized field. These two areas in particular (finance and legal) are both central and far reaching when it comes to M&A. Having deep expertise in these two areas in particular is absolutely critical to the success of any investment committee.

When it comes to the financial side of things, it's the CFO of an organization that is responsible for deciding where to allocate capital in order to maximize returns. This includes deciding what businesses to acquire, and at what price. Meaning, it's ultimately the CFO's responsibility to make sure that the company is not overpaying.

When acquiring a business, the CFO is also responsible for making sure that his or her own company is not exposing itself to any unwanted financial risks or liabilities. If there are any unwanted risks or liabilities, there needs to be a plan to manage them. On the legal side of things, it's the company's general counsel that bares a similar responsibility. Ensuring that the company isn't exposing itself to unwanted legal risks or exposures.

Make no mistake about it, it's ultimately the CFO and the general counsel that are responsible for the company's financial and legal decisions, regardless of whether or not advisors were involved. After all, when a deal is done, the advisors will likely have moved on to their next projects, but the CFO and general counsel will still be there to answer questions if something was missed or went wrong. These are the gatekeepers whose jobs it is to make sure that the company is making good financial and legal decisions, and the involvement of these individuals on the investment committee is an absolute must.

Investment Committee Protocols

It's not unusual for an investment committee to review and approve every single M&A transaction that a company does. Whether it's an acquisition, a joint venture, or entering into a partnership. The question though, for any of these things, is how deeply the committee wants to be involved? This is where the committee needs to define the process that it wants its teams to follow.

Does the committee want to be aware of, and in approval of, every deal throughout its entire process? Or, does it only want to be involved at certain touch points? For example, before anything gets signed like an offer or a contract. The answer will be different for every company depending on how well organized its process is, the experience level of its team members, and the committee's management style.

Generally speaking though, an investment committee should always be aware of, and in approval of, any deal where the buyer is devoting resources. Right from the beginning. This is because, the last thing a buyer should want, is to be spending time and money, at any level in an organization, only to have the investment committee question why you're doing it and kill it. Or worse, thinking you have a negotiated deal in-hand, but then once the investment committee takes a look, they're not OK with it.

In any case, it's a good idea to have a number of communication touchpoints with the investment committee throughout the life of a deal. Early on, to make sure it's a deal that the company wants to do, as well as throughout the process, so that when it comes time to seek an investment committee's approval for something, they're already up to speed and aligned. Because they've been part of the process all along. We'll cover more on key communication touchpoints and investment committee best practices as we continue through the book.

The Deal Team Leader

Someone has to lead the deal. From initially screening the deal and making sure it's something that the organization wants to do, to leading negotiations, navigating the due diligence process, and ultimately getting it to a close. This is the role of the deal team leader, sometimes referred to as a deal champion, or a lead negotiator.

It's not uncommon in larger organizations for there to be a designated business development group in-house, whose main role is to work on strategic growth initiatives like M&A transactions. If the buyer has a business development group in-house, it's likely that someone from this group, experienced in M&A, will lead the deal. Negotiating and navigating it through the M&A process.

Smaller companies though, who don't do deals very often, might not have such a person in-house. Afterall, it's a fairly specialized skillset where the person leading the deal needs to know how deals are structured, what drives their values, and how to negotiate. They also need to be familiar with the due diligence process, and how to handle issues when they come up. For situations where there is no such person in-house, there are buy-side advisors, such as investment banks and consultants, who specialize in this type of work.

From helping identify and screen targets, to structuring, valuing, and negotiating deals, these advisors are familiar with the M&A process and can help buyers who might not do deals very often. While it may not be ideal to outsource this role entirely, the ability to bring in an advisor who can help is certainly there if you need it.

In addition to all of the blocking and tackling that is involved with navigating a deal, one of the more critical roles of the deal team leader is to serve the needs of the investment committee. Because ultimately, it's the deal team leader that the investment committee will look to and hold responsible for following its process. Keeping them informed, seeking their advice, and getting their approvals when necessary.

In the eyes of the committee, it's the deal team leader that's responsible for executing. And often, as part of the investment committee's process, it's the deal team leader that's responsible for coordinating due diligence, a process that involves organizing the efforts of several cross-functional teams. We'll discuss more on the role of due diligence a little later.

In any given deal, there will be many different people entering and leaving the process as they each perform their individual roles on it. But it's the deal team leader that remains from beginning to end. Providing consistency and organization in the eyes of the seller, the investment committee, and the broader deal team members that are involved. Keeping track of many moving parts and organizing the efforts of many different people, all of whom need to be coordinated and working together. It goes without saying, that the deal team leader plays an important role, carrying the deal from start to finish.

The Deal Team

In the initial phase of a deal, there may only be a few key people involved at a relatively high level. This might be the deal team leader, the investment committee, and the business team leaders that will eventually own the business. In these early stages, this team is mostly focused on understanding the business, evaluating its strategic-fit, and deciding if it's a business worth owning. If it is, at what price and on what terms. Once there is an accepted offer, the deal moves into what is known as due diligence.

Due diligence is where a target company allows a buyer to do a deep-dive into its books, its records, its people, its processes, and everything else (within reason of course), so that the buyer can gain a deep understanding of what it is that he or she is buying, and get comfortable that there won't be any surprises after a deal closes.

This is the point in a deal where the team gets bigger, a lot bigger, to include all of the functional experts that will now be necessary to carry out the due diligence. Experts from finance, tax, legal, regulatory, HR, IT, risk management, treasury, and possibly other areas (depending on the nature of the business and the needs of the buyer).

Each of these experts play an important role in the transaction, looking at the business through his or her own unique lens, while also working with the broader deal team. It's these experts that know what to look for within their functional areas, and what questions to ask in order to identify any potential risks or liabilities that should be avoided. It's through this process that the collective team gains a deeper understanding of the business they're buying, while also flushing out any concerns or potential issues that might need to be addressed.

Functional Team Leaders

Organizations that are large enough to have a business development group in-house, will often have at least one person from each functional area that's deputized by the investment committee as the person who is responsible for overseeing due diligence on behalf of that functional area. For example, in finance there is a go-to person for financial due diligence, the same goes for tax, legal, regulatory, HR, IT, and others. There are several good reasons for this.

For one, it gives the investment committee comfort knowing that qualified people, with the right technical skills, are overseeing due diligence in each functional area. Asking the right questions and making sure that nothing important is being overlooked. It also gives the committee specific people to hold accountable, so things get done.

The deal team leader also benefits when there is just one person in charge of each functional area. You see, it's very likely that each functional area will require more than one person to perform the actual work. Meaning, that there could be multiple teams to manage. Too many workstreams and too many people for the deal team leader to keep track of. But by each functional team having just one point of contact, communication and organization becomes much more streamlined, manageable, and consistent from deal to deal.

Identifying functional team leaders well ahead of time, before you get to the due diligence stage of a deal, is very important. You see, it's not only enough to be a technical expert in a given field, such as say accounting, or tax. It's also important to understand the M&A process, how deals are structured, their terms, and what's important in the context of an M&A deal. As we said earlier, M&A is a highly specialized field, so having functional leaders with the right combination technical skills and experience in M&A is key in knowing what to look for and applying good judgement.

When it comes to knowing what to look for, there's only a limited amount of time in which teams are usually allowed to perform their due diligence. It's negotiable, but a seller will usually only tolerate between 30 and 60 days. There isn't enough time to dive into every detail and look under every rock. And a seller won't have the time or patience to entertain every question. They're busy answering lots of questions, from lots of teams, and they're usually spread-thin and short on patience. In order to execute a smooth due diligence process, where a buyer gets the answers they need without frustrating sellers, they need teams who know how to focus their efforts on what's important. Which only comes from the right combination of technical knowledge and experience doing deals.

When it comes to applying good judgement, once a potential issue has been identified, someone needs to make a call about what it means to the deal. Some issues will be ordinary business issues that really aren't worth worrying about, while others might require more work to figure out. Some might actually change the buyers view on the price and terms of the deal, and some might be reasons to walk away from the deal all together. Applying good judgement in a deal means having a sense of where an issue is likely to fall within this spectrum so that nobody is sitting on a ticking time-bomb and important issues are being dealt with quickly.

When functional team leaders know what to look for, it helps the buyer get through the process quickly. And when they know what issues are important enough to elevate, it can save the buyer time and money from pursuing a deal that may ultimately not be successful. If an organization doesn't have the right expertise in-house, for any functional area, it should definitely be seeking outside advisors for help.

Outside Advisors

It's almost standard practice for a buyer to engage lawyers and accountants to perform legal, financial, and tax due diligence in an M&A deal. This is not only due to the specialized knowledge that they bring, but it's also due to the heavy workloads that are usually involved with doing the work in these areas. And depending on the circumstances involved, other outside advisors might also be needed. Such as commercial, regulatory, HR, IT, and others. Ultimately though, it should be the decision of each functional team leader whether or not to engage an outside advisor for each functional area. Whether it's the business team leader seeking the assistance of a commercial advisor, or a functional team leader seeking the assistance of a due diligence provider. Each team leader should be making his or her own decisions as to what is best for their own area of responsibility.

In situations where there is no expertise in-house for a particular need, there really is no decision. It ought to be outsourced. In situations where there is expertise is in-house, the decision may vary depending on the specific facts and circumstances of each project. After all, some deals may be small and fairly straight forward. And if the internal team has the experience and the availability to cover it, it may make sense to do the work internally. Other deals though, might be much larger, more complicated, or have tight deadlines, and these might make more sense to outsource. In any event, the decision to outsource should really be made on a case by case basis by each of the individual team leaders. Depending not only on people's availability, but also the amount of work that's involved, and the qualifications and experience of the people that will be doing the work.

Defining the Process

Just to recap, every deal should have a deal team leader that navigates the deal from start to finish. This person needs to lead the negotiations, manage the due diligence process, and serve the needs of the investment committee throughout the deal. Working closely with the deal team leader from the very beginning of a deal should be the business team leaders that will ultimately own and operate the business. And supporting these teams, are the various functional experts who will perform the due diligence. Now that we've conceptually covered each of these groups, and the roles they each play, we need to define the process that these teams should be following when doing deals. Defining what needs to happen, when it needs to happen, and how it all needs to come together for the investment committee. This is what creates the guiding roadmap for a consistent and repeatable process on each and every deal that you do.

In order to define the process though, we need to understand the different stages of a deal and what should be happening in order to have a good buy-side process at each of these stages. This being said, regardless of how a deal originates, its lifecycle will usually exist across four distinct phases. These are the pre-LOI phase, the due diligence phase, the period between signing and closing, and then finally, closed deals. Each of these periods in a deal marks an important milestone, not only for what happens between the buyer and seller, but for what should be happening behind the scenes, each step of the way on the buy-side, which we'll discuss next.

Chapter 5: Pre-LOI Best Practices

A letter of intent (which is often referred to as an "LOI") is a document that puts in writing the proposed terms of a deal. Signed by both the buyer and the seller, it includes details about what it is that's being sold, the purchase price, the structure, and the key terms of a deal that a buyer and seller believe should be documented before they spend a bunch of time and money on due diligence and negotiating what will ultimately become the final purchase agreement. Just like it sounds, things get serious, and expensive, after you sign the LOI.

Getting to an LOI is an important milestone in a deal. It represents a meeting of the minds between a buyer and a seller on what the deal will eventually become. And while a letter of intent is usually considered to be a non-binding document, meaning that the two parties are not legally bound to actually going through with a deal yet, there's usually a good faith commitment when a letter of intent is signed that the two parties will now be working together with the intent of getting a deal done.

Everything leading up to the signing of an LOI is known as the pre-LOI stage of a deal. It's a stage that can last days, or even years, depending on how the deal originated and the circumstances that are involved. As a buyer though, regardless of how a deal originated, or how long it took to get to the point where you're now negotiating an LOI, it's important to make sure that any deals that move past this point have been fully vetted. Because, when a deal moves forward from here and into due diligence, as a buyer, you're going to be devoting a substantial amount of resources to it. Which means, now's the time to make sure that it's a deal your organization really wants to do. That there's alignment with the business team who will own it, and support from the investment committee who will eventually need to approve it.

The Pre-LOI Stage of a Deal

What happens in the pre-LOI stage of a deal? What sort of information should a buyer expect to get in order to make decisions at such an early stage? And what should an investment committee's role be in in deciding whether or not to move forward with an LOI?

Because each deal is likely to follow a different path, and each buyer is likely to have a different approach, the answers to these questions will be different from buyer to buyer and deal to deal. But generally speaking, by the time you get to the point where you're negotiating an LOI, you'll have already spent a good amount of time with the target company's management. And through a series of conversations, meetings, and sharing of information, you'll have already gotten to know a good amount about the target business, its management team, their vision for the future, and the seller's motivations for doing a deal.

By now, you should have also formed your own view about how attractive the target business is, and the strategic reasons for why you want to own it. Whether it's for geographical expansion, access to new products, buying out a competitor, or a supplier, by now you should be able to clearly articulate why you want it, what you believe you'll gain from it, and just how much of a priority it is. You should also have a feeling of whether or not there is a good cultural fit. Have you been working well so far with the team that will be managing the business? Do you trust them? Is there a common vision for how the business will be successful in the future? Assuming you've cleared all these hurdles, that it makes sense strategically, and that there's cultural alignment, you should also have a financial model that shows it's a deal worth doing, and at a price you can justify.

Does this sound like a lot? Because, it is. You see, the pre-LOI stage of a deal is where the vision is created for what the business will look like in the future. And it's where the structure, price, and key terms of a deal are negotiated. Getting to this point involves a healthy dialogue as well as a good amount of information sharing between both the buyer and the seller. Information that's not only about the business, but about numbers too. Enter, the non-disclosure agreement.

Non-Disclosure Agreements

When a buyer likes a business and has to decide whether or not to pursue a deal, that buyer needs information. Information that will help the buyer understand the business, evaluate the opportunity, and decide at what price a deal makes sense. This means the buyer needs both business and financial information. A seller's level of comfort though, in sharing this information, particularly in the pre-LOI stage of a deal, can vary. Some sellers might be completely comfortable sharing information. But others, might be concerned and hesitant to share anything that they consider sensitive just in case a deal doesn't work out.

From a negotiation standpoint, it's important that buyers respect when a seller has concerns about sharing sensitive information. But at the same time, especially as a deal keeps moving forward, a seller needs to appreciate that a buyer needs information to do their work and make decisions about a deal. There needs to be a balance, and when concerns come up, there needs to be an open dialogue between the buyer and seller as to why something's important. At times, both may need to bend a little to help find a solution so that the buyer can get what they need, and the seller can still feel like they didn't compromise anything that's sensitive.

When discussions about a possible deal evolve from what may have begun as casual conversations, to where it's now time to start sharing information, this is the point in a deal where a seller will usually ask a buyer to sign a confidentiality, or a non-disclosure agreement (referred to as an "NDA"). The basic purpose of an NDA is that the buyer agrees to keeping the information that's shared by the seller confidential. And the buyer won't use it in any way, other than to evaluate the potential deal that's being discussed.

In other words, it's intended to prevent the buyer from just taking the information and using it to compete against the seller. It defines things like what's considered confidential, how the information will be used, who the information can be share with (such as advisors), and how the information should be returned or destroyed in the event that a deal doesn't move forward.

It's often the first legal document that's signed between a buyer and a seller in a deal, and if you didn't already have a lawyer involved, now's the time to get one. As the case with any legal document, you should always have your attorney review it before signing. And you yourself should also read it, to make sure that you understand its terms. You should also raise your hand if you feel like any of the terms are too restrictive or overreaching, because in M&A, just about everything is negotiable.

Building the Financial Model

The buyer in an M&A deal should always have a financial model, even in the pre-LOI stage of a deal. A model that captures both the current and expected future financial performance of the business that's being acquired. This means having projected income statements, balance sheets, and cash flows. When done well, a model can capture a useful amount of detail and become much more than just numbers on paper. It can become a living tool that helps a buyer think about a business both operationally and financially. It can help a buyer develop a deep understanding of what drives a business, and what it takes to run it. It can also help the buyer organize their thoughts about where that business is going, and the financial impact that any future changes will have on it.

In the pre-LOI stage of a deal, the information that a buyer gets to build a model is usually very limited. This is completely normal in the early stages of a deal though, where the expectation is that the information should flow more freely after a price has been agreed and an LOI has been signed. But even before an LOI is signed, a buyer still needs a model, so that they can make decisions about a deal, including its price and terms.

To do this, as soon as a buyer has financial information, even if it's high-level information, they should begin running the model that will be used throughout the deal. Where information isn't available yet, there should simply be placeholders or assumptions that can be filled in later with better information. Once the LOI is signed, and the deal moves into due diligence, the flow of information usually improves, and the model can become much more complete.

When building a model for a deal, a buyer should not have to start from scratch. There should already be a template to start with. In fact, many buyers who do deals often, and many advisors who do deals for a living, have models that they've developed over time, and they've built templates from these models. Templates that are ready to go when a new deal pops-up. With a well-developed template-based model, information simply needs to be populated for the model to be up and running. This saves time and takes a lot of the guess work out of whether or not a model works properly. This isn't to say that a template-based model won't need to be tailored to the specifics of a deal, in fact all models need to be tailored in some way. But the basic functionality of the model should already be there, ready to go. And the mathematical dependability of a proven template-based model, means that a buyer doesn't have to worry so much about the basic functionality of it or formula errors.

We'll cover much more on models when we get to part three of this book. But for now, it's important to just keep in mind that as soon as casual conversations about a deal evolve into talking numbers, it's time to start thinking about getting the financial information you'll need to pull a model together.

Deciding on a Fair Price

Valuing a business is subjective. And while there are several valuation techniques that can help both buyers and sellers develop their own views on what a business should be worth, at the end of the day the price that's agreed in a deal will be a negotiated amount. It will be based on what the buyer is willing to pay, and what the seller is willing to accept. If an amount can't be agreed, there won't be a deal. If an amount is agreed, it should at last be reasonable and fair to both the buyer and the seller.

As a buyer, your financial model should be providing you with all the information you need to decide what a fair price should be. Once some numbers have been populated into a model, it should be telling you things like the purchase price multiples that you're thinking of paying. These can be used to benchmark against trends that might be taking place in the industry, or prices that others have paid for similar businesses (if you can find them). It should also be telling you your expected rate of return on investment, how accretive or dilutive the deal will be, and the enterprise value of the business based on its expected future cash flows. If you don't know what these things are right now, don't worry. We'll cover them in great detail when we get to part three of this book. For now though, you just want to keep in mind that it's usually a combination of these valuation metrics that help a buyer form a view on what a fair price should be for a business. Without metrics like these, a buyer is just guessing at what a business should be worth. And remember, as we said earlier, if you don't have a model that can justify the price, then you could be overpaying. Not something you want to be doing.

When negotiating price in the early stages of a deal, once you put an offer out there, if it turns out later on that it was too high, it could be very difficult, if not impossible to pull it back and still have a deal. So, once you have enough information, you want to start populating a model, so that you have some guiding metrics to think about before putting a price out there.

Drafting the Letter of Intent

The letter of intent puts in writing the proposed terms of a deal between a buyer and a seller. It's usually written by the buyer, addressed to the seller, and signed by both parties. It includes details about what it is that's being sold, the purchase price, the structure, and the key terms of the deal. From a buyer's perspective, when drafting the letter of intent, it's important to be as clear as possible on all the key terms. The structure, the purchase price, if there will be any purchase price adjustments, contingencies, and holdbacks or escrows. If you're not familiar with these terms yet, don't worry, we discuss them in detail when we get to part two of this book. For now though, it's just important to keep in mind that once you get to the LOI, you want agreement on all these key terms, so that expectations are aligned. Because, the last thing you want, is to be dealing with any misunderstandings or miscommunications after this point in a deal. For an example of what a letter of intent looks like, refer to Appendix

One in the back of this book.

When drafting the LOI, if there are any elephants in the room, meaning things that you're aware of, and concerned about, but that you haven't been able to address directly yet, you may want to call them out as items that need to be confirmed in your due diligence. Especially if they are things that could change your mind on the price or terms that you've agreed to so far. These could be financial issues, tax issues, or even possible violations of laws or regulations that you've become aware of and are concerned about.

If there are any issues like these, you need to be open about them, honest about them, and have a plan to deal with them as quickly as possible. And while it may not be something that you're going to full-out document in a letter of intent, it's certainly something you should be discussing with the seller. Especially if it could affect your view on price, or make you question if you even want to do the deal on those same terms. Don't just kick a can down the road if you have issues like these, because at some point, you'll need to deal with them. It may even make sense to do your due diligence on those items first, before you spend a bunch of money on other things like drafting agreements or performing due diligence in other areas. Just in case it ends up being what you feared, and it affects whether or not there's still a deal. In most situations of course, you don't have to deal with things like this, but on the rare occasions that you do, you'll be glad you dealt with them up front.

Exclusivity

While LOIs are usually considered to be non-binding documents, meaning that the buyer and seller are not legally bound to going through with a deal yet, there are usually certain provisions in them that are binding, and for good reason. For example, when a buyer decides to include an exclusivity period. Exclusivity means that for a defined period of time, the seller will not be allowed to solicit, negotiate, or enter into any other agreements with any other potential buyers. It's sometimes called a 'no-shop' provision. It's a commitment by the seller that gives the buyer a better sense of comfort that the seller is serious about doing a deal.

From a buyer's perspective, a seller's commitment to exclusivity is an important sign, because from here on out the buyer in particular will be devoting a substantial amount time to the deal, and spending a lot of money on lawyers, accountants, and other advisors to help get the deal done. Buyers are usually nervous about putting a lot of time and money into a deal unless they have exclusivity, because they don't want a seller stringing them along and using them as leverage to negotiate a better deal with someone else.

Practically, it's a real 'give' when a seller agrees to exclusivity. Because in doing this, they're no longer able to shop other offers for a better deal. It also means that the seller is putting all other offers (if there were any) on hold while they work toward completing a deal with only one buyer. It's for these reasons that a seller will usually try and make an exclusivity period as short as possible, like 15-30 days in some cases. It's a seller's way of motivating a buyer to get through their due diligence quickly, and get a deal signed. If they don't, the buyer can lose exclusivity and leave the seller open to revisiting any other discussions they may have had with other buyers.

From a buyer's perspective, you'd like the exclusivity period to be as long as you think you need to do your work. In some deals, if it's a sellers first time going through an M&A process, it can take a while for the seller to provide all the due diligence materials that the buyer will need. And, there could be some educating involved when it's time to negotiate the terms of the agreements. For situations like this, a buyer might need as much as 90-days to get through everything with the seller. On the other hand, some sellers are very sophisticated and might be very well prepared, so you may only need 30-45 days. It really depends on how experienced and prepared a seller is for what's ahead.

At the end of the day, it's going to be a compromise that takes into consideration how competitive the process is (in other words, where the seller wants to put pressure on the buyer to move quickly), and how quickly the buyer thinks he or she can realistically get through their work. If a seller is dead-set on having a short exclusivity period, and the buyer thinks it's a stretch to meet that time-frame, it should at least be understood that once exclusivity ends, it may need to be extended.

Investment Committee Approval

There are at least two times in a deal when the investment committee's approval is absolutely necessary before moving any further. The first time is before you sign an LOI, and the second time, is before you sign the final purchase agreement.

Before an organization ever signs a letter of intent to buy a business, it should make sure some boxes have been checked. Is the proposed deal something that the organization wants to do? Does the structure of the deal make sense? Is the price reasonable? Are the terms acceptable? Is the business team aligned with the financial model and supportive of the deal? Is the organization ready to commit the resources necessary to get the deal done? Concerns or doubts about any of these things should be addressed now, before entering into an LOI.

As the group that's responsible for overseeing the company's M&A process, deciding which deals the company should and should not be doing, and approving the price and terms of each deal, it's the investment committee that needs to be comfortable that these questions have been answered, and that the organization is ready to move forward.

Depending on the circumstances that may have led up to this point, the investment committee (or certain members of it) may or may not have been involved yet. If they have been involved, it should be relatively easy to make sure they're up to speed and supportive of the deal before moving forward. If they haven't, they'll need to be briefed, so that they can make a well-informed decision as to whether or not the team should be moving forward. Whatever the investment committee's involvement up to this point, getting their approval before signing an LOI is an absolute must, so that there is complete alignment and support for any deals that go past this point.

To help the investment committee make their decision, a document should be prepared. Not more than a handful of pages. It should provide enough background information on the business, and the deal, so that there is no confusion as to why the deal makes sense to do. It should summarize what it is that you're buying. Why the deal makes sense strategically. The quality and the experience of the management team that you're partnering with. The vision for the business going forward. The structure, purchase price, and all the key terms of the deal. It should also include any known risks or concerns that the team is aware of so that nothing important is being hidden or withheld from the committee as they make their decision. If the team would like the investment committee's guidance or input on something, that should also be included.

The model being used to analyze and value the business should also be available for the committee's review, and it should include all of the key valuation metrics we discussed earlier, showing that the price you've negotiated is reasonable and fair. Once these background materials have been provided to the committee, they'll usually need a call or a meeting with the deal team leader to discuss it. After this, the committee is likely to either take a pass (in which case the deal won't move forward), request that the terms of the deal are renegotiated, or approve moving forward with an LOI.

Prioritizing Deals

If a buyer likes a deal, before they commit to moving forward with an LOI, they need to decide if they're ready to commit the resources that will be necessary to getting the deal done. This doesn't only mean committing its internal people's time, but it also means committing to the cost of outside advisors and devoting the capital that will be necessary to making the actual investment. This is where prioritizing deals becomes real. Because it's at this point, that there are deals in the pipeline, ready to do, but resources are limited. So, buyers need to decide where those resources will be best used.

The fact of the matter is, organizations need to rank which deals should come first in terms of priority, and make sure that they're devoting resources to those deals that will have the best growth, the best returns, and the best accretion for their investment. Above all others in an organization, it's the investment committee that sees all the potential deals that an organization can do. So, it's the investment committee that's in the best position to set these priorities and make the sometimes-difficult decisions about where resources should be allocated.

Deciding if a target business is a 'must have' (meaning that you cannot risk losing it to a competitor), a business that you really want, or one that would just be 'nice to have' if you could get it at a good price, is the job of the investment committee. Looking at each deal strategically and financially and deciding which deals can best help the organization execute on its strategy to achieve its goals. It's the investment committee that should decide which deals ought to come first in line and receive the highest priority. We'll discuss more on how to measure the financial impact of deals for these purposes later in the book.

Chapter 6: Due Diligence Best Practices

During due diligence, a target lets a buyer to do a deep-dive into its books, its records, its people, and its processes, so that the buyer can develop a good understanding of the business they're about to buy and get comfortable that there won't be any surprises after a deal has closed. This is also the time when the buyer and seller will negotiate what will ultimately become the final purchase agreement. This, due diligence phase of a deal, begins when an LOI is signed and it ends when a buyer and seller have either signed a final purchase agreement, or decided they no longer want to do a deal.

The due diligence phase of a deal will usually last anywhere from 60 to 90 days. Which really depends on the circumstances that are involved, how well prepared a seller is for a process, and whether or not the buyer finds any issues as they do their work. During this time, the buyer will review a lot of information and ask a lot of questions about the business, its operations, and its financial performance. They'll confirm assumptions they made earlier in the deal, look for risks and exposures, buildup their model, and make plans for onboarding and integrating the business once the deal is done. All this, while negotiating the final purchase agreement. Just like it sounds, there's a lot of work that happens during the due diligence phase of a deal, on many fronts.

Ultimately, it's the buyer that decides how much due diligence they need to do in order to get comfortable. And it's the buyer that will do this work, either through its own internal teams or with the help of outside advisors. But even though this is the case, due diligence is still a lot of work for a seller. Because it's the seller that has all the information a buyer needs, and it's the seller that knows all the answers to a buyer's questions.

If you've ever been through a due diligence process before, you know that it can be a very intensive exercise for both the buyer and the seller. And while it probably goes without saying, the better prepared a seller is for a due diligence process, the smoother it can be. Whereas the less prepared a seller is for a process, the longer and more drawn-out it can be, for both sides.

Sometimes, if a process stretches out over a long enough period of time, deal fatigue can set in. Deal fatigue is a term for when people working on a deal begin to lose patience with each other, feeling like the deal is dragging out forever with no end in sight, and just wishing the whole thing would be over with. As a buyer, this is something you want to avoid as much as possible because it only makes it harder to do the work that needs to be done.

This is where having good advisors on both sides of a deal can help. On the sell-side, they can help by getting the seller prepared for due diligence. And on the buy-side, they can help by knowing 'when to say when' and deciding what level of due diligence is enough to be comfortable. But whether or not outside advisors are involved, a buyer can also help avoid deal fatigue by having a good M&A process. You see, buyers need to their work, but in order to not frustrate sellers, their work needs to be well-organized and efficient. In this chapter, we'll discuss a number of best practices that buy-side teams can use to help keep their processes well-organized and get their work done quickly.

Organizing the Team

Before an LOI is signed, there may only be a few key people involved in a deal at a relatively high level. Like the deal team leader, the business team leaders, the investment committee, and maybe a few others. But once there's a signed LOI, if it hasn't already been done, it's time to bring in the broader deal team. The broader deal team usually includes all the functional experts from finance, tax, legal, regulatory, HR, IT, and other groups that are all needed to perform the due diligence, plan the integration, and help execute the deal. From this point on, the deal needs to follow a structured process, so that the broader deal team is well-organized, communicating, and getting their work done in an efficient way where nothing important is being overlooked.

Kicking-Off the Due Diligence

To begin the due diligence process, the buy-side deal team ought to have a kick-off call (or a meeting) where the entire deal team can be briefed on the deal. For the kick-off, the team should usually be provided with a working group list of the team members that will be working on the project, and background materials to help them come up to speed on the business and the structure of the deal. This would include things like copies of the materials that were provided to the investment committee, the LOI, and any other background materials that would be helpful.

The deal team leader should kick things off by providing the team with an overview of the business that's being acquired and the strategic reasons for doing the deal. Just like the briefing with the investment committee, any issues or concerns about the deal should be shared with this group. If there's a plan to stagger the due diligence in phases to tackle any key issues first, this should also be discussed. But most of the time, now is when everyone will get the green light that it's a live deal and it's time to start the process. The deal team leader also needs to make clear during this kick-off, any rules of engagement, or guidelines that the teams should be following, as well as the timeframes in which they'll need to complete all their work.

Information Requests

Following the kick-off, if not already done, the next step in the due diligence process is for the buyer to send the seller its due diligence request list. The due diligence request list is usually a comprehensive list, organized by each functional area, that requests all the information that the buy-side team thinks they'll need to perform their work. Most buyers who do deals often will have a standard list, ready to go, that only needs minor editing before it can be sent to a target.

The target will often need time to get through the request list and provide its responses. Occasionally, a seller will have questions or issues with some of the requests where things either aren't applicable or can't be provided. But this is normal, and when it happens it should be discussed, so that the buyer can either take things off the list or work with the seller on a solution that makes sense. In any event, it can take days or sometimes weeks for a seller to respond to a buyer's request list. It all depends on how ready the seller is and the resources that they have devoted to the process.

Keeping Deals Confidential

When it comes to involving people in deals, some sellers will try and limit as much as possible the number of people they're bringing in. This is because they're trying to keep the deal a secret. Other sellers though, might be a little more willing to involve the different people that are all needed to answer a buyer's questions.

When sellers hesitate to bring people into a process, it can definitely slow things down, even when it's for a good reason. You see, it's possible that a seller doesn't want its people knowing about a deal just in case it doesn't work out. Or maybe they don't want its people to worry about their jobs. Whatever reason a seller has to not bring people into a process, a buyer needs to respect it, because it's still the seller's business. At the same time though, a seller needs to realize that the people who can answer a buyer's questions and provide the information they need, may still have to be available. It's a delicate balance that often needs to be worked through.

For anyone on a seller's team that is brought into a process, they need to be educated that what they're doing is highly confidential, and that it's not to be discussed with anyone who isn't involved. They need to know this from the very beginning, before it's accidentally leaked, and you end-up having rumors or gossip to deal with. And just as important as it is for a seller to want to manage leaks. The buy-side team should be just as cautious, and also treat deals as highly confidential. Documents shouldn't be left around for prying eyes to see and deals shouldn't be discussed with anyone that's not involved. From a buyer's perspective, there's also the risk that if a deal is leaked to the market, it could attract an unsolicited offer from a competing buyer.

At the end of the day, neither the buyer nor the seller want any disruptions to the business or the deal because of rumors, or poorly managed leaks. As for when the deal finally is announced, the buyer and seller should have a communication plan for that. Not just for managing communications with employees, but also for customers, suppliers, and any other stakeholders in a business where you'd want to get ahead of any rumors or any misconceptions about what the deal could mean for them.

At the end of the day, leaks can happen from either the buy-side, or the sell-side, and if they do, they can have negative consequences. Both sides should want to manage confidentiality and communications about deals on their own terms and avoid leaks as much as possible.

Online Data Rooms

Once a seller has prepared its responses to a buyer's information requests, the information is usually uploaded into a secure online data room that the buy-side team can access. More often than not, these data rooms will usually start-out being very lightly populated in the beginning of a deal. And as a deal progresses, they'll become much more populated over time.

On the seller's team, someone needs to be responsible for organizing and managing all of the information that's uploaded to the data room. It's an important role where whoever does this needs to understand how important it is that the data room be well-organized throughout the process. This usually works best when the data room is organized and populated in the same way that a buyer's requests are organized, by functional area. When a data room is well organized by functional area, it's easier for that buyer's different functional teams to find what they need. This also helps free-up a seller's time by not having to constantly tell people where to find things that have already been uploaded.

Allowing Teams to Work Directly

Once a seller has uploaded its information into an online data room, and the buy-side team has started to review it, the due diligence process becomes interactive. From here on out, each functional team from the buy-side, will now want to be working directly with their counterparts on the sell-side to get through their work. Businesspeople working with businesspeople, finance people working with finance people, tax people working with tax people… you get the idea.

These interactions tend to take place through a combination of site visits, meetings, and conference calls where the buy-side teams get to see with their own eyes how a business operates, ask questions, and request any additional information they'll need to do their work. When there are several functional groups all doing this at the same time, it's a lot to manage. And usually, it's just a faster and easier process for everyone involved if these functional groups are allowed to work directly with one another and not have go through some sort of an intermediary where bottlenecks can happen.

You see, sometimes a seller will have an investment banker or a business broker managing the sell-side process. For the most part, the role of these sell-side advisors is to help a seller find a buyer, navigate the due diligence process, and negotiate the best possible deal. They also help get documents in order, organize materials, and anticipate questions. A good sell-side advisor can really help a seller prepare for a due diligence process, especially when a seller has never been through such a process before. And as a due diligence process is happening, they can also do a good job of minimizing disruptions to a seller's business because of a deal. While a buyer may hate to hear it, a good sell-side advisor can also sometimes manage a buyer's requests if a buyer is asking for things that are overreaching or unreasonable. But for the most part, a good sell-side advisor, especially in the middle market, will help improve a process, and get buyers what they need.

While many investment bankers and business brokers do add value, some, unfortunately, can actually hurt the process if they are too controlling or unreasonable in how they chose to manage it. These types of advisors tend to limit a buyer's access to the sell-side team, cut them off from getting important questions answered, and try to short cut the process by pressuring a buyer into signing a deal without being able to do all their work. A bad sell-side advisor can not only slow things down but can be so difficult that a buyer will lose comfort if they aren't getting what they need and walk. If it's not a must-have business, a difficult sell-side advisor can absolutely kill a deal.

If this ever happens, or if a sell-side advisor is being dismissive about getting a buyer's important questions answered, then that buyer needs to be direct with the seller as quickly as possible, to let the seller know that the buy-side and sell-side teams can't afford such games. And that they need to work directly together if they're ever going to get a deal done. After all, the buyer is investing a lot of time and money in going through this process, and the seller needs to do their part by allowing the teams to work together whenever possible. It just goes faster that way.

Project Management

With multiple teams working on the buy-side of a deal in a short period of time, it can be difficult for any one person to keep up with everything that's going on. Let alone the deal team leader who already has a lot on his or her plate. For this person, keeping a finger on the pulse of how the teams are doing and if any big issues are popping up, is important. But it's also a lot to manage. This is where having a project manager help support the deal team leader adds a lot of value.

In organizations that are large enough to have a business development group, it's usually someone from this group that will help the deal team leader and play the role of a project manager. This person may already have been involved in the deal during the pre-LOI stage, helping run models and prepare investment committee materials, and more often than not, this person is also experienced in M&A. In situations where a buyer doesn't have a business development group though, and the deal is being led by an outside advisor, it's likely that the advisor will have someone from their own team playing the role of a project manager.

Whether it's an internal person or an external person, an effective project manager on the buy-side becomes an important person in the process. They help coordinate the teams, facilitate communications, and improve the overall flow of information. They stay on top of all the important events, milestones, and deadlines that are happening. And they keep the deal team leader informed if any important issues are popping up. Being well organized, a good communicator, and knowledgeable about the M&A process are all important qualities for this role.

On a day-to-day basis, the buy-side project manager will do things like make sure the teams have access to the data room, help coordinate site visits, and help organize meetings and calls between the buy-side and sell-side teams. They'll also sit in on meetings and calls to make sure that the teams are working well together and that the buy-side team is getting what they need. By being a part of the process in this way, they're also staying in tune with the progress that's taking place by each of the functional teams, and the demands that are being placed on the seller.

If for some reason a team from the buy-side needs to raise its hand that it's not getting the information they need, the project manager can be their main point of contact. And if the seller becomes overwhelmed by the number of requests they're receiving, and they don't know what to focus on first, they too can ask the project manager. Above all, the project manager facilitates good communications, a well-organized workflow, and helps make sure that the buy-side team is on-track for meeting their deadlines.

Team Communications

During the due diligence process, communications across the buy-side team needs to be open and smooth so that any issues or concerns that are identified can be dealt with as quickly as possible. After all, the last thing you want in a due diligence process is for any team member to be sitting on a ticking timebomb. Especially if it's something so damaging that it could change the deal or kill it. And you never want to be saying to your team, 'I wish I knew about this sooner,' especially if they did know about it sooner, but it was never communicated, and nothing was ever done about it. You see, when good communications are taking place, there shouldn't be any unexpected surprises at the end of a deal. Instead, any problems, issues, or concerns that the team identifies, should be discussed as soon as they're known about. This way, they can be dealt with while the deal is taking place. And hopefully, by the end of the deal, you've either already dealt with these things or you've come up with a plan to deal with them.

To help facilitate good team communications, there ought to be a number of team-wide touchpoints throughout a deal. The purpose of these touchpoints isn't for people to prepare a bunch of memos, or to talk for the sake of talking. On an active deal, when there's a lot to do, there's just no time for that. Instead, the purpose of these touchpoints, is so that the various functional teams can carve-out a little bit of time to update the deal team leader, and each other, on any problems they're having or issues they're finding.

For example, some team members may not be getting the information they requested or may not be getting access to the sell-side team members that they need to do their work. This could jeopardize the team's ability to complete their work on time. Or, one of the functional groups may have uncovered an issue, that could affect the buyers view on the value of the business or put the deal at risk. There are a countless number of things that could either be holding people up or create possible issues for a deal.

If something important hasn't yet been socialized because everyone is busy, and they haven't had a chance to connect, these touchpoints provide the time and place to do it. If it turns out to be something that should be taken off-line, or ends up not being an issue, so be it. But at least the team has a forum to touch base once in a while, and it's also a good way for the deal team leader and project manager to stay on top of the progress that's being made so that deadlines are met, and there won't be any surprises at the end.

The typical format for these touchpoints is for the deal team leader or project manager to first give an update on the deal from their perspectives. After all, these folks have a much more holistic view of what's going on in the deal than the individual functional teams do. Then, each functional leader can give an update for their groups. How things are going. If things are on track. If any problems or issues need to be discussed. If not, there's no need to take notes or take up anybody's time, only if there are issues that need to be discussed or followed-up on.

Before the touchpoints end, there should always be an opportunity to allow any team members a chance voice any concerns or issues that weren't discussed, or to ask any final questions. Going once, going twice, meeting ends. Keep it short and to the point. And the people that took follow-ups and to-dos, know what they'll need to discuss on the next call.

Of course, these team-wide touch points should never replace any of the informal conversations and communications that should naturally be happening between team members. Instead, they're intended to be a way to get the whole team together, to focus as a group. In some deals, where there are tight deadlines, having daily calls or meetings at the end of every day sometimes make sense. Whereas on other deals, if the timing is a little more relaxed, weekly calls or meetings might work better. In any event, it's the team's project manager that will usually decide and organize these touchpoints, based on whatever deadlines are involved.

Investment Committee Involvement

During the due diligence phase of a deal, it's a best practice for the deal team leader to keep the investment committee up to speed on how the deal is progressing. Keeping them informed, involved, and seeking their advice on any technical questions or issues where it's needed.

Keeping the investment committee informed, involved, and part of any important decisions that are being made is important for two reasons. First, it helps facilitate a smooth decision-making process at the end of a deal when it's time to request the committee's approval to sign agreements. And second, it helps make sure that the committee is supportive of any important decisions that are being made as a deal is happening, so that there isn't any second guessing after the fact, or re-trading of things later in the deal.

The level of a committee's involvement will be different from buyer to buyer, and deal to deal. It all depends on how deeply the committee wants to be involved, the committee's management style, and the confidence level that they have in their teams carrying out the work. There really is no set rule. Instead, it's up to the deal team leader's judgement and the investment committee's wants. But it's for this reason if nothing else, that above all others, it's the deal team leader that needs to know the process that the investment committee expects its teams to follow and when the committee wants to be involved.

Due Diligence Reports

As due diligence nears its completion, each of the individual functional teams will need to prepare and circulate their due diligence reports. Again, if the team's communications were tight during due diligence, then there really shouldn't be any surprises. But even though there shouldn't be anything new, reports still need to be written so that there are shareable documents and a paper trail that explains what work was done, the issues that were identified, and the team's recommendations.

A typical due diligence report from any one of the functional areas should cover things like the scope of due diligence that was performed, the details that were learned or observed from doing the work, and of course, the team's key findings and recommendations.

Depending on the circumstances of the deal, and the span of coverage for the individual functional areas, these reports can tend to be quite long and include a lot of details. Details that are unfortunately necessary for two reasons. For one, the reports sometimes need to be shared with a wide audience, including people that might not have been involved in the deal who still need to know what work was done, and the findings. The other, is for risk management.

As for sharing the report with a wide audience, it's highly unlikely that the functional teams' reports will be read cover-to-cover by the people who've been involved in the deal. Instead, these reports are more likely to be shared, read, and analyzed by people who were either only partially involved, or not involved at all. For example, an executive on the business team who needs to know what they're buying, or one that needs to come up with a transition and integration plan. Some of these people may not have been deeply involved up to this point. For them, it's important to have a well written document that provides enough detail so that they can get comfortable with the work that was done and to understand the issues that were identified. Having a report that can do these things helps its readers spend less time worrying if anything was missed, and more time focusing on the issues that matter. If a report doesn't have enough detail, the reader will have questions. Lots of questions.

As for the point on risk management, for anyone who prepares these reports it's important to remember that occasionally blow-ups do happen after a deal. It's unfortunate, but it's true. Not only that, but when there are problems after a deal they might not surface for months or even years after a deal closed when something eventually bubbles-up to the surface. How could this have happened? What did we know, when did we know it? Did the seller misrepresent something? Was it missed in due diligence? Did someone forget to follow-up?

In reality, a buyer never has perfect information. Instead, you do the best job you can with the information that you have. It's unfortunate, but true, that some people tend to have selective memories when things go wrong, and they'll tend to start pointing fingers rather than just fess-up and fix things. Maybe the issue was identified at the time of the deal, but then someone forgot to follow-up and fix it. Maybe the issue was considered immaterial. Or, maybe the issue didn't exist at the time of the deal and it happened after the fact.

Whatever the case, if something was identified in due diligence, or discussed as being an issue at the time of the deal, it needs to be documented. Not only to be able to point back to a report as proof of the matter, but so that things don't get missed. Remember, people are busy in the middle of a deal. They're doing a million things. And once people move on to the next two, three, or four projects, memories fade and details tend to be forgotten. So, when it comes to due diligence reports, they need to be thorough and clear. Especially if there is an issue to document. If an issue was identified, then regardless of how thoroughly it was discussed at the time of the deal, it's better to repeat it in a report so that it's not forgotten, rather than risk something being missed or not fixed down the road.

While a deep level of detail in due diligence reports is unfortunately necessary for the reasons we just mentioned, they can often be too much detail for a high-level executive who doesn't have a lot of time to read enormous reports, but still needs to make decisions. These executives are usually relying on their teams to be going through the details for them, and they only want to know what they need to know. For this reason, it's important that every single due diligence report, whether it's generated internally or externally, has a crisp, concise executive summary sitting on top of it. An executive summary that clearly pinpoints what the decision makers need to be aware of. What the key issues were, how the key issues were addressed, and if they weren't addressed, what's the action plan to dealing with them. This is what the executive decision makers need to know from each functional group.

Finalizing the Deal

It may go without saying, but the importance of issues that can be identified in due diligence, and the timing in which a buyer may want to address them with a seller, can obviously vary. From showstoppers that once identified can put an entire deal on hold, to the less severe items that a team may not want to bring-up with a seller until much later in the process. Once due diligence begins wrapping up though, it's time to address any open items that haven't been resolved yet. This includes deciding what's important enough to reopen negotiations, versus what's small enough that it can be dealt with after the deal has closed. Hopefully though, if you've made it this far in the deal, you're not sitting on anything that can't be resolved, and most of what's left can be negotiated so that even if each side isn't getting exactly what they want, they're at least finding a compromise that each can agree to.

This is also the point in a deal where the team will formalize its plans for onboarding and integrating the business, finalize its model, and review the final drafts of the purchase agreement, making sure that any questions, concerns, or comments have been addressed. Once all these things have been taken care of and the team believes it's ready to sign a deal there's one last step. Getting the investment committee's approval.

Investment Committee Approval

Once due diligence is complete, and the business and functional teams have all signed-off, the deal should be ready to go to the investment committee for their approval to sign the purchase agreement. But before doing that, the deal team leader should be going through a mental (and maybe even a physical) checklist of all the items that the investment committee is likely to expect.

- Were all the appropriate business and functional leaders involved in the deal?

- Are the business and functional leaders satisfied that enough due diligence was done, and that all the important items have been addressed?

- Has the buy-side financial model been reviewed and agreed to by all the appropriate business and functional experts?

- Are the business team leaders who will be responsible for the deal aligned and committed to achieving the results that are baked into the model?

- Have the buyer's legal advisors and general counsel reviewed and approved the purchase agreement?

- Are the price and terms of the deal consistent with what was envisioned when the LOI was signed? If not, what's changed? Is the price still fair and are the terms still reasonable?

If the deal team leader is uncomfortable on any of these points, it might be a good idea to retrace some steps and get comfortable before going to the committee. But if all is good, or the team has taken things as far as they can and need the committee's guidance, then proceed as planned.

To facilitate the committee's review, a document should be prepared, similar to what was done earlier in the deal. One that provides all the relevant information that the committee should know in order to make a well-informed decision. Ideally, it's a document that builds off of what was used earlier in the deal when the investment committee approved entering into the LOI. But now that diligence is done and the team knows a lot more about the business, the write-up should include the due diligence summaries from each of the functional areas, highlighting the issues that were identified, and explaining how those issues were resolved. If issues were identified that couldn't be resolved, these should also be communicated. Either with a plan of how the issues will be resolved, or if they can't be, what's the risk going forward.

Also, now that due diligence is done and the financial model is complete, the write-up should include all the final purchase price metrics, along with a summary of the final terms of the deal. The model should also be available for the committee to review. Most specifically, for the CFO's team to review. All of this should be clearly communicated for the committee so that nothing is being hidden or withheld from their ability to make a fully informed decision.

After the investment committee has had a reasonable amount of time to review the materials, it's more likely than not that they'll need a call or a meeting to discuss any questions, comments or concerns they have. Coming from all this, the committee will either approve the deal, ask the team to go back and renegotiate, or decide it's a deal that doesn't work and kill it. If approved by the investment committee, some organizations will have additional levels of approval, including the CEO's approval (if the CEO isn't already on the investment committee), and possibly board approval, depending on the size of the deal.

Chapter 7: Signing and Closing

Once a buyer and seller have finished negotiating a deal, and the documents are in order, they'll each sign the purchase agreement. Signing though, doesn't mean the deal is closed. The difference between signing and closing is that when a deal is signed, the buyer and seller are now committed to doing the deal as its defined in the agreement. It's not closed, because money didn't change hands yet. Closing is when the actual exchange of money takes place and the buyer assumes ownership of whatever it is that they're buying. These two events (of signing and closing) sometimes happen at the same time, but usually happen separately because of closing conditions.

Closing Conditions

A closing condition is some sort of an event or a requirement that needs to happen before a deal can close. For example, the buyer may have discovered an issue in due diligence that needs to be fixed before the buyer is willing to close. Or, the deal may be large enough that it needs the buyer and seller to file a pre-merger notification with the Federal Trade Commission (or the "FTC") under the Hart-Scott-Rodino Act (known as an "HSR" filing). With HSR filings, there's a minimum waiting period so that the government can review the deal before it closes. Or, there could be third-party consents that are needed in order to transfer important contracts in a deal.

There could be any number of closing conditions that could prevent a deal from closing until they're done. But by this point in a deal, both the buyer and seller want to close. The buyer wants to begin moving forward with its plans, and the seller wants its money. Which means, that both sides are usually pretty motivated by this point to follow-through so that the deal can close as soon as the closing conditions are met.

The Period Between Signing and Closing

The period between signing and closing can last days, weeks or sometimes months, depending on the amount of time that's involved in satisfying the closing conditions. During this time, the buyer is committed to buying the business. But they don't yet own it, operate it, or control it. There's a risk when you're committed to buying a business and things can happen that are outside of your control. So, whenever there's a gap between signing and closing, buyers need to do certain things, both operationally and legally, to protect themselves and make sure that there aren't going to be any surprises once the deal closes.

On the operational side of things, the business and finance teams in particular should be monitoring the performance of the business. They should be getting weekly and monthly operating reports, financial statements, and have conversations with the target about how the business continues to trend all the way up until closing. This way, the buy-side teams can continue to build on the relationships that were started in due diligence and stay up to speed on the operations of the business, in order to make sure that they're prepared to take ownership once the deal closes.

On the legal side of things, because again this is a legal transaction, there are certain provisions that need to be negotiated and included in the purchase agreement before signing. Provisions that not only make sure that the buyer will have the access it needs to monitor the business between signing and closing, but also so that the buyer is protected from the fact that they don't yet control the business. These include covenants, modifications to the seller's reps and warranties, and a material adverse change clause. We'll explain.

Covenants

Covenants are basically promises to do or not do something. In an M&A deal, when there's a delay between signing and closing, the buyer needs to negotiate covenants that will protect the buyer for the fact that the seller will still own and operate the business until the deal closes. These types of covenants usually include things like, having the seller continue to operate the business in the normal course. That the seller will continue to maintain its insurance coverage. That the seller won't make any significant changes to the business, make any significant purchases over certain dollar amounts, sell any assets, give employees raises, or sign any material contracts without first obtaining the buyer's consent. Also, that the buyer should continue to have access to the target's books and records so that they can monitor the business.

Negotiating these types of covenants not only gives the buyer a sense of comfort for what to expect between signing and closing, but it also helps make sure that the seller is aligned on how the buyer expects the business to operate. In going through the process of discussing and negotiating these covenants, the buyer has the chance to directly discuss these things with the seller and hopefully avoid any unwanted surprises down the road.

Reps and Warranties

Representations and warranties (which are often referred to as 'reps and warranties') are basically just statements that are made in a purchase agreement. For the most part, these statements are made by the seller and they say things like, the seller has the right and authority to make the sale. That there are no legal proceedings against the company. That the financial statements of the business are complete and accurate. That there are no undisclosed liabilities. And while reps and warranties can never replace the importance of a buyer doing good due diligence, they do help form the basis of what a buyer relies on when buying a business.

You see, a buyer never has perfect information, no matter how much due diligence they do. And while a seller may also not have perfect information, they usually know a lot more about the business than the buyer does. This is where reps and warranties help, by bridging the gap between a buyer's due diligence and what a seller knows, or should know, about the business that's being sold.

In due diligence, a buyer will usually identify all sorts of potential risks and liabilities. Once known, the buyer can negotiate and price those things into the deal. But for anything that wasn't identified, in other words, the unknown risks, a seller's reps and warranties will usually help provide that added sense of comfort, giving a buyer at least something to rely on.

In the event that something did pop-up after a deal closed where it turned out that any of those reps and warranties weren't true, it's called a breach. And when there is a breach, a buyer could have a claim against a seller, and the seller may have to make good on that claim. We'll discuss more on this when we get to part two of the book.

So, why did we bring this up now? Because, in deals that have a delay between signing and closing, buyers need to make sure that the agreements are clear, so that not only do the seller's reps and warranties need to be true when the deal is signed, but they also need to be true at the time of closing. This way, if there was ever a breach for something that occurred between signing and closing, the buyer still has a basis for making a claim.

Material Adverse Change

A material adverse change (or a "MAC") clause, which is sometimes referred to as material adverse effect (or an "MAE") clause, is a standard legal concept that's used in purchase agreements. It often serves two purposes. First, it can be used to set a materiality threshold for a seller's disclosure requirements. What does that mean? Well, it basically means that if something wasn't disclosed by a seller, but that it wouldn't have been material anyway, then the seller won't be on the hook for it. But another purpose, when there's a delay between signing and closing, is that it can give a buyer the ability to back-out of a deal if something so bad happens between signing and closing, that it causes a material adverse change to the business, or it has a material adverse effect on the business. It's sometimes referred to as a buyer's MAC-out.

If some unexpected event happens between signing and closing, and it actually causes a material adverse change to the business, having the ability to back out of the deal means that the buyer can either walk away completely, or use the threat of walking away to renegotiate the deal. In either case, it's a standard contractual protection in a purchase agreement that's intended to prevent buyers from having to go through with a deal if something really bad happens. At the same time, a MAC-out is something that a seller usually wants to limit as much as possible, because the seller wants the deal to go through no matter what. This is why MAC clauses are almost always heavily negotiated between the buy-side and sell-side lawyers.

Buy-side lawyers want a MAC-out to provide as much flexibility as possible for a buyer. They might define it in an agreement to say… 'any change, event, fact, or circumstance that has, or would 'reasonably' be expected to have, a material adverse effect on the business…' Doesn't that sound like it could mean just about anything?

A seller's lawyer will want to limit the buyer's ability to back out. So, a seller's lawyer will usually define a number of things that won't be allowed to qualify as a MAC-out in the contract. They'll specifically exclude things like changes to the economy, credit markets, political conditions, acts of war, and even general business conditions. They'll basically want to exclude anything that's outside the control of the seller or could otherwise be considered a normal business risk.

Sometimes, the MAC-out becomes so heavily negotiated, that it can 'loose its teeth.' As a buyer, there's no point in getting hung-up on this. Instead, if there's a specific concern that would cause you to lose sleep at night, or something that would make you not want to buy the business if it happened before closing, then rather than rely on a heavily negotiated MAC clause, discuss it specifically with the seller and call it out in the agreement as a condition to close. This way, if the issue you were worried about became true, there's a specifically agreed point clearly called out in the agreement as a reason that the deal doesn't have to go through.

Closed Deals

For the outside advisors that worked on a deal, closing usually marks the end of the project. But for the buyer, the process of onboarding, integrating, and operating the business is only just beginning. This is where the 'rubber meets the road' on why the buyer wanted to do the deal in the first place.

Remember earlier when we said that the fundamental question for whether or not a deal should be considered successful, is whether or not it produced its intended results? Well, now it's time to deliver on those results. And this is why it was so important to have involved the business team that would ultimately be running that business in the deal from the beginning. Getting their input, alignment, and support for the deal. On strategy, synergies, and plans for operating the business going forward. Because now, it's the business team that will be executing, on all of it.

Onboarding and Integrating

When a business is acquired, a buyer could decide to leave it alone and let it operate the way it always has, or they could want to make changes, sometimes a lot of changes. Changes to the business itself, its operations, the way it interacts with customers, its relationships with suppliers, its people's roles, who they report to, their processes, their systems, the list can go on.

When a new buyer steps in and intends to make changes to a newly acquired business, there's risk. Risk that things don't go well. Risk that problems pop-up, and that what was initially thought to be a short-term transition, drags out into a longer, more complicated process than it needed to be.

If not managed well, there can be disruptions to a business, and any disruptions to a business, especially after an acquisition, can cause issues with customers, suppliers, business partners, and employees. Unhappy customers can leave, and anxious employees can find new jobs. The last thing you want after you just bought a business is for any of these things to happen. So, when changes are going to be made to a newly acquired business, there needs to be a good amount of up-front planning, and good execution, with as little disruption to the business as possible.

Integration Planning

Well before you get to signing, early-on in a deal process, a buyer should be thinking about what it plans to do with the business after it's been acquired. Planning what changes will take place, if any, how those changes will take place, and when those changes will take place. It all needs to be well-thought-out, before a deal is signed, and in as much detail as possible. With realistic cost estimates and realistic timelines. And all of it, should mapped-out and reflected in the buyer's model that the business teams will commit to achieving.

In almost every acquisition, both the planning and roll-out of changes that need to be made to a business are done, not just by the business teams themselves, but also with the support of different functional groups. Finance, HR, IT, tax, legal, and others. Each group usually has its own role to play in both planning and implementing whatever changes need to happen. And yes, all of it, needs to be planned and coordinated in an organized way, so that once a deal closes, the newly acquired business doesn't get overwhelmed with whatever new changes are taking place by all of the different workstreams.

Integration Management

Making changes to a newly acquired business requires organization, attention, and focus. Attention and focus that sometimes the business teams may not have. That's because, after an acquisition, the business teams are usually so busy doing what they've always done that they don't always have time for managing an extra project or two. Especially now that they are also involved in operating a newly acquired business. So, when a buyer is planning to make more than a few simple changes to a business, changes that involve more than a few workstreams, an integration manager might be a good idea.

An integration manager's role is to provide the organization, attention, and focus that's needed to support and manage whatever changes are planned for a newly acquired business. Managing these changes in such a way that things get done, but with as little disruption to the business as possible. This allows the business teams to focus on what they need to do, which is onboarding and operating the newly acquired business, while the integration manager can make sure that all the planned changes are still taking place.

It's an important role, that to be effective, requires the right skillsets and experience. Remember when we said, earlier in the book that the skills required to buy a business, are different than the skills required to run a business? Well in a similar way, the skills required to manage an integration are different too. It's a skillset that requires a combination of operational experience, project management, and good communications. Ideally, it's someone from within the organization who has the institutional knowledge of knowing who to go to and for what. But like all other roles in an acquisition, if there aren't people in-house that have the skillsets to manage an integration, there are plenty of outside consulting firms that specialize in this type of work and can help.

Similar to how roles and responsibilities are designed when executing a deal, the same principles can often apply when managing an integration. So previously, where there may have been a centralized deal team leader supported by a business team and functional experts, there will now be an integration manager, supported by a business team and functional experts. And where the deal team leader would have reported to an investment committee, the integration manager can report to the newly combined business team's leadership, who sometimes might decide to setup an integration steering committee if the project is big enough.

Communications

Once a deal closes, and a business changes hands, there needs to be good communications right off the bat to the business' key stakeholders. Letting its customers, suppliers, partners, and employees all know right up front what to expect. What the long-term strategy is, what types of changes are expected, and what types of opportunities lie ahead in the newly combined businesses.

Getting out in front on these types of communications, and taking the lead in delivering these messages, not only helps put stakeholders' minds at ease with what they should expect, but it also helps get ahead of any rumors about the direction that the business is going. Setting the stage, and hopefully buying some goodwill, for whatever change is also about to happen.

Monitoring the First Year

The first few days, weeks, and months of owning a newly acquired business is a sensitive time. Because not only did the buyer just pay a lot of money for the business, but immediately, just by the fact that ownership changed hands, the business is going through a transition. Maybe the biggest one it ever has. As a buyer, you want to make sure this transition goes smoothly, that the business gets off to a good start, and that over time it performs as you would have expected.

As with all important business activities, the financial and operating performance of a newly acquired business should be monitored. Because no matter how well-thought-out plans were, how good communications are, or how solid the execution is, unexpected things can still happen.

Of course, many issues that pop-up can be learned about and dealt with in real-time as a business is transitioned and onboarded. But you can't only rely on what you see as you go through this process. And you don't want to wait until the end of a first quarter or a year when numbers are reported to see if things are performing as was expected. As a buyer, you need to keep an eye on performance in as real a time as possible, and at a minimum be looking at monthly financial results.

The monthly financial results of an acquired business need to be tracked and compared to the model that the team committed to achieving when the deal was signed. It's the only way to know if things are going according to plan. This isn't to say that your plan won't change. But the deal's model is your starting point. Every month, every quarter. For at least the first year.

Is the business performing how you expected? How are sales? Are operating expenses on-track? How's integration going? Are synergies on track? Did any unexpected issues or problems pop-up? If there's any reason why the business isn't performing, you'll want to know about it. This way, you can figure out what's happening and do something about it.

Not only is it good management to stay on top of how things are going. But it's also a way to keep an eye on the commitments that were made. So that when all is said and done, you'll know if the acquisition produced its intended results. If it didn't you should know why, so you can avoid from making that mistake again.

Part Two:
Structuring Deals

*'What are you buying, what are you paying,
and what are the terms?'*

Chapter 8: M&A Deal Structures

The structure of a deal basically refers to how a deal is put together in order to capture its terms and conditions. As a buyer, there are different structures to choose from when negotiating a deal with a seller. But before you can decide which one of these structures is likely to work best, you need to know the answer to three main questions. What are you buying, what are you paying, and what are the terms? It may sound straight forward, and it can be, but there's actually a lot that goes into answering these three questions.

For example, as it relates to the first question of, what you're buying. Are you buying the stock of a business, or are you buying the assets? Are you buying the whole business, meaning 100% of it? Or, are you buying something less than that? Are there pieces of the business that you don't want and would like to leave behind?

How about the second question of, what you're paying? How did you value the business? Will you be paying a fixed price for it, or will there be price adjustments for things that you don't know yet? What about the third question of what the terms are? As a buyer, are you getting enough protection in the deal just in case it turns-out that you didn't get what you thought you had bargained for?

Answering these three questions, actually involves a lot of financial, legal, tax, and other decisions that all need to be thought through. Economically and legally. Do you know what these are? And how do you know if you're making the right decisions?

Using a Common Deal Structure

In the middle market, deals can be structured in a number of different ways. Some of these structures are considered to be very common and widely used, while others can tend to be more customized and unique. For the highly customized deals, these tend to be more of the one-offs. In other words, a common deal structure didn't necessarily work for what the buyer and seller were trying to do, so they modified one. But for the most part, in the middle market, the overwhelming majority of deals are not one-offs, and will tend to use a common deal structure. Why? Because these common deal structures have been proven to work for both buyers and sellers time and time again.

In this part of the book, we'll explain what the most commonly used deal structures are for middle market deals. We'll explain the mechanics of how they work, and how the different components of these structures can help not only protect buyers, but also keep a deal's economics fair to both sides. We'll also explain the basic financial, legal, tax, and other issues that both buyers and sellers will often need to think through when answering the three main questions that need to be decided before choosing a structure.

By understanding the things that we'll talk about in this section of the book, once a buyer knows the answers to the three main questions of what they're buying, what they're paying, and what the terms are, it should be a fairly straight forward decision as to which structure should work best.

Also, by having a good understanding of some of the more commonly used deal structures and their main provisions, buyers will know what to watch-out for if a deal ever starts to stray from what's considered a commonly used structure, into something that's more of a one-off. Where if anything important is missed, or if any of the protections that a common deal structure would provide aren't there, it could end-up hurting you.

Commonly Used Deal Structures

In the middle market, stock deals and asset deals, valued on a cash-free, debt-free basis, with working capital adjustments are very common. Stock deals with locked-box mechanisms are also used, but these are much more common in Europe than they are in the U.S.

Do these terms sound like a foreign language to you? If they do, don't worry. In the next few chapters, we're going to explain them. What they are, how they work, and how to negotiate them.

Chapter 9: Stock Deals, Asset Deals, and Mergers

The first step in deciding how you want to structure a deal is choosing which 'type' of deal you want to do. This means deciding if you want to do a stock deal, an asset deal, or a merger. Each of these different types of deals have different characteristics that can be either positive or negative, to buyers or sellers, depending on the specific facts and circumstances that are involved. In this chapter we'll explain what stock deals, asset deals, and mergers are. We'll explain the basic differences between them, and we'll point-out some of the more common things that buyers and sellers should be thinking about when deciding which type of deal they want to do.

Stock Deals

In a stock deal, a buyer purchases equity in a legal entity and in doing so becomes an owner of that entity. The entity that's involved could be a C-corporation, an S-corporation, or a Limited Liability Company (known as an "LLC"). And while technically, corporations have stock and LLCs have membership interests, the concept of what happens when a buyer purchases equity is the same. So for purposes of this book, we refer to all deals in which a buyer purchases equity as a stock deal.

In a stock deal, a buyer purchases shares of stock (or in the case of an LLC, membership interests) directly from one or more of a target's selling shareholders (or in the case of an LLC, its selling members). Once this exchange happens between the buyer and the seller (or sellers), the buyer becomes an owner in that business. The legal entity itself doesn't change, only the ownership changes. And since nothing at the legal entity itself changes, the buyer becomes an owner in everything that comes with it. All its history, all its assets, and all its liabilities.

In a stock deal, a buyer can purchase all (meaning 100%) of the equity in a business, or they can purchase something less than that. Say 75%, or 50%, or 30%. Although generally, a buyer won't get control of a business unless they acquire more than 50% of it and can gain control over whatever voting rights exist.

Sellers usually prefer doing stock deals when selling their businesses. The first reason, although it depends on the type of legal entity that's involved, is that when a seller sells their stock to a buyer, for tax purposes, it's generally treated as long-term capital gains. As we'll discuss later, this can be a much more favorable tax outcome for a seller than when compared to an asset deal. The second reason sellers prefer stock deals, is that by selling their stock, they leave all the liabilities of that business behind with the legal entity. It's for these two reasons (favorable tax treatment and the ability to walk away from liabilities), that sellers tend to prefer stock deals.

Asset Deals

In an asset deal, a buyer purchases the specific assets that make-up a business, and assumes whatever liabilities are specifically agreed to. The way it works, is that instead of a buyer purchasing the stock of a legal entity (to acquire a business), the legal entity will sell and transfer the specific assets and liabilities that make-up the business, to the buyer. If there are assets or liabilities that the buyer doesn't want, those can be left behind in the legal entity that the seller will still own.

These deals are usually structured so that the buyer acquires 'all, or substantially all' of the tangible and intangible assets that are used to operate a business. Usually, this includes all of the accounts receivable, inventory, fixed assets, contracts, tradenames, and intellectual property. The employees of the business will usually come over too. And while a buyer could agree to take-on all of the liabilities that are associated with that business, in an asset deal a buyer will usually only agree to take-on specific liabilities, like its trade payables and accrued operating expenses.

Buyers usually prefer doing asset deals. The first reason is that buyers generally get better tax deductions in an asset deal, where they're able to deduct a much higher amount of depreciation and amortization expense (for tax purposes) than they would in a stock deal. We'll discuss more on this later. The second reason is that buyers usually have the ability to leave behind (or not assume) any unwanted liabilities. Although this isn't always the case, which we'll also discuss. It's for these two reasons (better tax deductions and the ability to leave behind unwanted liabilities) that buyers tend to prefer asset deals.

Mergers

In a merger, two legal entities merge into one, where one entity disappears, and a surviving entity remains. The surviving entity contains all the assets and liabilities of the two previously separate companies. Out of the three different types of deals (stock deals, asset deals, and mergers), mergers are by far the most complicated. From a legal perspective, from a regulatory perspective, and from a tax perspective.

First, they're governed by legal statutes, which in the U.S. depends on the state in which a business is incorporated. Second, there are different types of mergers, and depending on the type of merger used and the form of payment made to sellers, there can be different tax treatments. Making them taxable as either stock deals, asset deals, or potentially tax-free. And third, in a merger, a buyer's legal entity completely merges with the target. Meaning that all the assets and liabilities of the buyer's legal entity now become comingled with the target's. And because they are no longer separate legal entities, the buyer's assets become vulnerable to satisfying whatever liabilities the target brings over. It's because of this, that buyers will usually have to take an extra step of setting-up a merger subsidiary to merge with a target, so that the buyer's upstream assets are protected.

Mergers are very complicated. And when a deal is more complicated, it's more expensive to do because of all the time that lawyers, accountants, and others need to spend on it. So, why then are mergers used at all? Well, it's because one of the main benefits of doing a merger is that generally, a buyer doesn't need the approval of all a target's selling shareholders to do it. In a merger, because they're governed by statues, a buyer can generally work-up a deal with a target's management team, and once it's approved by that company's board of directors, it only needs a majority of the company's selling shareholders to approve it. This is why mergers are more common when a target is publicly traded. Because if it's publicly traded, and there's a large number of shareholders to deal with, then it may not be practical or even possible to get every single shareholder's approval. But by doing a merger, a buyer can negotiate a deal, and acquire 100% of the business.

Mergers are not that common in the middle market. Because in the middle market, many businesses are privately owned, and buyers are usually talking directly with a target company's selling shareholders. In these situations, stock deals and asset deals are much more common and practical. And they can be much more easily be tailored to the specific terms and conditions that a buyer and seller want to negotiate. With far fewer legal, regulatory, and tax complications. Because mergers are not that common in the middle market, and incredibly technical, this book doesn't focus on them. Instead, this book focuses on the much more commonly used stock and asset deal structures, because these represent an overwhelming majority of what actually takes place in the middle market each year.

Tax Considerations for Sellers

When a seller is selling all or even just a piece of their business, more likely than not, their number one goal is to maximize the amount of cash they'll be able to walk away with from the deal, after paying their taxes. But depending on the legal entity that's involved, the difference between doing a stock deal and an asset deal can have very different tax consequences for a seller. This is especially the case when the seller's entity is a C-corporation.

When a seller sells stock in a C-corporation, they only pay tax once, on the gain that they realize from the sale of their stock. But because C-corporations are taxable entities, if a seller of a C-corporation does an asset deal, they end-up paying tax twice. First on the sale of the assets, and then again on the distribution of proceeds to the selling shareholders. It's what's known as double taxation.

Here's how it works. When a seller of a C-corporation does an asset deal, the C-corporation first sells and transfers its assets to the buyer. The C-corporation has to pay tax on any gains it realizes from the sale of those assets at the corporate level. Then, when the proceeds from that sale are distributed to its shareholders, those shareholders pay tax on the distributions at the individual level.

It's because of these two layers of tax (at whatever rates apply in the specific tax jurisdictions involved), that sellers of C-corporations can end-up paying much higher taxes in an asset deal than they would in a stock deal. Because again, in a stock deal a seller will only pay tax once on the gain that they realize from the sale of their stock, and it's usually at a more favorable long-term capital gains rate. This difference in tax treatment is usually the number one reason why sellers of C-corporations prefer doing stock deals.

S-corporations and LLCs, for the most part, don't tend to have this problem with double taxation. Unless, in the case of an LLC, they made an election to be taxed as a C-corporation. But assuming that's not the case, these are what's known as pass-through entities. Pass-through entities don't pay tax at a corporate, or entity level. Instead, their profits and losses pass-through the entity and their owners only pay tax once at the individual level.

It can get very complicated, where certain events can trigger different tax treatment, but for the most part, when it comes to asset deals and pass-through entities, some gains will be taxable as ordinary income, and the rest will be treated as long-term capital gains. But, there's no double taxation. This makes the difference that a seller will pay in tax between a stock deal and an asset deal much less of a problem in a pass-through entity. In fact, in some cases, like with LLCs, there are special tax rules and the tax treatment of a stock deal could end-up being exactly the same as an asset deal for both the buyer and seller anyway.

When it comes to taxes, things can get very complicated, and the consequences of choosing between an asset deal and a stock deal can make a real difference for a seller in terms of how much money they're going to walk away with. This is why, sellers should always have their tax advisors provide guidance before agreeing to a deal structure. This way, they can evaluate whatever tax treatment applies to their specific situation and compare what their after-tax proceeds would be if they decided to do a stock deal or an asset deal.

As a buyer, you want to make sure this is ironed-out early on a deal, before an LOI is signed. Because the last thing you want, is for a seller to change their mind later in a deal, especially if due diligence is almost done, and agreements have already been drafted.

Benefits of Asset Deals for Buyers

For buyers, asset deals usually provide much better tax deductions than stock deals. This is for two main reasons. The first reason is that in an asset deal, buyers are allowed to 'step-up' the value of any tangible assets that are acquired, to their current fair market values. These tangible assets are basically a business' physical assets like its inventory, buildings, and equipment. By being able to step these values up from their previous carrying amounts to their current values, a buyer will usually get better depreciation deductions (for tax purposes), going forward.

The second reason, and this is usually a big one, is that in an asset deal, a buyer can amortize and deduct (for tax purposes), the value of all the intangible assets and goodwill that are acquired. This basically means that for tax purposes, they get to deduct whatever purchase price was paid in excess of the tangible assets that were acquired.

Remember, in a stock deal when a buyer purchases stock, nothing changes at the company level. Only the ownership changes. So, for tax purposes, all the pre-existing asset values remain the same, and they continue to depreciate and amortize the way they always have. But in an asset deal, these are all newly acquired assets for tax purposes. So, the buyer gets to reset their values. When these values are reset, they're usually being reset at higher amounts than the target was carrying them at. This is because the target probably already depreciated and amortized these things for a while, which made their carrying values lower than their current values. When a buyer gets to step these values back up to something more current, it usually means they get a higher basis in those assets, and better tax depreciation deductions because of it. And whatever purchase price is paid in excess of those tangible assets (meaning any amount that's paid for the intangible assets and goodwill), that gets amortized and deducted over a period of 15-years in an asset deal, which can be a very significant tax benefit.

So just to recap, because this is an important point, what really ends up happening in an asset deal, between being able to step up the value of the tangible assets, and then being able to amortize and deduct the intangible assets and goodwill, is that for the most part, the entire purchase price in an asset deal is either depreciated or amortized for tax purposes. A very good thing for buyers when they can get it.

Net Operating Losses

One thing we didn't mention yet about stock deals, is that while it generally is the case that nothing changes at the company level, there are certain exceptions. One exception is when a corporation has net operating losses (also known as "NOLs"). An NOL is when a corporation has net operating losses (for tax purposes) in any given year.

Prior to recent tax changes, those losses could be carried back two years, to get an income tax refund (if the company was profitable in those two years), and they could be carried forward for up to 20 years to offset future income taxes. A few years ago, as part of the Tax Cuts and Jobs Act of 2017, these rules changed. Now, you can no longer carry losses back to get a refund, but you can carry those losses forward indefinitely and use them to offset up to 80% of taxable income each year until they're fully used.

NOLs are often seen in situations where the owners of a business invested in that business over time to grow it. Sometimes, incurring years of operating losses (at least for tax purposes) until the company became profitable. In those situations, the NOLs that built-up over time could be quite valuable in terms of shielding the company from having to pay future income taxes.

In stock deals, when a new buyer takes control of a business, Section 382 of the U.S. tax code places restrictions on that buyer's ability to use those NOLs. Where basically, the amount of NOLs that can be used each year gets limited. There's a formula involved that determines the limits. It doesn't mean that the NOLs go away completely, but because they are going to be limited, they're usually not as valuable to a buyer going forward.

In an asset deal, these NOLs don't come over to the buyer. Instead, they remain behind in the seller's legal entity where the seller can potentially use those NOLs to offset any gains that might be realized by doing an asset deal. The calculations can be complicated and will obviously depend on the specific circumstances that are involved. But because of the limitations that are placed on NOLs for buyers, whenever NOLs are present, and the pros and cons of doing a stock deal versus an asset deal are being debated, the buyer and seller should be having their tax advisors look at those NOLs and figure out what value if any there is in preserving those NOLs by doing a stock deal, versus using those NOLs by doing an asset deal.

When Stock Deals Make Sense

So far, we learned that sellers tend to prefer stock deals, and buyers tend to prefer asset deals. Both, for tax reason. But occasionally, a buyer will prefer a stock deal too. It has to do with the ability to transfer assets. You see, in an asset deal, all of the individual assets that are being purchased need to be assigned and transferred to the buyer. Every single one. This includes contracts, permits, licenses, intellectual property, everything. But in some countries, and in some regulated industries, transferring these assets can take a very long time. Sometimes, certain assets can't be transferred at all. In these types of situations, when assigning and transferring assets is a problem from a legal or a regulatory perspective, buyers will often prefer doing stock deals. So that they can acquire a business quickly, and with all the assets that come with it.

Another more common situation though, as far as when a stock deal is going to make sense, is when a seller just won't do an asset deal. Afterall, the seller owns the business, and unless they have to sell to you and only to you, they're going to decide the terms on which they want to do a deal. You can try all you want to negotiate an asset deal, but if a seller will only do a stock deal, as is often the case with the seller of a C-corporation, it means you're either doing a stock deal or you're not doing a deal.

Usually though, a seller's preference to do a stock deal should not be an issue. Afterall, stock deals are very common. Buyers just need to make sure that whether they're doing a stock deal or an asset deal, that they're modeling the correct amount of taxes that they'll pay. We'll explain more about this later in the book. And if you're wondering about exposures to past liabilities, stock deals can still provide mechanisms that will allow buyers to leave behind unwanted liabilities. It's done by getting indemnifications from a seller. We'll discuss this later in the book too.

When Asset Deals Make Sense

Asset deals make sense for both buyers and sellers in many different situations. One such situation, is a carve-out. Let's say for example that there's a seller who owns and operates several different businesses. But all of those different businesses are owned and operated through only one legal entity. Now let's say that the seller wants to sell one of those businesses. In a situation like this, a stock deal probably won't work, because the business that the seller wants to sell isn't housed in its own legal entity. It's part of a bigger group. So here, an asset deal would probably make the most sense. Because in an asset deal, the specific assets, and liabilities that make-up the business can be carved-out, sold, and transferred to a new buyer. By carving out and selling the assets and liabilities that make up the business, the seller's legal entity and all its other operations can be left behind with the seller. This is what's referred to as a carve-out.

Another situation where an asset deal makes sense, is when a buyer really wants to avoid past liabilities. Let's say for example that the seller ran a business, where in the past, they didn't pay all their taxes. Or maybe, they violated some rules or regulations that they should have been following. Because of these things, there could be potential liabilities for past taxes, fines, penalties, or worse. If these things are significant, a disciplined buyer would not want to assume the risk of having to deal with them. So, if in spite of finding these things a buyer still wanted to acquire that business, the buyer would need to structure a deal that leaves those unwanted liabilities behind. In this case, an asset deal might work. Because generally speaking, in an asset deal, a buyer can acquire the assets it wants, assume only the specific liabilities it's willing to accept, and leave all the unwanted stuff behind. Unless that is, if successor liability applies.

Successor Liabilities

The ability to leave unwanted liabilities behind in an asset deal, generally is the case. But, it's not always the case. You see, it actually depends on the nature of the liabilities that are in question, and the legal jurisdiction that's involved. It's called successor liability. And it's where a buyer's lawyer will need to provide guidance because the laws around successor liabilities are different from country to country, and state to state.

In general, when it comes to things like product liabilities, employment related liabilities, taxes, and environmental liabilities, successor liability could apply. If it does, it means that even in an asset deal, a buyer may still be responsible. So, if you're buying a business, even if it's an asset deal, you still need to do your due diligence.

You need to know what potential liabilities could exist, and you need to know where you have exposure. If it turns out that an asset deal won't provide you the protection that you thought you would get, and you still want to do the deal, then you'll need to quantify the exposures, deal with them head-on, and negotiate a structure where the seller will indemnify you if those things materialize. We'll explain how this is done later in the book.

Alternative Tax Elections

Occasionally, a buyer will prefer doing an asset deal for tax purposes, and a seller will be OK with it, but a stock deal still makes the most sense because the target has a lot of contracts, licenses or other assets that could be difficult, or maybe even impossible to transfer in an asset deal. In a situation like this, if the buyer would have preferred doing an asset deal for tax reasons, and the seller would have otherwise been OK with it, there might still be a way to do a stock deal for legal purposes, but get asset deal treatment for tax purposes.

When the target entity is a corporation, it's called a section 338(h)(10) election, named after that section of the U.S. tax code that created it. A section 338(h)(10) election allows a buyer and a seller to do a stock deal legally, but then make a specific tax election that will treat it like an asset deal for tax purposes. If the deal qualifies, the buyer gets the step-up and all the other depreciation and amortization benefits that go along with doing an asset deal. To qualify though, the buyer needs to be a corporation that's acquiring at least 80% of the target, and the target either needs to be an S-corporation, or a corporation that is part of a consolidated group. In other words, the target can't be a stand-alone C-corporation. As long as all the selling shareholders agree, the election can be made, and the stock deal will be treated like an asset deal for tax purposes.

Sometimes, in situations where a seller agrees to do a 338(h)(10) election, it means they'll end-up paying higher taxes because of the asset deal treatment. When this is the case the buyer and seller will usually study the benefits of doing a 338(h)(10) election before deciding to do one. This way, they can make sure that there's more benefit to doing one, in terms of tax savings to the buyer, than not doing one. And just so the seller isn't any worse off, once the benefits have been quantified, the buyer might be willing to increase their purchase price. Sometimes they'll even share in the value of some of the benefits so that they're both ending up better off than they otherwise would have been if they didn't do the election. We'll explain how tax benefits are valued later in the book.

In situations where the target entity is an LLC, different rules apply. With these, if a buyer is acquiring 100% of an LLC, it will generally be treated like an asset deal for the buyer anyway. No special election necessary. But, if a buyer is acquiring less than 100%, the LLC will need to make what's called a section 754 election, which allows the buyer to treat their investment in the LLC as if it were an asset deal for tax purposes.

Advice on Negotiating Structure

Now that we've covered the basics of stock deals and asset deals, you can see, it's not always a straightforward decision as to which type of deal is going to make the most sense. Many factors are involved. The type of entity. What kinds of tax treatments apply? If there are contracts, or assets that would be difficult or impossible to transfer in an asset deal. If there are past liabilities that the buyer wants to avoid. And of course, the seller's preferences. All these things come into play. It comes down to what's practical, what liabilities there are, and tax treatment. It's not only the buyer's decision, it's the seller's decision too. And a lot of what drives the seller, is tax treatment.

In any event, deciding which type of deal to do is the first step in structuring a transaction. There's a lot of thought that should be put into it up front as soon as the buyer and seller start thinking about what a deal might look like. And while the concepts in this chapter are intended to be helpful, they are really only the high-level basics that a buyer and seller should be aware of when starting to piece together a deal.

When you start getting into the details, there could be situations where facts or circumstances can trigger different legal and tax treatment. So, once conversations start evolving from a high-level discussion about which type of deal to do, into something that's more definitive, like a written term sheet or a letter of intent. It's time for both the buyer and the seller to bring in their financial, legal, and tax advisers, so that the overall structure of the deal can be planned out in as much detail as possible up front, and they can avoid from having any unexpected surprises later in the deal.

Chapter 10: Cash-Free, Debt-Free Deals

Earlier in the book, we said that stock deals and asset deals, valued on a cash-free, debt-free basis are common deal structures in the middle market. Then, we explained what stock deals and asset deals are, and the basic differences between them that buyers and sellers should be thinking about when deciding which type of deal they're going to do. In this chapter, we'll explain what it means to be valued on a cash-free, debt-free basis, and conceptually why deals are done that way. In the next chapter, we'll continue the conversation by explaining what a net debt adjustment is, and how that works to settle-up whatever cash or debt actually does exist in a business at closing.

A Primer on Valuation

There are many ways that a buyer can value a business. In the middle market, where many target companies are privately held, it's usually based on a combination of different valuation metrics. Things like purchase price multiples, the calculated enterprise value of a business based on its expected future cash flows, rate of return on investment, and how accretive or dilutive a deal will be. We'll explain more about these different valuation metrics later in the book, but for now, it's just important to keep in mind that it's usually a combination of these things that help a buyer decide what a fair price should be.

Regardless though, of how a buyer decides to value a business, or which combination of valuation metrics they decide to use, the value of a business is almost always based on some measure of its earnings, or some expectation about its future earnings. But it's not just any measure of earnings. Because as a buyer, you want to be using a measure of earnings that represents the underlying business you're buying. This means separating the earnings that are generated by the actual operations of that business, from things that don't necessarily belong or represent those operations, like its capital structure.

Defining the Capital Structure

The capital structure of a business is the amount of cash, short-term investments, debt, and equity that a business has on its balance sheet. It basically represents the result of all the past financial decisions that were made in a business. Decisions on how to fund it, and how to finance its activities.

It could be that a business is sitting completely flush with cash, maybe some short-term investments, and absolutely no debt. Or, it could be that a business has no cash, and it's completely saddled with debt. Either way, its capital structure (meaning how it's capitalized) is the result of the past financial decisions that were made by its owners. Because, it was those owners who chose to fund it through either debt or equity. And it was those owners who chose to either leave cash in the business or take it out.

When there are things like gains or losses from short-term investments, or interest expense related to debt that are flowing through a business' earnings, those things don't necessarily exist in that business because of its operations. They exist because of the funding and financing decisions that were made in the past. These are two different things. This is why buyers will exclude the effects of a business' capital structure when valuing its operations. So that it's clear what those operations are actually worth, separate from its capital structure.

We'll get into the mechanics of how this is done for valuation purposes later in the book. But for now, it's just important to know the concept of why we separate a business' operations from its capital structure when valuing a business. Because what we're really doing, is valuing its operations separate from whatever funding and financing decisions were made in the past by its owners. This is what it means, when a business is valued on a cash-free, debt-free basis.

Doing Deals on a Cash-Free, Debt Free Basis

When a buyer values a business on a cash-free, debt-free basis, it pretty much means exactly what it sounds like. The buyer is valuing the business as if it had no cash or debt in it. Again, the concept is quite simple in that the buyer is placing a value on the underlying operations of that business, regardless of its capital structure. This value is often referred to as the 'headline price' of a deal, or the 'enterprise value' of the business.

When a deal is valued on a cash-free, debt-free basis, it means that the buyer is willing to pay a headline price of 'x' for the business. Based on the value of its operations. But it also means that the seller will be responsible for paying off any debt that the business has. If there happens to be any cash left over after paying off the debt, the seller will get paid for it. But if there's not enough cash in the business to pay off the debt, then it will have to come out of the seller's proceeds from the deal. In the next chapter, we'll explain the mechanism that makes this all happen, which is called the net debt adjustment.

The Benefits of Doing Cash-Free Debt-Free Deals

Cash-free, debt-free deals are very practical. From a seller's perspective, if it's a competitive situation, meaning that there are several buyers making offers, having a headline price from each buyer helps make the process of comparing different offers much more straightforward by seeing who is offering the best headline price.

From a buyer's perspective, there are two good reasons to like cash-free, debt-free deals. First, as a buyer, you're probably going to want to change the capital structure of the business anyway. So why not decide the price you're willing to pay for the business and let the seller clean up the old stuff? And second, there's probably going to be a lot of time that passes between the moment that a price is agreed, and when a deal finally closes.

From agreeing on a price, to negotiating the LOI, doing the due diligence, and then eventually negotiating agreements and closing, a lot of time can pass. And in all that time, the amount of cash and debt in a business is probably going to change. It could change a lot, and for any number of reasons. But in a cash-free, debt-free deal, it doesn't really matter. Because the headline price stays the same, and the net debt adjustment, which we'll discuss in the next chapter, provides a

93

mechanism that settles-up whatever cash or debt actually does exist in the business at closing.

Chapter 11: The Net-Debt Adjustment

When a deal is valued on a cash-free, debt-free basis, the capital structure still needs to be dealt with. Settling the business' debt and paying the seller for whatever cash is left over at closing. This is done through the net debt adjustment. The way a net debt adjustment works, is that the headline price, or the enterprise value of the business that's negotiated, becomes the actual purchase price that the buyer will pay for the business. This purchase price though, isn't necessarily the final amount of proceeds that the seller will walk away with. Instead, this purchase price gets increased for the amount of cash and decreased for the amount of debt that's in the business at closing. The seller gets credit for the cash but gets dinged for the debt. It's the net of these two amounts that represents the net debt adjustment.

What the net debt adjustment does, is it takes the enterprise value of the business and adjusts it to arrive at the equity value that the seller should be entitled to. To say it differently, enterprise value, minus net debt, equals equity value. So basically, through it, the seller gets paid for the value of their equity.

An example might help. Let's say that you were looking at a business that you valued at $100 million on a cash-free, debt-free basis. If that business actually had no cash or debt, and you were buying 100% of it, the seller would be entitled to $100 million. But in a different scenario, if that same $100 million business had $20 million of net debt because the seller decided to fund a portion of that business with debt instead of equity, then the seller would only be entitled to $80 million. In other words, $100 million of enterprise value, minus $20 million of net debt, equals $80 million of equity value.

Net debt adjustments are commonly used and accepted. Where things tend to get a little complicated though, is when it comes to how a buyer and seller choose to define what should be included as debt. You'd be surprised, but it's not always straightforward as to what should be or shouldn't be included. There can be a lot of grey areas. And because anything that the buyer wants to treat like debt will reduce the seller's proceeds, you'd better believe that if it's not a clear-cut debt item, it's probably going to be negotiated.

Defining Debt

When it comes to defining debt in in an M&A transaction, some things are almost always included. Things like interest bearing loans, bonds, notes payable, and other long-term debt-like obligations. In other words, the things that you would normally think of as being debt.

In an M&A transaction, if there are any unpaid dividends, those are usually treated like debt too, just so a seller doesn't go declaring a bunch of dividends that a buyer would then have to pay after the deal closed. For these types of items, most M&A lawyers will already have a standard list of what they'd like to see included as debt in the transaction agreements.

Sometimes though, there are special items. Things that you wouldn't necessarily think of as being debt. But they're still treated like debt for purposes of a deal. These items usually fall into one of three different buckets. First, there could be obligations that were created by what were really financial decisions made by the seller. Second, there could be legacy liabilities from things that happened a long time ago, but still haven't been paid. And third, there could be things that a buyer just isn't willing to accept, because they either weren't factored into the buyer's valuation, or it just wouldn't be fair for the buyer to pay them.

Examples of these types of items, which are almost always included as debt in a deal, are accrued interest, finance lease obligations, liabilities related to hedging activities or financial instruments, unfunded pension obligations, unpaid employee severance, restructuring liabilities, past due payables to suppliers that have been stretched well beyond their normal terms, payables to related parties or affiliates that have been under the sellers discretion to pay or not to pay. You see, it's not only the types of things that you would normally think of as being debt.

Income tax liabilities that relate to the time when the seller owned the business are also usually treated like debt. Unless, there's already a specific provision in the agreement that deals with income taxes. Because after all, a seller really ought to be paying their own income taxes.

The list of items that can be included as debt can sometimes be very extensive, and heavily negotiated. The way to think about it though, is that a buyer's valuation is usually based on a measure of earnings that values a business based on its operations, separate from the effects of its capital structure. If that valuation didn't consider cash payments that need to be made for things that aren't part of its normal operations, then a buyer is probably going to want to treat those things like debt so that it's captured in the deal. We'll cover more on valuation when we get to part three of the book.

At the end of the day, when it comes to defining what's considered debt in a deal, it comes down to a buyer doing their due diligence, identifying the items that matter, and having thoughtful negotiations based on experience, what's considered to be market, and what's fair. For an example of what a typical definition of debt looks like in a deal, refer to Appendix Two in the back of this book.

Debt Versus Operating Liabilities

When it comes to defining debt for purposes of a deal, these items shouldn't be confused with what makes up a business' normal operating liabilities. Normal operating liabilities usually include things like payables to suppliers that aren't yet due, accrued payroll, accrued rent, and all the other operating expense type items that are normally incurred in a business but aren't yet due for payment. These types of liabilities are different than debt. Because generally speaking, these types of liabilities relate to a business' normal ongoing operations. Which get paid or settled in the normal course of business when they're due. These types of liabilities are always present when a business conducts its normal day-to-day operations, and they're part of what makes up its working capital.

In most M&A deals, when debt is defined, it almost always excludes the short-term liabilities that are associated with a company's working capital. And working capital gets treated separately in a purchase agreement, through its own adjustment, which we'll discuss in the next chapter.

Negotiating Debt and Debt-Like Items

Now that we've explained how cash-free, debt-free deals work, and the sorts of items that are often included as debt in a deal, you can see that it's not always straight forward. There's a certain amount of judgement as to what should be or shouldn't be included as debt. This is why buyers and sellers can sometimes be thinking about debt differently. If they are, and there are any misunderstandings about what will be treated like debt in a deal, it can cause big issues later in the process when a seller realizes what's happening. Especially if that seller hasn't been through an M&A process before, or if they don't have a good financial advisor that's telling them what to expect.

This is why, when a buyer and seller are discussing the concept of doing a cash-free, debt-free deal, it's on the buyer to be completely up front with how they're viewing debt, and what they think should be included. Any items that are known or believed to exist in a business that the buyer would think of as debt should be clearly communicated. Especially if there's a big-ticket item that someone wouldn't normally think of as being debt. This way, there shouldn't be any confusion, and there shouldn't be any misunderstandings. By addressing it early, if there are any disagreements, they can be dealt with upfront.

As a buyer, if there's any doubt about having a meeting of the minds on what should be included as debt in a deal, you can always include a proposed definition of debt in the letter of intent. This way, it's in writing for the seller and the seller's advisors to review and no one can be accused later in the deal of re-trading terms.

Chapter 12: The Working Capital Adjustment

This may come as a bit of a surprise, but there's a problem with doing cash-free, debt-free deals, and it's a big one. Remember how it works. The purchase price that a buyer pays, gets increased for the amount of cash, and decreased for the amount of debt that's in a business at closing. And that's fair. But because of how it works, sellers are incentivized to have as much cash, and as little debt in the business as possible to maximize their payout. That's the problem. You see, a seller still controls a business all the way up until closing. And there are things that a seller can do to squeeze cash out of a business, so that they can increase their payout. The problem is, these things can both damage a business, and make things more expensive for a buyer.

Let's say for example, that right after signing a deal, a seller incentivized its customers to pay-up faster, stopped buying inventory, and stopped paying all its bills. In the short-term, these things would absolutely increase a company's cash, because the business would still be collecting from its customers, and it wouldn't be paying any bills. The seller could stockpile this cash, use it to pay down debt, or take it out of the business. In any of these cases, it would increase their total payout in a cash-free, debt-free deal. The problem is, it's only temporary and it's designed to benefit the seller, not the business. If a seller did this, and the deal closed, the buyer could be stepping into a business that doesn't have a lot of receivables to collect, could be short on inventory, and could have a lot of past due payables that are owed to its suppliers.

If inventory levels are too low, there could be problems meeting customer orders. If payables are stretched too far, there could be unhappy suppliers ready to cut that business off. A buyer might not only get stuck paying more to a seller for all the cash they squeezed out, but they might even have to inject more cash into the business to get inventory levels back up and pay suppliers. That's the problem with cash-free, debt-free deals. The seller still controls the business and they can game the system if they want, to maximize their payout.

If a seller ever gamed the system this way, it would obviously be unfair. That's because, no buyer should ever have to pay more for a business, just because a seller decided to pull some strings. Especially if those strings were actually hurting the business. But that's how cash-free, debt-free deals work. Which means, a seller is almost always going to be incentivized to do this. The question becomes, how does a buyer prevent it? This is where working capital adjustments come into play, and it's why working capital adjustments are almost always necessary when doing a cash-free, debt-free deal. So that a seller can't game the system.

What is Working Capital?

Working capital is a combination of the short-term assets and liabilities that a business creates as it goes through its day-to-day activities. Short-term assets that include things like accounts receivable from customers, inventory, and prepaid expenses for things like rent and software licenses. And short-term liabilities that include things like accounts payable to suppliers, accrued payroll, and other accrued operating expenses that the business will eventually have to pay.

These kinds of short-term assets and liabilities are created by a business as it goes through its normal day-to-day activities. Serving its customers, buying from suppliers, and compensating its employees. Which by the way, is different than debt. Because debt, can be paid off. But working capital is always there, every day. In fact, there's a cycle to working capital. As receivables get collected, they get replaced with new receivables from more recent sales. As inventory gets sold, it gets replaced with new inventory that will be used to fill future orders. And as payables get paid, they get replaced with new payables from more recent activity. As long as the business is interacting with customers, suppliers, and employees, its working capital will constantly cycle, and will always be there. Day after day, and year after year.

Measuring Working Capital

In an M&A deal, the working capital of a business is normally calculated by taking its current assets (excluding things like cash) and subtracting its current liabilities (excluding things like debt). The net of these two numbers is its net working capital. In other words, it's a business' short-term assets, minus its short-term liabilities, excluding cash and debt. We'll explain why cash and debt are excluded in a minute. But for now, just keep in mind that for purposes of an M&A deal, working capital is meant to capture things like a business' accounts receivable, inventory, payables, and accrued operating expenses. Because these are the sorts of things that a seller can manipulate if they want, to squeeze cash out of a business.

Here's an example, let's say that a business has $10 million of current assets (excluding cash), which is mostly made up of receivables and inventory. And let's say that it has $6 million of current liabilities (excluding debt), which is mostly made up of payables to suppliers and accrued payroll. Its net working capital would be calculated by taking the $10 million of current assets and subtracting the $6 million of current liabilities. So here, net working capital would be $4 million. If this $4 million happened to be the business' normal level of working capital, meaning that it's usually always somewhere around that amount, then it's probably what a buyer would expect that business had, right up to closing.

The Working Capital Adjustment

In an M&A deal, the working capital adjustment increases or decreases the purchase price of a business, up or down, based on the amount of net working capital that exists in a business at closing. The way it works, is that a buyer and seller agree on what a normal level of working capital is for a business, in general. And then, they agree on the amount of net working capital that should be in the business at closing. This number is called the working capital target.

If the business' net working capital at closing, is below the target, it means the buyer got less working capital than was agreed, so the purchase price gets reduced by that amount. If the business' net working capital at closing is above the target, it means the buyer got more working capital than was agreed, so the purchase price gets increased by that amount.

Let's say for example that a buyer and seller agree that a particular business has a normal level of working capital that's usually somewhere around $4 million. And based on that, they agree on a working capital target of $4 million. Now let's say that between signing and closing, the seller decided to stop buying inventory. Pocketing about $1 million. What would happen? Well, if the business continued fulfilling its customers' orders, inventory would go down, meaning that working capital would also go down, and fall below the target by $1 million. So here, the buyer would pay $1 million less in purchase price, and they could use that money to catch back up on inventory.

Let's use another example. Let's say this time the seller stopped paying its suppliers. Also, to the tune of about $1 million. What would happen? Well, if the business continued to operate, it would start racking-up bills. So, its payables would go up. Meaning that its working capital would go down, once again falling below the target. Here, the buyer would again pay $1 million less in purchase price, which they could then use to pay the suppliers, and get them current.

Now let's try it from a different angle. This time, instead of the seller trying to game the system, something good actually happens. Let's say that the business signed up a new customer. But to service that new customer, the business needs an additional $1 million of inventory as soon as possible. If a seller put cash into the business in order to stock-up on that new inventory, what would happen? Inventory would go up, meaning that working capital would go up, and this time go above the target. Here, the buyer would pay $1 million more in purchase price and the seller would get paid for the investment of that inventory. Which is fair, because it's the right thing to do for the business, and the buyer got that inventory.

A working capital adjustment actually serves two purposes. First, it protects buyers from the risk that a seller will squeeze cash out of a business. And second, it pays sellers for continuing to invest in the business, even though they're about to sell it. Generally, it's a concept that most can agree on. Where things tend to get complicated though, is when it comes to negotiating the working capital target. You see, every business is different, and there's no set formula for what a target should be. Instead, it's something that involves analysis, judgement, and thoughtful negotiations. As you can imagine, given how the adjustment works, a buyer will tend to want a higher target, to protect his or her interests. And a seller will want a lower target, so they can get paid. At the end of the day, it really just needs to be fair. In the next chapter we'll explain how to calculate and negotiate a working capital target.

Chapter 13: Working Capital Targets

Agreeing on a good working capital target is important, because if a target's not good, someone won't be happy. And if someone's not happy, there could be a dispute after the deal has closed. Think about it this way, if a target is set too high, working capital will probably come in below the target. If that's the case, the seller won't be happy because they'll get paid less. On the other hand, if a target is set too low, working capital will probably come in above the target. If that's the case, the buyer won't be happy because they'll have to pay more.

So how do both a buyer and a seller come-up with a target that isn't too high, isn't too low, and it's fair to both sides? The answer? Someone needs to do an analysis that shows why a target makes sense. It could be someone from the buy-side, or it could be someone from the sell-side. But whoever does it, they need to know what they're doing. Because the buyer, the seller, and their financial and legal advisors are all going to have to understand it, get comfortable with it, and agree on a target. If people can't understand it, they won't get comfortable with it, and they won't agree.

Once a buyer and seller have gotten comfortable, and they've agreed on a target, that target and a definition of how working capital should be calculated at closing are then written into the agreement. When the deal closes, working capital at the time of closing will be calculated exactly how it's defined in the agreement. Generally speaking, whatever the difference is between the working capital that's calculated at closing, and the target number that's in the agreement, that's the purchase price adjustment.

Without going into too much detail yet, once a target number has been agreed to, it's important that both the buyer and seller pay close attention to the definition of how working capital should be calculated at closing. Because, as we'll discuss in this chapter, working capital can be a very subjective term, and it can be defined in a number of different ways. Sometimes things are included, or not included, for very specific reasons. This is especially the case in an M&A deal, which is why you want to make sure that however it's defined in the agreement, it's exactly how it's intended it to be calculated at closing.

In this chapter, we'll explain all of this. We'll provide best practices that should be followed whenever building a working capital analysis. We'll explain the sorts of items that should be kept in and kept out of a working capital adjustment. And, we'll share advice on how to negotiate working capital targets that are fair to both the buyer and the seller. Understanding all of these things, the analysis, the target, and how to define working capital in an agreement, can help you not only negotiate good targets, but also help you avoid what can be very costly disputes if for any reason someone isn't happy after a deal closes.

The Working Capital Analysis

A well-built working capital analysis does three things. First, it helps define which assets and liabilities should be included, or not included, in the working capital adjustment. Second, it helps the buyer and seller form a view on what a normal level of working capital is for a particular business. And third, it helps the buyer and seller agree on a target.

Usually, the analysis begins by showing all of the pieces that make up a company's working capital. Meaning its receivables, inventory, payables, and accrued operating expenses. It shows how all those things add-up to net working capital in total, and it shows how all those things have trended over time. Ideally, the analysis shows all of this for every month, or if monthly data isn't available every quarter, for at least the past two years, and it goes forward for whatever forecast information is available.

Why go back two years? The reason is that two years allows you to not only see trends in the business, where working capital may have been growing, flat, or shrinking over time, but it also allows you to see if there's any seasonality in the business. Where things like receivables or inventory might tend to peak or valley at certain times of the year, bringing working capital up or down with it.

From here, the analysis is tailored specifically to the deal, where things either need to be removed because they don't belong in the adjustment, or the analysis needs to be improved in some way, so that the buyer and seller can get comfortable with the trends they are seeing.

Once a company's net working capital has been laid-out in a nice, clean schedule, where you can see all of the pieces and a normalized trend, a buyer and seller can usually get comfortable pretty quickly and agree on a target. For an example of what a working capital analysis looks like, refer to Appendix Three of this book.

So, what are the things you would need to be aware of if you ever had to build or review someone else's working capital analysis? And more importantly, what are the things that you would need to watch out for so that a target isn't accidentally set too high, or too low?

To begin with, the analysis would need to show all of a company's current assets and current liabilities exactly as they've trended over time. This is important because at some point, other people will review the analysis, and they'll need to be comfortable that it came from a reliable set of numbers. Meaning that it came directly from the company's balance sheets, exactly as they've been reported in the past. But then, three things need to happen.

First, anything that shouldn't be included in the working capital adjustment for purposes of the deal, needs to be taken out. These need to be presented clearly in the analysis so that anyone who reviews it knows exactly what's been removed. Then, operating metrics that can help the buyer and seller understand why things have trended the way they have, or how they're expected to trend in the future, should be added in. And finally, if anything seems out of whack, or if the data wasn't so great, the analysis might need to be 'adjusted' so that you can see what things would have looked like if everything was clean. We'll discuss all three of these points next.

Once these things have been done, you're left with a normalized trend of working capital that includes the things you want and keeps out the things you don't want. From here, it's much easier to visualize what a target should be, and how it should be defined in the agreement.

What Should be In, What Should be Out

There are lots of sources that will tell you there's a standard definition for working capital. They'll say it's a company's current assets, minus its current liabilities. Without getting too technical, this basically means anything that's either already cash, can be converted into cash, or is likely to be settled in cash, within a year. And for some purposes that's fine. But, not in an M&A deal. You see, in an M&A deal, working capital can be whatever you want it to be. If you decide that working capital shouldn't have cash, short-term debt, or anything else that would otherwise be included in someone else's definition of working capital, then it's OK. You don't have to include those things, and you can define working capital however you decide it should be defined for purposes of the deal.

Remember what a working capital adjustment is trying to do. It's trying to prevent a seller from squeezing cash out of a business. If you keep this in mind, you'll have a good sense for the sorts of items that should be kept in your definition of working capital, and the sorts of items that it's probably OK to keep out. If there's an item that relates to the business' short-term operating cash flow, you'll probably want to keep it in. If there's an item that doesn't relate to the business' short-term operating cash flow, or if it's already being dealt with somewhere else in the agreement, then you'll probably want to keep it out.

So, what are we talking about? The sorts of things that would stay in a working capital adjustment, would probably include what we already discussed. Accounts receivable, inventory, prepaid assets, payables, and accrued operating expenses. The sorts of things that a seller could manipulate if they wanted to. But what should be kept out?

Usually, for purposes of a deal, there are three things you'd want to keep out. First, would be anything that's already being taken care of somewhere else in the deal, so that there's no double counting. This usually means cash, debt, and income taxes. Second, would be non-operating assets, and third would be non-operating liabilities. These three things aren't always straight forward, so we'll discuss all three.

Avoiding Double Counting

For any items that are already being taken care of somewhere else in the deal (like cash, debt, and usually income taxes), these things generally need to be taken out of the working capital adjustment, to avoid double counting. What do we mean by double counting? Well, let's use cash as an example. Remember, in a cash-free, debt-free deal, the purchase price of the business gets increased for the cash and decreased for the debt, through the net debt adjustment. This means that these items are already being taken care of in the deal. But now, if we also left cash in the working capital adjustment, and for some reason working capital went up because of an increase in cash, then the buyer would be paying twice for that increase in cash.

Here's how. First, the buyer would pay, dollar for dollar, for all of the cash that was left in the business, through the net debt adjustment. Then, the buyer would pay again for the 'increase' of cash that caused working capital to go up. This is what we mean by double counting. It's being counted twice in the agreement. And when something is being counted twice, it means that someone is probably going to pay twice. This same logic can apply to anything that's being double counted in an agreement.

Let's use a different example. Let's say that a certain debt item was left in the working capital adjustment, and for some reason that specific debt item went up. This would cause working capital to go down. Here, the seller would first get dinged, dollar for dollar, for that specific debt item, through the net debt adjustment. Then, they'd get dinged again for the 'increase' in that debt item that caused working capital to go down.

So wherever anything is being dealt with somewhere else in an agreement, like cash, debt, or income taxes, it needs to be looked at very carefully. More likely than not, it needs to be taken out of the working capital adjustment, to avoid double counting.

Excluding Non-Operating Assets

Earlier, we mentioned that a working capital analysis begins with all of a company's current assets and all of its current liabilities. Things are then removed or adjusted in order to come up with a normalized trend that can be used to decide on a target. During this process, assets are often identified that a buyer might not care about, and a seller might not want included in the target. These are usually a company's non-operating assets, and if a buyer and seller both agree, these assets can be kept out of the working capital adjustment all together.

The kinds of non-operating assets that would fall into this category might include things like loans receivable from shareholders that the buyer doesn't want to have to worry about collecting after the deal closes. Risky short-term investments, or personal assets like a seller's prepaid country club membership that ran through the business. These types of assets might have always been on a company's books in the past, but they may not be necessary to the business going forward. Sometimes, there might even be assets that won't transfer to the buyer anyway, for legal reasons.

When these types of assets are identified, and it's agreed that they should be kept out of the working capital adjustment, they're usually taken out of the normalized trend that's being developed for working capital, so that the trend only includes the true operating assets of the business.

As long as the target number that's decided doesn't include those things, and the definition of how working capital should be calculated at closing also doesn't include those things, then any changes in those assets won't hurt the buyer or the seller, because they'll be completely excluded from the adjustment. If the seller wants, they can liquidate those assets and take the cash out of the business or leave them there. In either case, the buyer won't pay more, and the seller won't get less, at least not through the working capital adjustment.

Excluding Non-Operating Liabilities

Just like there can be non-operating assets you that want to take out of a working capital adjustment, there can also be non-operating liabilities. Usually though, these liabilities are either debt, or they have the characteristics of debt. They can include things like short-term loans, bank borrowings, finance lease obligations, basically anything that will be defined as debt for purposes of the deal. With these items, once they're included in the definition of debt in the agreement, they'll be handled through the net debt adjustment. Which means, they should be removed from the working capital adjustment to avoid double counting.

Removing these debt and debt-like items from the working capital adjustment, is done in exactly the same way as the non-operating assets were removed. They're taken out of the normalized working capital trend that's being developed, so that it only includes the true operating assets and liabilities of the business. And again, as long as the target that's decided on doesn't include those things, and the definition of how working capital should be calculated at closing also doesn't include those things, then they won't affect the working capital adjustment.

Sometimes though, there are liabilities that a buyer and seller just don't see eye-to-eye on, in terms of whether they should be treated like debt or working capital. Things like overdue payables to suppliers, payables to related parties, and deferred revenue. Clearly, a buyer would like to treat all these things like debt, so that they can get dollar for dollar purchase price relief through the net debt adjustment. But a seller wouldn't. A seller would probably make the argument that carrying those liabilities was always part of the business' normal operations, and they should be left in working capital.

Unfortunately, these types of situations do pop-up, and they can be very subjective, where no one answer will apply to all situations. Sometimes it'll look more like debt, sometimes it'll look more like working capital. It really depends on the specific facts and circumstances that are involved, followed by thoughtful negotiations of course.

But let's say, that there was actually a liability that a buyer just wouldn't accept, and the seller wouldn't agree to treating like debt in the deal. Here, a buyer can still try to get purchase price relief through the working capital adjustment. The way this works, is that once a liability has been identified, if it's not going to be treated like debt, it can be kept out of the working capital target that's being set. But it can be kept in the definition of how working capital should be calculated at closing.

By keeping a liability out of the target that's set, it makes the target relatively higher. And by keeping it in the definition of how working capital should be calculated at closing, if that liability is still there at closing, it will cause working capital to be lower than the target. In other words, there will be a shortfall, and the buyer will pay less because of that liability being there at closing. So even though the item didn't get treated like debt, the buyer was still able to get purchase price relief through the working capital adjustment.

Now of course, this all depends the specific facts and circumstances involved, how a target is developed, and how a definition of working capital is negotiated. But even in a situation where a buyer may not be able to get the full amount of that liability excluded from a target, they still might be able to get something if a seller is willing to compromise.

Operating Metrics

Once a working capital analysis has been prepared, and all the things that don't belong have been removed, the buyer and seller still need to get comfortable with the trends they're seeing, so that they can visualize and agree on a target. This is where operating metrics can help. Operating metrics that are specific to working capital include things like days sales outstanding, which is a measure of how long it's taking a company to collect its receivables. Days inventory on-hand, which is a measure of how much inventory a company is carrying relative to its sales. And days payables outstanding, which is a measure of how current a company is in paying its bills.

With metrics like these, trended over time along with the working capital numbers themselves, it helps paint a deeper picture. It allows a buyer and seller to not only see trends, but to also ask questions as to why things are trending the way they are, and what's driving the numbers. Why are receivables taking longer to collect? Why are inventory levels climbing relative to sales? Why does it look like payables are being stretched? Answers to these types of questions not

111

only help buyers and sellers understand what's happening in the business, but it helps them form a more comfortable view of where working capital seems to be trending.

Normalizing Adjustments

Earlier, we mentioned that a typical working capital analysis captures monthly or quarterly data that goes back for about two years. This is so that you can see trends and if there's any seasonality in the business. Unfortunately though, monthly, and quarterly data isn't always perfect. Especially in the middle market. This is because a company's accounting could be inconsistent, or there could be anomalies, one-time events, or changes taking place in the business. When it comes to these sorts of issues, it's not uncommon to make what are called 'normalizing adjustments' to the working capital analysis. This way, you can see what the data and trends would have looked like if everything was clean, consistent, and as close normal as possible.

Most of the time, the accounting issues, events, and changes in a business that are having an effect on its working capital will be identified in financial due diligence. This is where accountants who specialize in M&A will scrub a company's financials as part of the work that they do. It's this financial due diligence team that will usually adjust the working capital analysis so that you can see what things would have looked like over time, again, if everything was clean, consistent, and as close normal as possible. Smoothing out any noise in the data, so that you're left with a fairly normalized trend.

Negotiating the Target

Once the working capital analysis has been prepared, it's going to tell you certain things. It will tell you if working capital tends to be flat, within a range, or if it's been trending up, or down. It will also tell you if there's any seasonality in the business where it tends to peak or valley at certain times of the year. Every business is different, so each will have its own unique set of facts and circumstances. In most situations though, it's at this point that a buyer and seller can look at an analysis, see a trend, and agree on a target.

The target number itself could be agreed in a number of different ways. It could be based on the amount of working capital that exists in the business today, it could be based on a trailing twelve-month average, or it could be based on a projection of where it looks like working capital will be at closing. It really just depends on what the analysis is saying, and what the buyer and seller are both comfortable with.

Usually, a buyer and seller will agree on a standard working capital adjustment. This means, that there will be a dollar for dollar purchase price adjustment, up or down, based on the amount of working capital that exists in the business at closing, compared to the target.

What happens though, if a buyer and seller aren't on the same page with setting a target? Maybe when they look at the analysis, they see a lot of growth, but it's hard to say how that growth will continue to trend. Or maybe, they see unpredictable swings. Or maybe, it's been shrinking.

For these types of situations, when it's hard for a buyer and seller to agree on what a target should be, there are alternatives. Ways that a target can still be set, but the mechanics of the adjustment can be tailored to fit the situation. Two of these alternatives, are minimums and collars.

Working Capital Minimums

Let's say that there's a high growth business, and along with that growth, the business' working capital has been trending up. Month after month, quarter after quarter, and year after year. It's up because receivables have grown with sales, and inventory has grown to keep up with customer demand.

A buyer might look at this and want to set a working capital target based on where they think it's going to be at closing. In other words, they want to set it higher than where it is today because they're expecting the growth to continue. The buyer might be thinking that if the target is set too low, and working capital grows beyond it, then they'll end-up having to pay more. It might be that the buyer doesn't want to pay more, because they feel like they've already baked that growth into their purchase price.

A seller might not see it this way and might not be comfortable setting a working capital target any higher than where it is today. After all, if the target is set too high, and they don't hit it, the seller will get less. Even though, they didn't do anything wrong. In this type of situation, a working capital minimum might make sense.

The way a minimum works, is that instead of setting a target, and then having a dollar for dollar purchase price adjustment up or down, a minimum is set. If working capital comes in below the minimum, it's a shortfall, and the seller will be paid less. But, if working capital comes in above the minimum, there is no purchase price adjustment. With minimums, a seller can be more comfortable committing to an actual level of working capital, meaning where it is today. And if closing is only a month or so away, then a buyer is still protected from having cash squeezed out of the business.

Working Capital Collars

What if, working capital tends to swing quite a bit each month. It's up, it's down, up again, down again, you get the idea. Maybe there are real business reasons behind it, where the timing of certain things makes it jump up and down from month to month. Or, maybe the accounting is a little sloppy. Sometimes, this is just how it is. When this happens though, it can be hard for anyone to say what a specific working capital target number should be. Because if it really does jump around in an unpredictable way, then you'd just be leaving it to chance that the target number would actually be hit. And if it's not hit, then whoever's on the wrong side of it, is either going to pay more, or get less. When this kind of a situation happens, and a buyer and seller are both a little uncomfortable setting an exact target, a collar might make sense.

The way a collar works, is that a target is still decided, but rather than it being a dollar for dollar purchase price adjustment for any amount over or under the target, a range is used.

So, let's say for example that a working capital target of $10 million was agreed to, but because of the unpredictable swings in working capital every month, the buyer and seller agreed to having a collar of plus or minus $2 million. This means, that while there's a target of $10 million, there's range of plus or minus $2 million in either direction before any purchase price adjustments would kick-in. In other words, as long as working capital came in between $8 million and $12 million at closing, there would be no purchase price adjustment.

It's only if working capital ends-up outside of the collar that there would be an adjustment. And usually, the adjustment will only be for the amount of working capital that comes in above or below the collar. So, in the example we just used, where there's a range of $8 million to $12 million, if closing working capital were to come in at $15 million, the adjustment would be $15 million, minus the $12 million upper-end of the range. So, a $3 million purchase price adjustment where the buyer pays more. The same math would apply in a situation where working capital came in below the range. So, if working capital came in at $6 million, the adjustment would be the difference between that $6 million and the $8 million lower-end of the range. So, a $2 million adjustment where the seller gets less.

Defining Working Capital

Once a buyer and seller have agreed on a target number and the mechanics of the working capital adjustment, that target and a definition of how working capital should be calculated at closing need to be written into the agreement. It's very important at this stage of a deal that both the buyer and seller review very closely both of these two things. Making sure that the target number is what was agreed, and that the definition of how working capital is intended to be calculated at closing is accurate.

As we said earlier in this chapter, when the deal closes, working capital at the time of closing will be calculated exactly how it's defined in the agreement. Whatever the difference is between the working capital that's calculated at closing, and the target number, that's the purchase price adjustment. Which means, that if anything were unintentionally not captured correctly in the agreement, it could create an unintentional difference between the working capital that's calculated at closing and the target number. Not something you want to happen if you can avoid it.

This is why it's important to have both the buyer and seller's legal and financial advisors review these items. Any particulars around the mechanism in terms of dollar for dollar adjustments, minimums, and collars also need to be reviewed, so that these things are exactly as they're intended to be. For an example of what a definition of working capital will sometimes look like in an M&A deal, refer to Appendix Four of this book.

Chapter 14: Locked-Box Mechanisms

In a traditional cash-free, debt-free deal, the net debt and working capital adjustments are calculated and settled after the deal has closed. This is because, these adjustments are based on the amounts of net debt and working capital that exist in the business at the time of closing. Which means, they can't be finalized until after closing when numbers are available. Because these adjustments take place after closing, they're often referred to as closing adjustments, or post-close adjustments. And it can take a while for these numbers to be calculated, reviewed, and then finally settled, after a deal has closed.

What happens though, if you're a seller, and you're not too crazy about the idea of signing a deal, and then having to wait until after the deal has closed to finalize the numbers? Afterall, it will affect your final proceeds. What if you want the deal to have a fixed price, right up front, so that you know exactly what you'll be walking away with before you even sign? Well, there's a way, and it's called a locked-box mechanism.

With a locked-box, the purchase price of a deal is fixed at the time of signing, and there are no closing adjustments. Basically, the way it works, is that a buyer still comes up with an enterprise value for the business, they still calculate a net debt adjustment, and they still calculate a working capital adjustment. But the difference, is that with a locked-box, instead of waiting until closing to apply these adjustments, the buyer values the business and applies these adjustments at a point in time that already happened. It's called the locked-box date, and it's the date that's used to fix the price that the buyer will pay for the business.

Having a fixed price at the time of signing, is obviously a good thing for a seller. They get price certainty. But what about the buyer? The buyer is now signing a deal to buy a business at a fixed price, where there won't be any closing adjustments. Uh oh, do you see where this might be going? If there aren't any closing adjustments, and the seller still owns and controls the business all the way up until closing, couldn't this once again be creating a situation where a seller could run-up a bunch of debt and squeeze out a bunch of cash from a business before the deal has closed? Yes, they could. Unless, there were specific protections in-place that would prevent this from happening. Which is why in a locked-box deal, instead of having closing adjustments, there are specific buyer protections called leakage provisions which are intended to prevent any 'value' from 'leaking out' of a business, until the deal has closed.

In this chapter, we'll explain how locked-box deals work, how they're priced, and the kinds of protections that a buyer needs when doing a locked-box deal. We'll also discuss the types of situations where locked-box deals might not work, and some of the finer details that are sometimes overlooked early on in a deal when a buyer and seller are thinking about doing a locked-box.

Choosing a Locked-Box Date

The locked-box date that's chosen for a deal is very important. Because, that's the date that the buyer will use to value the business and fix the price that they're willing to pay for it. It's also the date after which the buyer will want protections, so that no value leaks out of the business until the deal has closed.

When it comes to deciding a locked-box date, it's important to remember that the purchase price will be fixed, and there will be no adjustments. This means, that the buyer will need a very reliable set of financial statements to value the business and its equity, as of that date. Not just income statements, but balance sheets too. In fact, the balance sheet that's used to value the equity of a business at a locked-box date is so important that it gets its own term called the 'reference balance sheet'. We'll discuss how the reference balance sheet is used to value the equity of a business in a minute. But as you can imagine, from a buyer's perspective, if these financial statements are what you're going to use to fix the price of a deal, they'd better be right. Because if they're not, meaning that they're not accurate or complete, then it could be a problem.

If a target company's financial statements are audited as of the locked-box date, then that can usually help give a buyer a pretty good sense of comfort in relying on those financial statements. But what happens if a lot of time has passed since the date of a company's audited financial statements? Or, what if the business has never been audited?

If a lot of time has passed since the date of a business' audited financial statements, then those financials might not be so accurate anymore. Why? Because the more time that passes, the more things can change in a business. So, using old financials for a locked-box date might not work so well. In a situation like this, if a lot of time has passed since a business' financials were audited, then a buyer may still use those financials as part of their due diligence, but they may not want to use them to set the locked-box date. Instead, it probably makes more sense for the seller to prepare updated financials for purposes of setting the locked-box date. If not with a refreshed audit, then they should at least be prepared on the same basis as the audited financials were.

What if a business has never been audited? Well, if that's the case, then a buyer is going to have to use their own judgement as to whether or not they'll be able to get comfortable enough with that company's financials to even do a locked-box deal. You see, sometimes a company can have very good record keeping and very good accounting, even if they're not audited. But sometimes they don't have good record keeping and they don't have reliable accounting. If a buyer isn't going to be able to get comfortable enough with a company's financial statements to do a locked-box deal, then a locked-box probably won't work, and a traditional deal with closing adjustments probably makes more sense.

Assuming though that a locked-box date is ultimately chosen, a buyer is also going to want protections from that date forward, so that no value leaks out of the business. Without getting into too much detail, this basically means that a target company needs to have good enough accounting in-place that it's able to track all of its business activities after the locked-box date. All the way up until the deal has closed. This means being able to track normal course business activities separately from what will ultimately be defined as leakage in the deal, which we'll discuss later. If it can't do this, then it's also going to be a problem.

As a buyer, you do sometimes look at business that don't have great accounting. So, if you're looking at a business, and it's not going to be able to provide a good balance sheet to use for a locked-box date, and it doesn't have good enough accounting to track normal course business activities separate from what will ultimately be defined as leakage, then you may not want to do a locked-box. Instead, you might prefer doing a traditional deal with closing adjustments.

Fixing the Price

If you recall from earlier in the book, a buyer typically values a business on a cash-free, debt-free basis, so that they're valuing the underlying operations of that business, separate from its capital structure. This is called the enterprise value of the business. In a traditional deal, when the deal closes, the buyer applies a net debt adjustment (to settle-up the capital structure), and a working capital adjustment (based on a normal level of working capital), to arrive at the final amount that's paid to the seller.

In a locked-box deal, these two adjustments (the net debt adjustment and the working capital adjustment) are referred to as equity value adjustments. That's because, they're used to calculate the equity value of the business as of the locked-box date. To say it differently, enterprise value, minus net debt at the locked-box date, adjusted for working capital at the locked-box date, equals equity value at the locked-box date.

You see, the valuation process for buying a business in a locked-box deal, is exactly the same as it is for a traditional deal. The only difference is that instead of waiting until closing to adjust the enterprise value for the net debt and working capital adjustments, it's done at the locked-box date. Based on the numbers that come from the reference balance sheet.

As far as the net debt adjustment goes, the reference balance sheet is used to tally-up the cash, debt, and the debt-like items. And as far as the working capital adjustment goes, the buyer and seller still do a working capital analysis to agree on what a normal level of working capital should be for the business. But instead of setting a target and waiting until closing, they'll compare that normal level of working capital to the amount of working capital that's on the refence balance sheet. The amount that working capital on the reference balance sheet is over or under the normalized amount, that's the adjustment.

After adjusting the enterprise value of the business for net debt and working capital as of the locked-box date, that's the equity value of the business, and that's what becomes the fixed price that the buyer pays at closing.

Preventing Leakage

In a locked-box deal, one of the more obvious risks for a buyer, is that the price is fixed as of the locked-box date, and it could be months after that date before the deal actually closes. Just like in a traditional deal, the buyer doesn't own or control the business until the deal has closed. Meaning that, the seller is still in-charge. And just like in a traditional deal, there are things that a seller can do to game the system, increase their payout, and make things more expensive for a buyer.

If you remember, in a traditional deal, a seller could game the system by squeezing cash out of the working capital of a business. They could either stockpile this cash, use it to pay down debt, or take it out of the business. If they stockpiled the cash, or used it to pay down debt, it would increase their proceeds through the net debt adjustment. Or, if they took it out of the business, they would get to keep it. That's why in a traditional deal, to prevent these things, there was a working capital adjustment.

Locked-boxes are a little different. In a locked-box, if a seller pulls strings to increase the amount of cash or decrease the amount of debt in a business, they don't get paid for it. Because the price is fixed. The only way a seller gets more in a locked-box deal, is if they actually take cash or some other sort of value out of the business before the deal has closed. If they do that, they'll still get the fixed purchase price, and they'll also get to pocket whatever they took out of the business. The question becomes, how does a buyer prevent this from happening? In a locked-box, this is referred to as preventing leakage.

Leakage is a term that basically refers to any leakage of value that comes out of a business after the locked-box date. It's intended to capture any transfer of value to the sellers. Things like distributions to shareholders, payments to related parties or affiliates, management fees, or any other transactions or payments that would be transferring value to the seller, or sellers, as opposed to running the business in the normal course of operations.

In a locked-box deal, there's a specific provision in the purchase agreement that will define exactly what qualifies as leakage. Along with this, the seller should also be providing a representation that there won't be any leakage, and an indemnification if any leakage does occur.

While usually, you don't expect there to be any leakage, a buyer and seller will occasionally agree on having some. For example, a previously scheduled dividend payment, or bonuses to managing shareholders. With these types of items, if they're known to be happening, the buyer and seller can agree on them, and they don't have to count as leakage. They'll be exceptions. This is called permitted leakage. It would technically be leakage, but it's something the buyer and seller have specifically agreed to allow. So, it's permitted. In these situations, whenever there is going to be permitted leakage, it's important that it's scheduled-out in very exact terms and amounts and included in the agreement so that there's no misunderstanding. As long as the items are very specifically identified and quantified, the buyer can factor these things into their fixed price.

In theory, by preventing any leakage of value after the locked-box date, the buyer is getting exactly what they valued on the locked-box date. Because nothing of value was transferred out of the business. This is what gives rise to the term locked-box. All of the value and all the cash, other than any permitted leakage, remains locked in a box until closing.

The Value Accrual

If you're a seller doing a locked-box deal, and you're happy with the fixed price that you've negotiated, you're probably feeling pretty good. But what if the deal won't close for a while. Technically, you still own the business and you're still running it. But after the locked-box date, you can't take any profits out of it. If you do, it could be considered leakage and you'd have to pay it back.

So, what happens to all of the profits that are generated by a business after the locked-box date if the seller isn't allowed to take them out? Should the buyer get those profits? As a seller, if you did a traditional deal, you'd probably be entitled to keep those profits and all the cash that those profits generated, right up to closing. But by doing a locked-box, are you now leaving something on the table? Meaning, all those after-tax profits that were generated between the locked-box date and closing? You might be. That's why in a locked-box deal, there actually is an adjustment for this. Except, they don't call it an adjustment, it's either called a value accrual, or an interest charge.

The value accrual, which is also known as an interest charge, is usually intended to represent the cash flows that the seller would have otherwise been entitled to in a traditional deal. It's usually calculated by taking the expected free cash flow that the business would have generated, and could have paid to its equity holders, from the locked-box date to closing. And expressing it, in the form of an interest rate that's applied to the purchase price. The buyer then pays this amount of interest as an additional charge on top of the fixed price.

Unfortunately, calculating the interest charge is almost always based on using forecasts and estimates. Which means, it's not always going to be precise. But, because it's the buyer that will be paying it, it's the buyer that needs to get comfortable with it. Sometimes this isn't an issue because signing and closing aren't that far apart, and the business is fairly predictable in terms of how much cash it generates. When this is the case, a buyer can usually get comfortable pretty quickly by looking at the current run-rates of the business and not having to rely too heavily on forecasts. But sometimes, this isn't the case.

If it's a situation where there's going to be a long delay between signing and closing, or the company doesn't really have a good handle on its forecasting, or the business is going through changes, it can be much more difficult for a buyer to get comfortable enough to set an interest charge, or at least set one that a seller would also agree to. When this happens, and it looks like a buyer and seller aren't going to see eye-to-eye on how an interest charge should be calculated, then again, a traditional deal with closing adjustments may be the better approach. It really is something that needs to be thought through early on in a deal, so that expectations can be set right from the beginning, and the right structure can be chosen.

Chapter 15: Indemnities and Other Terms

Earlier in the book, we said that when it comes to structuring deals, a buyer needs to be able to answer three main questions. What are you buying, what are you paying, and what are the terms? To answer the first question of what you're buying, we explained how you can either buy the stock of a business or its assets, and we explained the basic differences that buyers and sellers need to be thinking about when deciding which type of deal they're going to do.

To answer the second question of what you're paying, we explained how businesses are valued on a cash-free, debt-free basis, and how net debt adjustments, working capital adjustments, and locked-box mechanisms work in determining the actual purchase price you'll pay. Now, to answer the third question of what the terms are, we need to take things one step further. Because whether you're doing a stock deal or an asset deal, or one with traditional closing adjustments or a locked-box, you're going to need protections. Just in case it turns-out that you didn't get what you thought you had bargained for.

What if, after you bought a business, you discovered liabilities that you didn't expect to find? Or, something that you thought you could rely on when doing the deal turned out to not be true? Or, the seller didn't take care of something that they said they would? We're not talking about fraud, that's a totally different issue. We're talking about things that you weren't aware of at the time of the deal. Or, things that you didn't find in due diligence. Or, things that the seller was supposed to have taken care of but didn't.

Whatever it was, we're talking about things that a buyer just didn't fully know at the time of a deal. But rather than being scared of the unknown and not doing a deal, the buyer made a decision. A decision that was either based on what they knew at the time, or what they thought they could rely on from the seller. But unfortunately, something didn't go right.

As a buyer you never have perfect information. In fact, sellers rarely have perfect information either. You know what you know, but you may not know what you don't know. So how do you protect yourself if something was missed in due diligence, something you relied on turned out to not be true, or the seller simply didn't follow up on something? This is where indemnifications, escrows, and holdbacks come into play. Giving a buyer security in a deal, just in case.

In this chapter, we'll explain what indemnifications, escrows, and holdbacks are, and some of the more common terms that are often associated with them. But before we do, we'll need to go through a little refresher on what reps, warranties, and covenants are from part one of the book. Because these are the things that a buyer needs to rely on and hold a seller accountable for when doing a deal.

Reps and Warranties

As we said before, no matter how much due diligence a buyer does, they never have perfect information. And while sellers may also not have perfect information, they sure know a lot more about their business than the buyer does. This is why it's standard market practice that sellers will provide buyers with representations and warranties (or 'reps and warranties') in the sale of a business.

Reps and warranties are statements that a seller makes about a business that's being sold. These statements are written into the purchase agreement between the buyer and the seller. They say things like, the seller has legal authority to make the sale, the company is compliant with all applicable laws, the financial statements of the business are complete and accurate, and that there are no undisclosed liabilities. A seller will also make representations that these statements are true, at both the time of signing, and the time of closing.

These statements become an important part of the purchase agreement for two reasons. For one, they help a buyer bridge the gap between what they learned in due diligence and the seller's knowledge about the business. And two, they provide something that the buyer can rely on contractually if something goes wrong. You see, if it turns-out that any of the seller's reps and warranties aren't true, it's called a breach of contract. If a breach is discovered before a deal closes, it could allow a buyer to say, 'you're already in breach of this contract' and walk away or renegotiate the deal. On the other hand, if a breach isn't discovered until after a deal has already closed, and the buyer ends-up suffering a loss because of it, the buyer can point to those statements in the agreement and say to the seller 'this statement wasn't true and I suffered a loss because of it, now you need to make me whole.'

In other words, the reps and warranties form the basis of a claim that a buyer can make against a seller to be made whole for any losses or damages that resulted from that breach. If this is the case, the seller may have to make good on the buyer's claim and compensate the buyer for the losses.

Let's say for example, that in the reps and warranties section of a purchase agreement, a seller made the statement that there were no undisclosed liabilities. But then, not too long after the deal closed, the buyer discovered a very large, very material liability that was actually never disclosed. It turned out that the liability was quite valid and owed to a third-party. It was something that clearly occurred during the time that the seller owned the business, and technically, it should have been recorded on the company's books and disclosed to the buyer, but it wasn't.

If this were the case, it would look like there was a breach, and the buyer would have a claim against the seller. If so, there should be an indemnification provision in the contract, which we'll discuss in a minute, that would provide the mechanism for the buyer to recover whatever loss was suffered as a result of that breach.

Covenants

A covenant is a promise to do, or not do something. In M&A deals, covenants can be made by both buyers and sellers, and they can apply to the period between signing and closing (which are referred to as pre-close covenants), or they can apply to the period after closing (which are referred to as post-close covenants).

Pre-close covenants come into play when there's a delay between signing and closing. When this is the case, a buyer will usually want covenants from a seller to be protected for how the seller will continue to operate the business until the deal has closed. For this, a seller will usually agree to things like continuing to operate the business in the normal course, maintaining insurance coverage, and basically not making any big changes to the business.

Pre-close covenants can also include things like having the seller obtain third party consents for transferring important contracts in a deal, helping obtain regulatory approvals for the deal to close, or fixing things that were identified in due diligence. As for post-close covenants, these can include things like covenants not to compete, or promises that the seller will help transition the business to the buyer over some period of time.

From a buyer's perspective, covenants don't only help make sure a deal will close, but they also help protect a buyer's longer-term interests. Such as in the case of a seller helping transition a business, or not compete. And similar to how a breach of reps and warranties can cause a buyer losses and damages, a breach of covenants can also cause losses and damages.

Indemnities

As a buyer, what happens if a seller breaches a rep, a warranty, or a covenant? Or, if they owe you money for a liability that they agreed to pay? You probably have a claim. But, how do you get paid for that claim? Do you have to go to court? Do you have to sue? Not if you have an indemnity. Especially if it's one with an escrow or a holdback attached to it. We'll explain.

An indemnity is a contractual obligation where one party agrees to compensate another party for losses or damages. In an M&A deal, when a buyer acquires a business, it's standard market practice that a seller will usually provide a buyer with indemnities for a range of items. These will often be used to cover any losses that a buyer suffers as a result of breaches in reps, warranties, covenants, or any other special items where a seller specifically agrees to provide an indemnity. A purchase agreement will often contain an indemnification provision that captures all of the indemnities a seller is making to a buyer.

Let's say for example, that a buyer was acquiring a business, and during due diligence the buyer discovered a significant potential liability. For this example, let's say it was from an ongoing lawsuit that was taking place. But because the lawsuit wasn't yet resolved, it wasn't yet clear if the potential liability was going to be real or not. Here, the potential liability was disclosed, otherwise the buyer wouldn't have learned about it. But once it was disclosed, if the buyer didn't want to take on the risk of assuming that liability, there's only two options. Either reduce the purchase price for the risk of now having to deal with that item or ask the seller for an indemnity.

If the seller agrees to provide an indemnity for that item, the buyer will be protected, and the seller will be responsible. You see, an indemnity provides the ability to shift risk from one party to another. This shift of risk, works the same for any item that's covered by an indemnity where the party that's providing the indemnity picks up the tab.

The indemnification provision of an agreement should capture all of the indemnities that are being made in a deal. It should also capture the terms that the buyer and seller agree on for those indemnities, so that the buyer has a clear path to make claims for any losses that they believe should be covered.

Limitations

Usually, sellers don't want buyers coming back to them with claims years after a deal closed, and they don't want their indemnities to be unlimited in terms of the amount of dollars that they're willing to cover either. It's for these reasons that sellers will always want to negotiate limits on their indemnities. Limiting the amount of time in which a buyer can make a claim, and the amount of losses that they're willing to cover. These time limits are referred to as survival periods, for how long the indemnity survives, and the dollar limits are referred to as caps, meaning that an indemnity is capped at a certain amount. These and other terms that are used to limit a seller's indemnities, are usually included in the indemnification provision of an agreement.

Survival Periods

The survival period of an indemnity defines the timeframe in which a buyer can make a claim for any losses or damages that he or she believes should be covered. Generally speaking, buyers like longer survival periods, and sellers like shorter survival periods. Usually though, survival periods will depend on the types of indemnities being made, where certain indemnities will have longer survival periods than others. This is why indemnities are often grouped into different buckets. Buckets that are used for setting survival periods, caps, and other terms, which we'll discuss. Three commonly used buckets for purposes of defining these terms are the fundamental reps, the general reps and warranties, and specific indemnities.

Fundamental Reps

Some indemnifications relate to reps and warranties that are considered to be so important, so fundamental to a deal, that a buyer never would have done a deal if he or she knew that they were not true. For example, a seller's authority to make the sale, or the business' ownership of the assets that are being sold. Clearly, if a buyer knew that these things were not true, they would not have done a deal. These are called 'fundamental reps.'

Fundamental reps take on a special meaning in the context of a deal, in that they are so important, the indemnifications related to those reps will often have an unlimited survival period. When this is the case, it means that a seller's indemnifications to a buyer for those items are indefinite, or more practically speaking, they'll last as long as whatever statute of limitations would apply to the particular items that gave rise to a claim.

Usually, when it comes to fundamental reps, sellers don't have any issues providing unlimited survival periods, because they usually know at the time of doing a deal whether or not those fundamental reps are true. And let's face it, if there is any concern that a seller can't back a fundamental rep, like whether or not they own the assets they're selling, then there's probably an issue that needs to be dealt with before that deal can move any further.

Because of the importance that fundamental reps have, it's usually a highly negotiated point as to what is, or is not, considered to be a fundamental rep. Once agreed though, they should be clearly identified in the agreement.

General Reps and Warranties

Separate from any reps and warranties that are identified as being fundamental, are the 'general' reps and warranties. Examples of these would include things like the financial statements of the business being complete and accurate, that there are no undisclosed liabilities, and that there's no ongoing litigation.

Usually, the indemnities on general reps and warranties do have survival periods. Which means, there's often some negotiation as to what the appropriate survival periods should be. To be fair, whatever survival period is agreed between a buyer and a seller on the general reps and warranties, they should at least allow for enough time so that the buyer would know if there was an issue or not. Afterall, the whole point of indemnities is that a seller is providing a buyer with some level of security in a deal.

Survival periods on general reps and warranties will often range anywhere from 12 to 36 months, although 18 to 24 months is probably the most common that you'll see in the middle market. It really depends on the specific facts and circumstances that are involved, and what level of comfort a buyer has that there won't be any surprises.

For example, if a company is audited by a reputable accounting firm, and they have good legal records, and there aren't any regulatory issues, and there weren't any specific concerns coming out of due diligence, then a fairly standard 18-month survival period would probably make sense. But if a company was never audited, the record keeping wasn't all that great, and the buyer feels a little nervous that something might pop-up a year or more later, then a slightly longer survival period might be more appropriate.

Specific Indemnities and Covenants

Sellers will often provide specific indemnities. For example, a specific indemnity to cover the seller's unpaid income taxes, or a specific indemnity to cover a specific liability that was negotiated.

When it comes to taxes in particular, these are usually subject to statutes of limitations in whatever tax jurisdictions apply. This means that taxing authorities have some period of time in which they can come back to a company years later and seek payments for unpaid taxes. It's for this reason that tax indemnities in particular, will usually have their own survival periods that last at least as long as the statutes of limitations that are involved, plus an additional six months or so to allow for any claims to be discovered.

Other specific indemnities though, for specific liabilities that are negotiated, or covenants, usually either have an unlimited survival period, or they're negotiated on a case-by-case basis. It really depends on the specific items that are involved and the intent of the parties.

Indemnity Caps

When negotiating indemnity survival periods, sellers will also want to negotiate caps on their indemnities, setting a limit on the amount of losses that they're willing to cover. For example, in a deal where there are indemnities for fundamental reps, general reps and warranties, tax, and maybe even one or two special items. Each of these buckets, will either have an individually negotiated cap, or be subject to an 'overall' cap that sets a total limit on the entire amount of dollars that a seller is willing to cover in a deal. Usually, these caps are either expressed as a percentage of the purchase price, or as stated dollar amounts.

Fundamental reps are usually not capped. Instead, these will often be subject to whatever 'overall' cap is negotiated for a deal. In many situations, this will be the entire purchase price of the deal.

General reps and warranties usually do have a cap. But, the amount of cap will often depend on the size of the deal and dollars involved. For example, in a $100 million deal, a 10% cap on the general reps and warranties (meaning a cap at 10% of the purchase price), would give a buyer $10 million of protection. In some situations, this might be just fine and completely in-line with market terms. But in a much smaller deal, say it's only a $10 million deal, a 10% cap would only be $1 million of protection. Here, a buyer might not be comfortable with only $1 million of protection. Because if the company was never audited, or didn't have good record keeping, or it was questionable if the company was compliant with all the rules and regulations that they should have been, then a buyer might be expecting issues to crop-up after a deal and want a little more than a 10% cap. This is why caps in smaller deals will usually be set at a higher percentage of the purchase price than they would in a larger deal. To cover the absolute dollars that are involved.

To give you a sense, at the higher end of the middle market, it would be fairly common to see a deal with a 10% cap on the indemnity covering general reps and warranties. But at the lower end of the middle market, it wouldn't be unusual to see a cap anywhere from 20% of the purchase price, all the way up to 50% or more, depending on the specifics involved.

When it comes to things like tax, special indemnities, and covenants, these are usually not capped, or if they are, they're subject to the overall cap, or some other specifically negotiated amount.

Deductibles and Baskets

Let's say that you were a seller, and you recently sold a business for $50 million. As part of the deal, you agreed to provide the buyer with indemnities on the general reps and warranties. Now let's say, that not too long after the deal closed, the buyer started sending you claims. Lots of claims. And some, were for really small amounts. A little here, a little there. It's happened every month since you've closed the deal, and you feel like you're being nickeled and dimed.

You feel like it's a nuisance more than anything else by having to constantly look at claims and deal with them. You thought the buyer would only come back to you if they found something big enough to matter, but the small stuff? What a pain. You're wondering how long this will carry on and you're wishing there was a way that you could have prevented from being bothered with such small things. Actually, you could have, by using deductibles and baskets.

In an M&A deal, a deductible, which is also referred to as a basket, represents an amount of losses that a buyer has to incur before being able to go back to a seller with a claim. In other words, it's a threshold that needs to be passed. In the case of a 'true' deductible, a buyer accepts the risk of any losses up to that amount. For every dollar of losses that a buyer incurs after a deductible has been reached, the seller will be responsible, all the way up to the cap on that indemnity. For example, in a situation where an indemnity was subject to a $50,000 deductible, the buyer wouldn't be able to make any claims until his or her losses exceeded that $50,000. After that, the seller picks up the tab.

Sometimes, a buyer and a seller will agree to what's called a 'tipping basket.' A tipping basket is when a deductible is set, but it's as if the losses pile up in a basket until they reach the deductible. As soon as they exceed the deductible, the whole basket tips over, and the seller is responsible for all of the losses that were incurred. All the way back to dollar-one.

Tipping baskets are sometimes used because a seller wants a high deductible, whereas of course a buyer wants a low deductible. A tipping basket is sometimes used as a way to bridge the gap. You see, a buyer might be willing to accept a higher deductible, if the risk for doing that is made up by having a tipping basket. Because, once the basket tips over, all of their losses are covered. Sometimes, sellers will also try and negotiate minimums, or de minimis claim amounts, where they'll try and set a threshold for the size of any individual claims that can be made.

Generally speaking, deductibles, baskets, and de minimis amounts, are all intended to help sellers avoid from having to deal with a lot of small and immaterial claims, and it forces buyers to accept some level of risk in a deal. If you think about it though, all businesses have some level of risk. Including the risk that small things can and sometimes will slip through the cracks. That's basically what a deductible is intended to cover. Deductibles though, don't usually apply to all indemnities. In the case of general reps and warranties, yes. Afterall, the general reps and warranties are basically covering normal business type items. But with things like fundamental reps, taxes, or any special indemnities where the expectation or intent is that the seller should be fully responsible. Deductibles, baskets and de minimis amounts don't usually apply.

Buyers need to be aware of these terms, so that when deductibles are being negotiated, it can be clear as to which indemnities they apply, and wherever they do apply, that they're reasonable given the size of the deal.

Escrows and Holdbacks

As a buyer, if for some reason you ended up having a legitimate claim after a deal closed, you want to make sure that you'll be able to collect. But what happens if there are multiple sellers in a deal, and after the deal closed, the money went in different directions? What if all the money got spent? What if a seller disappeared or went bankrupt? The money's gone. How do you collect then? Believe it or not, these things do happen.

You see, indemnifications are only as good as the money that's behind them. There are no guarantees that you'll be able to collect, and it can be a very long and costly process to try and get what you believe you're owed. So, how do you prevent from being in a situation where you have a claim, and you have an indemnity, but you're struggling to collect? Two common ways that buyers can avoid this are with escrows and holdbacks.

An escrow is where an amount of money is placed in a third-party bank account, where a third-party escrow agent oversees it. The money is there for the purpose of settling claims and other obligations after a deal has closed. It's funded from the purchase price. So instead of a seller getting all of their proceeds at the time of closing, a portion goes into an escrow account. The funds are then used to settle whatever that escrow is intended to cover. Sometimes it will be used for settling closing adjustments, but usually it's intended for settling claims on a seller's indemnifications. Escrows provide buyers with security in a deal, so that the money is there if it's needed.

A holdback is similar to an escrow, except that with a holdback, the money doesn't go into a separate third-party account, the buyer holds on to it. The money is still used for the same purposes that it would have been used if it were in escrow. Except that, it's held with the buyer.

As far as the amount of dollars that are involved, and the length of time that these funds are typically set aside in escrow or as a holdback, it can vary. It really depends on the size of the deal and the obligations that the funds are intended to cover.

Usually though, in a typical deal, an escrow or a holdback will mirror the terms that were negotiated for the indemnifications covering the general reps and warranties. In other words, they'll be around 10% of the purchase price, and held for around 18 to 24 months. Unless, there's a special indemnification that has an escrow or a holdback attached to that. For those, the terms can be longer. And just like the indemnification caps that are negotiated in a deal, the percentage of purchase price that's often set aside in an escrow, or as a holdback, will tend to be higher in smaller deals, in order to cover the absolute dollars involved.

Chapter 16: Rep and Warranty Insurance

Let's say you're a buyer negotiating a deal, and the idea of having an escrow isn't sitting well with the seller. Or if it is, they aren't agreeing to the amount of escrow that should be set aside. What if you're a seller, and you don't want 10% of your deal's proceeds sitting in an escrow account for the next 18 to 24 months earning some measly amount of interest? Isn't there a way that a seller can get more of their money up front, but a buyer can still get the protection they need for the things they might not know about? Actually, there is, it's called rep and warranty insurance.

Rep and warranty insurance is an insurance policy that covers a buyer's losses from breaches in reps and warranties in a purchase agreement. These policies can either be taken out by a buyer (as a buy-side policy), or a seller (as a sell-side policy). And while it may not completely eliminate the need for any escrow, it can help reduce the amount of escrow. In some cases, reducing it from 10% of purchase price, down to 1% or less.

Unfortunately though, rep and warranty insurance doesn't cover everything. So, when rep and warranty insurance is going to be used in a deal, it's important that buyers understand what's covered, and what's not. Because anything that's not covered by insurance, and won't be covered by the seller, it will be the buyer's risk.

In this chapter, we'll explain what rep and warranty insurance is. We'll explain what it covers, what it doesn't, and why buyers may still need indemnities and escrows, even when rep and warranty insurance is being used. Finally, we'll discuss how pricing for this type of insurance usually works and how buyers can go about getting it if they're interested.

What is Rep and Warranty Insurance?

Rep and warranty insurance is an insurance policy that can be taken out by either a buyer, or a seller, to cover losses from breaches in the fundamental and general reps and warranties of a purchase agreement. Usually, these policies provide survival periods of 6 years for fundamental reps and 3 years for the general reps. As an insurance product, these policies have actually been on the market for quite a while, but it's only been over the last decade or so that they really began to gain traction in the U.S.

Part of the reason that rep and warranty insurance has become a more popular lately, is that in the past, it wasn't seen as a very buyer friendly product. In fact, earlier versions of the product would exclude coverage for just about any item where 'facts or circumstances' could 'reasonably' have given rise to a breach. The problem was, in an M&A deal, that language could be interpreted to exclude coverage for just about anything. So back then, the product wasn't considered very useful. Eventually though, insurance carriers realized this, and the policies evolved to where they will now cover just about any breaches in reps and warranties, within a defined limit of course, that aren't actually known to be breaches at the time of entering the policy.

This subtle shift from excluding anything that could have 'reasonably' given rise to a breach, to what's 'actually known' to be a breach, gave buyers much more confidence in the product. And since then, it's become much more widely used. As the product has continued to gain attention in the marketplace, it's also attracted competition from insurance carriers that want to offer it. This combination of more use in the marketplace, more competition from carriers, and not to mention more claims data that's now being tracked, has all helped reduce prices for the product overall, to where it's now seen as a very practical option when structuring deals.

What's Covered and What's Not

Rep and warranty insurance doesn't cover everything. It's really only intended to cover losses for unknown breaches in the fundamental and general reps and warranties of a purchase agreement.

It doesn't cover things that are already known to be in breach, breaches in covenants, or special indemnities. And it won't cover any high-risk items that an insurance carrier specifically excludes because they think it creates a higher level of risk or exposure.

In other words, it will cover your basic fundamental and general reps and warranties, but not the things that are specifically excluded. You see, in insurance, exclusions are items that are specifically not covered by a policy. It's a way that carriers narrow the definition of what they will and will not cover. This way, they can be more precise with the risks they're taking on and the pricing that they're offering. With rep and warranty insurance, exclusions are pretty standard for things like under-funded pension obligations, asbestos related liabilities, and environmental issues. But sometimes they'll also exclude things that a buyer might have thought would be covered by a rep and warranty policy. For example, findings from due diligence.

Sometimes, findings from due diligence can suggest that a target may already be in breach of something, for example that they might be in violation of a contract with a customer, or that they don't have proper licensure in all the states in which they do business, or that there is a potential accounting or tax issue. There could be any number of things that might suggest there's already a problem. With these, an insurance carrier might see them as being a higher level of risk and exclude them.

When it comes to exclusions, buyers need to pay close attention. Because while some items will be standard with any carrier, some items could be more subjective and specific. It could just be that the insurance company needs more information to get comfortable, or it could be that something really is a concern, and the insurance company won't cover it under the rep and warranty policy. If this is the case, and a buyer isn't willing to accept the risk for whatever those exclusions are, that buyer can either adjust their price or get a special indemnity from a seller. Possibly one with an escrow or a holdback attached to it. In fact, this can be done for any specific risks that rep and warranty insurance won't cover.

By understanding what's covered and what's not, buyers can

identify important gaps, and if necessary, negotiate special indemnities with holdbacks or escrows to support them. Sometimes, separate insurance policies may even be available for specific items, though these would be separate from a rep and warranty policy. And depending on the risk for the items involved, the pricing would be likely to reflect that exposure.

Coverage Limits

All rep and warranty insurance policies have coverage limits. This means that they'll only cover losses up to a certain amount. Most policies provide coverage up to around 10% of the purchase price. If a buyer wants more coverage than that, additional coverage can sometimes be purchased. For situations though, where a buyer is concerned about the amount of coverage that insurance will provide, and they either can't get additional coverage, or don't want to buy additional coverage, that buyer can still negotiate a backstop indemnity from a seller. In other words, a seller would still be on the hook for any losses that the buyer suffers in excess of the insurance coverage.

For example, in the case of fundamental reps, in a traditional deal without insurance, the indemnity would usually be capped at the total purchase price of the deal. But now with insurance, coverage may only be capped at 10% of the purchase price. If a buyer didn't feel comfortable with that amount of coverage, they could still negotiate a backstop indemnity from the seller. So that if there was a catastrophic loss, once the insurance coverage hit its limit, the seller would still be responsible for whatever insurance wouldn't cover up to the indemnity cap that's negotiated.

The Cost of Coverage

The cost of a rep and warranty insurance policy depends on the amount of coverage that's being purchased. Usually, most policies will provide coverage for around 10% of the purchase price. Which by the way, is more or less what would be placed in escrow in a deal that didn't have insurance. At the time of writing this book, premiums tend to range from around 2.5% to 3.5% of a policy's coverage amount.

For example, in a deal with a $100 million purchase price, if a buyer was seeking $10 million worth of coverage (to cover around 10% of the purchase price), they could expect to pay a premium anywhere from $250,000 to $350,000. Of course, this would depend on a number of factors, one of which is the amount of retention, or deductible, being taken on. We'll explain.

Retention Amounts

The retention amount in a rep and warranty policy is basically just another term for its deductible. It's the amount of losses from breaches in reps and warranties that a buyer and seller are willing to cover themselves, before being able to collect from insurance.

A typical retention amount on a rep and warranty insurance policy is usually around 1.0% of the purchase price in the deal. So, in a $100 million deal for example, the retention amount would probably be around $1 million. This means, that the buyer and seller would together bare the risk on the first $1 million of losses from any breaches. Usually, the buyer and seller agree to split the retention amount. So, if the retention was $1 million for example, the buyer would usually accept the first $500,000 of losses, and the seller would accept the next $500,000 of losses. Once the $1 million retention has been reached, insurance will kick-in.

Sharing the retention amount, where the buyer picks up the first half and the seller picks up the second half, is a similar concept to the way a traditional deal works without insurance. Because there, a buyer usually accepts a deductible anyway. But now, with insurance, instead of a seller being responsible all the way up to the indemnity cap, they're only responsible for losses up to their share of the retention amount. Because insurance will cover the rest. Unless of course, there are special indemnities involved.

One final point worth mentioning, is that as a buyer, it's important that sellers are still responsible for some amount of losses. In other words, not being able to simply walk-away from a deal without any recourse. By still being responsible for their share of the retention amount, they still have skin in the game and something to lose if any of their reps and warranties turned out to be inaccurate, or not true. By still being on the hook, there's still an incentive to pay close attention to the agreement and to get those reps and warranties right.

The Effects on Escrows and Holdbacks

In a traditional deal, one that doesn't have any rep and warranty insurance, a seller will usually leave around 10% of the purchase price in escrow for 18 to 24 months. But now, in a deal with rep and warranty insurance, a 10% escrow is no longer necessary. Unless there's a special indemnity involved. But setting that aside for a minute, and assuming that insurance will cover what the buyer needs it to cover, the only amount of escrow that the buyer will now need from a seller is their share of the retention amount. Because insurance will cover the rest.

This is why, unless there are special indemnities involved, rep and warranty insurance can generally allow sellers to reduce the amount of sale proceeds they leave in escrow from 10% of the purchase price down to around 0.5%. Covering only their share of the retention amount. This allows a seller to get more of their money up front, while still providing the buyer with the protection they need for things they might not know about.

For sellers that either don't want to wait for their money or are simply too nervous to leave their money in escrow because they've never been through an M&A process before, the cost of obtaining rep and warranty insurance may be worth it to them. This is why in most situations, sellers are either willing to pay for the entire cost of the insurance, or they're at least willing to split it with a buyer. Of course, this all depends on negotiation, but generally speaking the benefits of freeing up all that cash 18 to 24 months sooner than if it were in escrow, clearly benefits the seller.

How to Obtain Quotes for Coverage

Insurance carriers have an underwriting process that they need to go through before they can issue insurance coverage. So typically, the way the process works, is that a buyer or seller will first begin with a

142

broker, one that specializes in rep and warranty insurance. The broker will help the buyer or seller obtain competitive quotes from different insurance carriers. This involves sharing drafts of the purchase agreement and background materials on the business, so that there's an appreciation for the type of business involved, and the reps and warranties being made.

Once quotes have been provided, the broker will help the buyer or seller select the best carrier to work with. And just like everything else in M&A, being a broker for rep and warranty insurance is a highly specialized area, so having a qualified and experienced broker is important. The broker can help the buyer or seller not only compare quotes for prices, but also compare the coverage that's being offered by the different carriers, to understand any exclusions that are being called-out.

It's important to weed out and select the best carrier early-on in a deal. Because once that decision has been made, and the deal is getting closer to signing, the carrier will need to go through their underwriting process, and this can be very involved. The typical underwriting process involves the carrier reviewing all the due diligence work that's been performed and having calls to walk through the due diligence findings with the teams that performed the work. Once everything is finalized, the policy is ready to go, and will usually be signed and bound at the same time that the deal is executed.

It May Not Work on Lower-Middle Market Deals

Rep and warranty insurance isn't free, you pay for it, and unfortunately, sometimes, in the lower-middle market, the cost of insurance isn't worth it. The reason for this, at least at the time of writing this book, is that many carriers don't provide coverage for less than $5 million. Which means, that with some of the smaller deals, where the purchase price may only be $10 million or so. If a buyer only wants protection for 10% to 20% of the purchase price, meaning $1 million to $2 million of coverage, then they may have trouble finding a carrier willing to provide that coverage.

If they do want insurance, they may have to pay a minimum level of a premium based on what it would cost for $5 million of coverage anyway. Here a premium could cost as much as $175,000, which may not be worth it to that buyer and seller. Something else to consider, is that with some smaller targets, an insurance carrier may not even be willing to provide coverage if the due diligence isn't clean or the company has never been audited.

So, while it may not make sense to use, or even be possible to use rep and warranty insurance in some of the smaller deals, if it is something that a buyer and seller are interested in, then they should still talk to a broker. Because, at least at the time of writing this book, the market continues to evolve, and it's very likely that carriers in the near future will develop products that are aimed specifically at serving the lower end of the middle market.

Part 3:
Valuing a Business

'At the end of the day, it will come down to what a buyer is willing to pay and what a seller is willing to accept.'

Chapter 17: Having a Disciplined Approach

In an M&A deal, having an agreement on price is by far the number one issue, because without that, there's no deal. Valuing a business though and getting a buyer and seller to agree on a price, isn't always easy. You see, there's no set rule for how a business should be valued. It's subjective, and it involves a lot of judgement, especially when it comes to valuing a privately owned business.

While there are different valuation methods that buyers and sellers can use to decide what they think a business should be worth, generally speaking, they all have flaws in some way, and they all depend on assumptions. Assumptions by the way, are really just ways of explaining through numbers what a person thinks about a business. Like how much it will grow, and how much profit it will make. But this is why valuing a business is so subjective. Because it's the methodologies a person decides to use, and the assumptions they decide to make, that determine its value. And because every business is different, there's no exact science to it. It's an estimate.

The truth is that a person can very easily increase or decrease the estimated value of a business on paper by just using different methodologies and applying different assumptions. All of which could be very reasonable. But this wouldn't necessarily mean that the business was actually worth anything more or anything less to someone who was about to either about to buy it or sell it. So, while a valuation on paper can be very useful in terms of helping someone decide what they think a business should be worth, you don't know for sure until there's actually a buyer and a seller that are willing to do a deal at that price.

The reality is, that no matter what some valuation says on paper, at the end of the day, it will come down to what a buyer is willing to pay and what a seller is willing to accept. Until there's an agreement on that price, a buyer and seller will probably have their own views on what they each think a business is worth.

Eventually, the price that's paid in an M&A deal will be a negotiated amount. The buyer will have a bid, the seller will have an ask, and if they both want to do a deal, they'll probably end-up somewhere in between. The buyer of course won't want to overpay, and seller of course will want the highest price they can get. So obviously, this is where the negotiations happen. Hopefully though, at the end of the day, the buyer has a valuation that can justify the price that was agreed.

In this part of the book, we'll explain some of the more commonly used valuation methods for when it comes to doing deals in the middle market. We'll explain what they are, how they're used, and some the drawbacks and benefits that each of them have. Because even though it's true that they each have flaws, it's also true that when used together, they can help complement each other, so that a buyer is better able to work through some of those flaws and get a better sense of comfort in deciding what a fair price should be for a business.

Before we go into details though about how businesses are valued, we do need to talk about the role that people play in the valuation process, and why it's important that buyers have a disciplined approach to valuing the businesses they buy.

Avoiding Biased and Emotional Decision Making

As we'll discuss in this part of the book, valuation is a very subjective exercise. Which basically means that it's up to people to decide what a business should be worth. The dangerous part of this, is that if a buyer or even a buyer's advisor really wants to justify paying a high price for a business, whether it's intentional or not, they could probably do it by just picking and choosing the information they wanted to focus on, and the assumptions they wanted to use, in order to support a high valuation. Of course, this wouldn't necessarily prevent a blow-up from happening after a deal if it turned out that the buyer actually did overpay.

For the most part, it comes down to the simple fact that people are only human. And setting honest mistakes aside, sometimes their bias and emotions can play a role in the decisions they make. Whether it's intentional or by mistake, bias and emotions can cloud a person's judgement. This is why buyers in particular need to have checks and balances in place when it comes to valuing the businesses they buy. In other words, it shouldn't only be up to one person's judgement to decide. Buyers need to have a disciplined approach that's transparent, objective, and free from any bias or emotions that could be clouding its people's judgement.

What do we mean by bias? In short, we're talking about a belief or a view that someone who is usually, but not always, a decision maker, develops early on about why a deal is important and maybe even at what price. In a way, it's a mental shortcut or an easy way to rationalize making a quick decision. It could be based on a person's experience or judgement, but it's usually based more on intuition than analysis.

These types of decisions can be OK when people need to make quick decisions. For example, at an early stage of a deal when deciding whether or not to enter into an LOI. But if left unchecked, it can become an issue later on in a deal. You see, if a decision maker develops a biased view, or becomes too convinced early on about why a deal is important, or why it's worth a certain price, they may not be as open minded as they should be throughout the rest of the deal process. This is called confirmation bias, and it can be a problem if, or when, there's conflicting information.

You see, people who tend to develop biased views early on to support a decision, can also tend to seek out information that confirms their initial decisions. And they can be less attentive, or even sometimes dismissive, when there's conflicting information that's not consistent with their initial views. It can happen to a person without even realizing it. And by the way, it's not only decision makers that can fall into this kind of thinking, anyone can.

People that work on deals need to be aware of these sorts of tendencies, so that they're consciously staying open minded and paying attention to all of the information that's learned throughout a deal process. Including information that might not be consistent with their initial views. Whether they're positive, or negative.

You see, a quick decision to move forward with an LOI at an early stage of a deal is one thing. But making a final decision when it's time to sign an agreement and write a big check for a business, is quite another. Believe it or not, it actually does happen that as a deal moves from the pre-LOI stage, where you don't have a lot of information, through the due diligence phase, where you learn a lot more about a business, that you do sometimes learn the business either isn't what you thought it was, or it's not worth the price.

Good decision makers need to make sure that they're staying open minded throughout a deal, and that they're willing to change their minds if that's what's needed. The bottom line is that a buyer's final judgement should always be reserved until there's enough information to make a well-informed decision.

How about the role that emotions play? When emotions are involved, people can very easily get caught-up in a deal. And whether it's intentional or not, they can find reasons for why a deal is too important to lose, and why it's worth paying a high price.

It could be that they're feeling a lot of pressure to get a deal done. Or, it could be that they're overconfident in themselves, and maybe not nervous enough about all the things that could go wrong. And while feeling pressure to get a deal done and being overconfident may be two very different things, the risk from both of them is that people will either chose to ignore important facts in order to get a deal done, or they'll just plow through a deal with blinders on and not really take the time to think through all of the risks that might be there.

The truth is, that there will be high pressure situations and there will be exciting opportunities. But if a deal is important enough that there's a willingness to pay a high price for it, the last thing a buyer should want is for its people to ignore important facts, or not consider all the risks. In fact, it should be just the opposite. Because if a deal is important enough that a buyer is willing to pay a high price for it, that buyer should also want to make sure that there won't be any surprises after they close. Because there probably won't be a lot of room for error.

The Importance of Having a Disciplined Approach

If we accept the fact that valuing a business is subjective, which it is, and we recognize the reality that people's judgment can sometimes be affected by bias and emotions, which it can. Then we can appreciate why buyers need to have an objective way of valuing the businesses they buy. As a buyer though, the question becomes, how do you do this? How do you remain objective when it comes to deciding what you should be willing to pay? The answer is by having a disciplined approach.

Buyers need to have a framework, a model, and a process that involves the right people in helping them decide very objectively what a fair price should be. And they should know how to set limits on how far they're willing to go, so that they know when a deal is getting too expensive and it's time to walk. It doesn't mean that a buyer should never be willing to pay a high price. It just means that buyers should be honest with themselves about what a business is really worth and the risks they're taking on, so that they're making well-informed decisions.

With all this being said, over the course of the next few chapters, we'll explain the different valuation methods that buyers can use to develop their own frameworks for valuing businesses. As we do, it will become very clear how important it is that a buyer has a model that includes input from the different functional teams within its organization. Not only to help predict the expected financial performance of a business going forward, but also to help value it.

In part four of the book, we'll explain how the results of a buyer's financial due diligence, specifically the quality of earnings, can also help buyers make sure that they're considering all the facts they should before making any final decisions on price. This way, by having a framework, a model, and a process that includes input from the entire team, a buyer is much more likely to stay objective and make well-informed decisions.

Chapter 18: Valuation Methods

In the middle market, many of the businesses that are bought and sold each year are privately owned. They're either owned by a small group of people like its founding members, a family, a private equity group, or they're divisions of larger companies. When any of these things are the case, and a business is not publicly traded, there's usually not a lot of outside information that's available to value them.

If a buyer wanted to value a publicly traded company, there would be stock prices to look at, audited financial statements, regulatory filings, and lots of other sources of information that could give the buyer a very clear sense of how that business was already being valued by other investors. But with a privately owned business, you don't usually get these things.

When a buyer wants to value a privately owned business, for the most part, they'll still use the same valuation methods that they would if it were publicly traded. But they'll usually have to use different assumptions to value it. We'll explain what these are a little later, but for the most part, they're different because investing in a privately owned business is usually more risky.

Valuing Privately Owned Businesses

From an investor's standpoint, a privately owned business will usually sell at a discount when compared to a publicly traded company. Why? Because they're more risky. Why are they more risky? Well, sometimes they don't have all the things that a publicly traded company might. For example, they might not have audited financial statements. They might be smaller and not as diversified. They can be more dependent on the management teams that run them. The way they do things may not be very sophisticated, or even up to the level of what a public company's standards might be.

And because a private business isn't publicly traded, a buyer doesn't really know how that business would be valued by other investors. And because its stock isn't traded, if a buyer decided they wanted to sell their investment and take their money out of the business, it could take some time to do that. Put all these things together with some other things that we'll talk about a little later, and you'll see why, generally speaking, investing in a privately owned business usually just involves more risk.

Commonly Used Valuation Methods

When valuing a privately owned business, a buyer will usually want to use a combination of different valuation methods. This is because, as we said earlier, any one method by itself is likely to have flaws. But by using a combination of methods, a buyer can work through some of those flaws when deciding a value. In a sense, triangulating between the different methods, to decide the right price. As a result, a buyer can be a lot more confident in the price they finally settle on.

Some of these more commonly used valuation methods, that we'll discuss over the next few chapters, include purchase price multiples, the enterprise value of a business based on its expected future cash flows, a buyer's rate of return on investment, and how accretive or dilutive a deal will be. We'll explain each of these methods next.

Chapter 19: Purchase Price Multiples

Whether you're talking about real estate, cars, or businesses, there's a basic concept that similar assets tend to sell for similar prices. Their market prices. But before we get into how this concept specifically applies to businesses, let's use real estate as an example. Because real estate, is something that we're all pretty familiar with.

We can all relate to the fact that certain houses, in certain areas, will tend to sell for certain prices. Their market prices. Each price may be higher or lower because of the exact location or specific condition that a house is in, and it may go up or down with the market, but generally speaking, at any point in time, there's a way that you can get your arms around what a house is worth, because of what similar houses in an area may have sold for.

A big house that's in good condition and in a good location, is probably going to cost you more than a small house that needs a lot of work in a worse location. But, to get a sense for what each of those two houses might be worth, you could go online. You could find what two, three, and four-bedroom houses have sold for in each of those areas. What you find may not be perfect, but it could give you a sense for what each of those two houses might be worth, because of what others have paid for similar houses in the past.

That's it, that's the concept. Similar assets tend to sell for similar prices. It's driven by what buyers are willing to pay, and what sellers are willing to accept. Because, that's what defines the market.

When this concept is applied to valuing businesses, it's sometimes called different things, like precedent transactions, comparable transactions, or comparable multiples, but they all mean the same thing. If you can find information on the sale of similar businesses, it can give you a sense for what the business you're trying to value might be worth. It won't be perfect, and there are challenges with doing it.

But you can get an idea, because of what others have been willing to pay in the past. Two ways this kind of analysis is done for businesses are by comparing revenue multiples and EBITDA multiples.

In this chapter, we'll explain what revenue and EBITDA multiples are, and how to prepare a comparable transactions analysis. We'll also discuss some of the challenges that are involved when doing this kind of an analysis, and why you wouldn't only rely on this when valuing a business. Because just like buying a house, if some else paid a certain price for theirs, it doesn't mean the one you're looking at is worth the same amount.

Revenue and EBITDA Multiples

Earlier in the book we explained how businesses are valued on a cash-free, debt-free basis, and that it's done this way because buyers want to value the actual operations of a business, separate from its capital structure. This value that's placed on a business is called the enterprise value, and it represents the total price that a buyer is willing to pay for a business. One way to measure how expensive or not this price is, is with purchase price multiples.

Two of the most commonly used purchase price multiples, when it comes to valuing a business, are revenue multiples and EBITDA multiples. These multiples represent nothing more than the price that a buyer was willing to pay for a business (its enterprise value), compared to those two amounts (its revenue and its EBITDA). We'll go into detail on what EBITDA is, and why that's so important in a minute, but before we do, let's go over how these multiples are calculated.

A revenue multiple is calculated by taking the enterprise value of a business and dividing it by the annual amount of revenue that the business generates. Similarly, an EBITDA multiple is calculated by taking that same enterprise value and dividing it by the annual amount of EBITDA the business generates. So for example, if a business sold for $100 million, and it generated $50 million of revenue and $10 million of EBITDA, then the revenue multiple that was paid would have been 2.0 times revenue, and the EBITDA multiple that was paid would have been 10.0 times EBITDA.

When the purchase price of a business goes up compared to its revenue and EBITDA, the multiples go up. And when the purchase price of a business goes down compared to its revenue and EBITDA, the multiples go down. In a way, a higher multiple means a deal is more expensive, and a lower multiple means a deal is less expensive.

By using multiples, it puts the price of a deal in context no matter how big or small the business. And to know if a set of multiples are high or low for a particular deal, they can be compared to the multiples that have been paid for other, similar businesses. And they can be compared to market trends too. We'll explain how this is done a little later, but first let's talk about EBITDA and why that's so important.

What is EBITDA, and Why is it So Important?

EBITDA stands for earnings before interest, tax, depreciation, and amortization. It's probably one of the most important financial terms in M&A. Some people say it's a measure of a company's cash flow, but that's not exactly true. To be more accurate, it's a measure of a company's profitability. But not just any measure of profitability, because EBITDA intentionally leaves out certain things that either don't relate to a business' underlying operations or can create challenges when trying to make comparisons between different companies.

In its most simple terms, EBITDA is a measure of a company's sales, minus its operating expenses. But those operating expenses don't include interest, tax, depreciation, or amortization. Why? Because interest expense is directly related to a business' capital structure. Which can be different from company to company because of the different financing decisions that have been made. Income taxes are related to the tax structure of a business. These can be different from company to company because of the different tax structures that have been used. And, depreciation and amortization expense, which we'll discuss later, are not actually cash expenses. And these tend to be different from company to company because of past acquisitions.

155

So, while EBITDA is not exactly a measure of a business' cash flow, it is a measure of its profitability. And more importantly, it's a straightforward measure of profitability that captures the operating expenses you want but leaves out the things you don't want. This way, you can make better comparisons between different companies. It's because of the things that EBITDA doesn't include that make it such an important measure in M&A. And as we'll discuss later in the book, pretty much everything that falls outside of EBITDA is probably going to change after a deal anyway.

Comparable Transactions Analysis

A comparable transactions analysis provides a summary of the purchase price multiples that buyers have paid for businesses in the same industry, and with similar characteristics, to a business that you're trying to value. The whole purpose of doing this type of an analysis is to see what kinds of multiples others have paid for similar businesses in the past and to get a sense for what a fair multiple might be for the business you're about to buy.

Let's say for example, that you did some research and found some comparable transactions of businesses that were acquired in the same industry, which had similar characteristics, to a business that you were trying to value. To prepare the analysis, you would research each one to understand who the buyers were, what the target companies did, and whatever other information you could find. Not only on the buyers and the targets, but also on the deals. You see, you'd want to find out whatever you could about those deals, and the prices that were paid, in order to make comparisons to the business that you were looking at. This would include trying to understand what each buyer's motivations might have been for doing their deals.

You'd want to sort the transactions by size, to see what makes sense, or what you could gleam from the information. You'd want to look at the range of multiples and the average multiples that were paid. And you'd try to understand, as much as you could, what drove the different prices that were paid. Along the way, you'd probably want to weed-out any deals that you just couldn't get your arms around, or where the multiples just didn't make any sense, especially if they seemed like outliers that were skewing your analysis.

But let's say you did all this, and you managed to find about five or so comparable transactions. These are referred to as 'comps'. And let's say that once you analyzed the data, it looked like all of the comps seemed to have sold somewhere around 1.5 times sales, and around 9.5 times EBITDA. All other things being equal, and not having any other information to go by, you might assume that the business you were trying to value, if it really was similar to those other businesses, might also be worth around 1.5 times sales, or 9.5 times EBITDA.

That's it, that's the concept. By seeing what kinds of multiples have been paid for similar businesses, you can get a sense for the kinds of multiples that might apply to the business you're trying to value. For an example of what this type of an analysis looks like, refer to Appendix Five.

Finding Comparable Transactions

The first step in preparing a comparable transactions analysis is obviously, finding comparable transactions. Unfortunately though, it's not that easy to do. This is because, even if you can find information on transactions that involve businesses in the same industry, there are lots of reasons why companies are different, and why they would be worth more or less to different buyers. Afterall, businesses have different reputations, brand power, intellectual property, technology. They're different sizes. Some could be growing more or less than others, taking, or losing market share, have better or worse margins. All sorts of things. And sometimes, a specific buyer just might have been willing to pay more, sometimes a lot more, than you or anyone else could justify. All of these things play into the prices that have been paid and how comparable the transactions really are to the business you're trying to value.

When you prepare a comparable transactions analysis, you need to keep all of these things in mind. Because all businesses are different, and all deals are different. This is why the comps you find probably won't have all sold for the same multiples. Some will be more, some will be less, and as part of doing this analysis, it's important to try and understand the reasons behind the multiples that were paid.

Why did some pay more? Why did some pay less? And maybe some multiples you find are so outrageous that you just wouldn't want to include them in your analysis. As we go through this part of the book, we'll revisit some of these points, because they're some of the main reasons why you wouldn't only rely on a comparable transactions analysis when deciding what the value of a business should be. It's a benchmark, a comparison, it'll give you a sense of what's market. But because it's not based on the underlying fundamentals of a business, it's not the only thing that you should be using to decide your price.

To find data on comparable transactions, there are different sources. Starting with the most obvious, there's public information that you can find online, from when a publicly traded buyer acquired a business. Sometimes they won't disclose much, especially if a target was privately owned. But sometimes they will, and you can find a good amount of information on both the target and the deal. The hard part is finding it because it involves spending the time and doing the research.

In addition to what you can find online, there are also proprietary databases you can subscribe to. These are provided by companies that collect and analyze this type of information, and for a fee you can access it. Some of these companies even specialize in collecting private company transaction data. We'll discuss in a minute why that's so important. But if you're not looking to gather the information yourself, or subscribe to a service, investment bankers and M&A advisors that you might have relationships with can also be a good source of this information.

Differentiating Public from Private Targets

When you're identifying the comparable transactions that you want to use in your analysis, it's important to differentiate transactions that involved public company targets from those that involved private company targets. You see, before a deal, a public company will often already be trading at a higher multiple than what a private company would even sell for. And then, when a buyer comes along to acquire it, they'll usually pay a premium on top of that in order to get a deal done. It's because of this, that multiples paid for public companies don't usually make good comparisons to what's paid for private companies.

If you're wondering why a public company would already be trading at a higher multiple than what a private company would sell for, then think about it this way, they're traded. Their stocks are liquid. People can get in one day, get out the next day, speculate, and take risks. Traders and investors can take positions, trade on momentum, diversify, and hedge their investments across an entire pool of securities. Not to mention, there's a lot of psychology in the stock market where people will simply make bets on the future movement of a stock. But when you're actually buying a privately owned business, the whole thing, it's a totally different story.

First of all, publicly traded companies are usually held to a high standard in order to be listed. They have audited financial statements, they have to make regulatory filings, and they're usually professionally managed. Not always, but usually. So generally speaking, there's a bit of a premium for that. Second, privately owned businesses are not liquid. You can't just buy a position one day and then sell it the next. Instead, when you buy a privately owned company, your money is going to be locked up for a while. If you want to exit, it takes time to do that, and not to mention, there can be a cost to it. There's a discount for that lack of liquidity. And third, when you're writing a big check to buy an entire business, one that you can't exit quickly, your attention to the risks that are specific to that business become much more concentrated.

Your money is going to be locked up. It's not the same as if you were spreading your risk across a diversified pool of securities in an actively traded market where you can exit quickly if things go south. Here, the fundamentals of that individual business become much more important. It's size, it's position in the market, it's competitive risks, its economic risks, it's margins. Things that need to be fixed or brought up to standard, how dependent the business might be on the people that run it. When you're investing a lot of money in a not so liquid investment, it becomes much more about the fundamentals of that business and how much cash flow it will generate.

And if you're wondering about the premiums that buyers of public companies will often pay on top of what a target was already trading at, these are also not comparable to private companies. Because a lot of the time, when one public company buys another public company there are synergies where the two combined businesses will no longer need to have two corporate overhead structures, two boards of directors, two headquarters. You get the idea. These are big costs that can be cut pretty quickly. On the other hand, when a private company is acquired, sometimes costs actually need to be added in order to bring the business up to a buyer's standards. So instead of a premium, there may even be a discount.

All of these things are reasons why, generally speaking, public company transactions do not make good comparisons to private company transactions. The risk profiles are different, there's a lack of liquidity, the cost structures are different, and the premiums and discounts are different. All of these things affect the multiples that a buyer would be willing to pay and make for bad comparisons. So, when you're trying to value a privately owned business, you want to make sure that you're getting comparable transactions of other privately owned businesses. They may not be perfect, but they're much more likely to be comparable.

Analyzing the Data

Once the data has been collected, and homework has been done on the background of each deal, the analysis can begin. First, you'd want to make sure that you take out any transactions you feel don't belong in the analysis. This way, you can focus on what you believe are the most comparable deals. Then, you'd want to organize the data from each transaction into a schedule, one that summarizes the key statistics. The name of the target, the name of the buyer, when the deal took place, the purchase price that was paid, the size of the target. If you have metrics around growth rates and margins, those are also useful. And of course, the revenue and EBITDA multiples that were paid for each of the businesses that were acquired. Once again, for an example of what this type of analysis looks like, refer to Appendix Five.

When looking at the different multiples that were paid, you generally want to see if there were any deciding factors that you can gleam from the information. Things like size, because generally speaking, bigger businesses tend to have more scale, and so they go for higher multiples. Businesses with better growth also tend to go for higher multiples. Same goes for businesses with better margins because there's less risk. But numbers aren't the only things that tend to drive prices. Remember, it's people that decide the price they're willing to pay for a business. And there could very well have been qualitative reasons, strategic reasons, even personal reasons, why a buyer might have paid a higher multiple than what you can see in the numbers alone.

It could be that the business had a very good reputation and a powerful brand name that carried a lot of value. Maybe it was the number one player in its space. Maybe there was a new product or a technology that the target had developed. Or, it could have been that the buyer viewed the deal as being strategically important, maybe even defensive, and they needed to do it to stay relevant. Maybe there were synergies. There could be any number of reasons why a price was paid beyond the numbers you're seeing. Which is why doing the homework is so important. After all, you're trying to use this information to make comparisons to a business that you're trying to value. And there could be reasons beyond the numbers you're seeing as to why a transaction is, or is not, a good comparison. It's very subjective.

Size and Industry Multiples

What if you managed to find a handful of comparable transactions, but you weren't sure if they were giving you a good rule of thumb? Or, what if you just couldn't find any good comparable transactions? Either way, it's a good idea to also look at industry multiples as another benchmark.

In the same way you can research multiples that have been paid for individual businesses, either through publicly available information, or through subscription services, you can also research the overall market multiples that buyers have been paying for businesses of different sizes, and in different industries. As a buyer, it's just another way to get a sense for what's market. And again, if you weren't looking to gather this information yourself or subscribe to a service, investment bankers and M&A advisors can also be a good source of information.

Good market data can not only show how multiples tend to increase with the size of businesses, or how they differ between industries, but can also show how multiples have been trending over time. You won't get specifics, but it's another rule of thumb that can help a buyer get a sense for what's market.

Market Trends

Just like the economy, the stock market, and the housing market, the M&A market is also cyclical. Its activity is driven by economic conditions, innovations in technology, the regulatory environment, the availability of financing, all of these things. And just like the prices of stocks and houses can get driven up, and sometimes overheated during the boom times, so can the multiples that are paid for businesses.

When you combine a good economy where the outlook is strong, with access to capital and low interest rates, you have an environment where competition for deals can tend to drive prices up. This is especially the case in auctions where buyers need to compete for deals. In an auction, if a seller has a good business to sell, they can put a lot of pressure on buyers to increase their prices if they want to win the deal. And sellers can hold out, especially if the business is doing well and the seller isn't under any pressure to sell it.

When this happens on a wide scale, and in the boom times it does happen on a wide scale, it's referred to as a seller's market, and prices can tend to rise in these conditions, especially if it lasts a while. But why do they rise? Well, there could be any number of reasons when you look at individual deals, but if you look at the overall market, what generally happens is that when business conditions are good, some buyers start to pay more. Either because their outlook on the business is strong, or they have access to cheap capital, or they're just not pricing in as much risk as they would if the economy wasn't as good. As this continues, the market heats up, and buyers begin paying more to win deals. That's how multiples rise.

On the other hand, what happens if, or when, there's a slowdown, or when buyers are a little less certain about the economy? Or even worse, what if there's a recession? Or, a depression? In that kind of an environment, some businesses will take a hit to their top and bottom lines because there's a pullback in their industry. This wouldn't be a seller's market anymore. Because once buyers aren't as optimistic, or the businesses they're looking at aren't doing as well, or buyers have less visibility into how a business is going to perform, they'll start pricing more risk into their deals because there's less certainty.

Higher risk means lower prices. And in a slowdown, if buyers don't have access to the same level of capital they once did in the boom times, either because the banks have pulled back or some other reason, then you've got an environment where multiples will tend to come down, because buyers simply aren't willing to pay as much.

You see, just like the price of stocks and houses can go up and down with market conditions, so can the multiples of businesses. And if you did some research online to look at the multiples that have been paid for businesses over time, you would see waves of activity, where multiples both expand and contract. If you go back far enough, you'd see these trends repeat over and over based on a combination of the things we mentioned. Economic conditions, innovations in technology, the regulatory environment, interest rates, the availability of financing. It all plays a role.

So why are we bringing this up? We're bringing it up because, when you're looking at multiples, whether they're comparable multiples that you've identified on your own, or industry multiples. It's important to also understand current market conditions and where you are in the overall cycle.

The Problem with Multiples

While comparable transactions and industry multiples can help a buyer get a sense for what's market, there are still limits to how useful the information really is. This is because even if you can find comparable transactions for a deal, the fact of the matter is that all

163

businesses are different, and all buyers are different. And with different brand names, margins, growth rates, and technologies, some businesses are simply worth more than others. In the same way, some buyers are simply willing to pay more than others.

It's because each business is different and each buyer is different, that comparable transactions and industry multiples really won't tell a buyer what a specific business should be worth. They're benchmarks. They're good for making comparisons and estimating a range, but they're not precise. You see, just like buying a house, the one you're looking at could be better or worse than the comps. And just because a buyer before you may have paid way too much, it doesn't mean that you should.

So, if what we're saying is true, and it really is the case that multiples are nothing more than a benchmark, then what should you be basing your valuation on? Well, to get right to the point, you should be basing it on a model. One with projections and estimates that are specific to the business you're trying to value. One that allows you to capture the fundamentals of that business. A model really is the only way to do this.

When you base your valuation on a model that captures your expectations about how a business will perform, and the earnings that business will generate, the multiples become more of an output from that model. An output that can then be compared to the comps and industry multiples that you're seeing as a sanity check to see how close, or not, you are to those benchmarks. We'll discuss how this is done over the course of the next few chapters.

Chapter 20: Discounted Cash Flow Analysis

There's a concept in valuation that the value of a cash generating asset, like a business, should be equal to the net present value of its expected future cash flows. The way this concept is applied in an acquisition, is by using a model where the buyer will both predict and place a value on the expected future cash flows that a business will generate.

A typical buy-side model will capture both the current and expected future financial performance of a business that's about to be acquired. It will project income statements, balance sheets, and cash flows. And, it will include all of the changes that a buyer expects to happen in that business, both now and going forward. The typical model will run these projections out for about five years or so into the future, and it's what provides the numbers that are then used to calculate the net present value of that business based on its expected future cash flows. This entire exercise of projecting out the financial performance of a business, and then discounting its cash flows back to a present value is what's referred to as a discounted cash flow analysis (or a "DCF").

Valuing a business using a DCF is without a doubt one of the most widely accepted and commonly used valuation methods available. Especially when it comes to valuing privately owned businesses. But, just like there are challenges when using comparable transactions to value a business, there are also challenges when using a DCF. And, there are reasons why you wouldn't only want to use a DCF for valuing a business without also having other ways of sanity checking the values that a DCF was calculating.

In practice, a model that's used to value a business is usually very detailed and very heavily driven by assumptions. These assumptions are used to both project the financial performance of a business and also discount its cash flows back to a present value. Some of these assumptions are commercial, some are operational, and some are financial. They're all subjective, and sometimes very technical. And with some of these assumptions, only a very slight change in them can have a very big impact on the value that a DCF will calculate for a business. In fact, it's because of how sensitive a DCF can be to certain assumptions, that some buyers don't put much faith in them. Instead, buyers like these will tend to rely on purchase price multiples or return on investment calculations, because those things can be much more straight forward.

So, why then would a buyer want to use a DCF? Well, one of the main benefits of a DCF is that it allows a buyer to capture their own views on the fundamentals of a business. Commercially, operationally, and financially. It helps a buyer think about the current state of a business, where it's going, what drives its value, and where the risks are. And, it allows a buyer to actually calculate the enterprise value of a business themselves, from the ground up, using their own assumptions. Once a buyer has calculated an enterprise value using a DCF, they can then compare that value to the amount of revenue and EBITDA that the business generates and calculate for themselves the multiples they'd be willing to pay for it.

A buyer can even compare the multiples they'd be willing to pay for the business with the multiples that others have paid in comparable transactions, or an industry. And they can see how close, or not, they are to those other benchmarks. You see, by using a DCF in combination with other valuation methods, like comparable transactions, industry multiples, and even rate of return calculations (which we'll discuss later), a buyer is simply providing themselves with more information to make better decisions.

In this chapter, we'll explain how DCFs work. In the next chapter, we'll take the discussion a step further to explain where some of the risks are when using a DCF to value a business, and ways that buyers can sanity check the values that their DCFs are calculating when deciding what a fair price should be. This way, buyers can know the right questions to ask in order to get comfortable with their DCF calculations.

Building the Model

In order to calculate the net present value of a business based on its expected future cash flows, a buyer first needs to estimate those future cash flows. For this, a buyer needs a model. When a model is done well, it can help a buyer develop a very deep understanding of a business. This is because, a model provides a framework for how a business operates, like what drives its sales and what it takes to run it. It can also help capture and quantify a buyer's thoughts about where a business is going and the financial impact that any future changes might have on that business. A good model captures all of these things, and it's what helps a buyer estimate the future cash flows that a business will generate.

As we said earlier in the book, when a buyer wants to build a model, they should not have to start from scratch. There should already be a template. This is because most buyers who do deals often, and most advisors who do deals for a living, already have models that they've developed over time. And from those models, they've usually built templates that are ready to go when a new deal pops-up. Again, it doesn't mean that a template-based model won't need to be tailored to the specifics of a business or a deal. But with a template-based model, the basic framework should already be there, ready to go, so that information simply needs to be populated for that model to be up and running. This doesn't only save time, but it also takes a lot of the guess work out of whether or not a model works properly, which we'll discuss in a minute.

With this being said, the question becomes, who should be running the model? The answer is that whether it's a template-based model, or one that a buyer builds from scratch, it needs to be someone who knows what they're doing. You see, there can be an incredible number of inputs, assumptions, links, and formulas that all need to work together in a model. It takes knowledge of how to build models, accounting, finance, and business operations. And unless the person who's running the model knows how it needs to work in order to reflect all these things correctly, then there's a good chance that they could unknowingly miscalculate something, change something, delete something, or cause an error that other parts of the model depend on.

If that were the case, it could cause an error that might not be noticed until after a deal when numbers start getting reported and people begin to realize that the model was wrong. If this ever happened, it would be a problem. So, whether a buyer is using a template-based model, or building one from scratch, the person that's running it, really needs to know what they're doing. You don't want someone figuring it out for the first time on a live deal.

Usually, in larger organizations where there's a business development group in-house, it will be someone from this group, or sometimes someone from the finance group, who has the experience to run the model. Smaller organizations though, who may not do deals very often, may not have this expertise in-house. For these types of buyers, there are advisors and consultants who can help.

Once a model is built, whether it's a template-based model, or one that was built from scratch, they should all have to go through a review process. This is because people are only human, and everyone makes mistakes now and then. With a model, it's no different. Which means, there could be bad links, formula errors, or other things that just weren't calculated correctly from an accounting or financial perspective. If something was wrong, and it was left unchecked, it could mean that the buyer will miss their numbers after the deal has closed because something was wrong in the model. These types of errors are completely preventable.

It's not to say that accidents won't ever happen, or that assumptions won't be wrong, but as far as the basic functionality, logic, accounting, and mathematical dependability of a model go, these things should always be correct. So, whether you use a proven template-based model, or one that's built from scratch, the person that's running it needs to know what they are doing, and there should always be a quality review process.

What the Model Should Include

A typical model should include at least three years of historical financial information for a business and have projections that run out about five years or so. The reason historical information is important, is because this is what provides the baseline for how the business has been trending and is currently performing. This baseline should be what's used to build projections into the future.

The typical model includes all of a company's sales, costs of sales, and operating expenses. And, it should show all of these things in a good amount of detail. Everything that's necessary to calculate and project the financial performance of that business, from sales all the way down to EBITDA. Every year, for five years. And, any positive or negative synergies, or purchase accounting adjustments, or anything else that's expected to affect those numbers, should also be included. This part of building a model is usually done between the business team who needs to make assumptions about how the business will perform, and the person who's running the model.

Once the performance of the business from sales down to EBITDA has been projected, all of the other expenses that are necessary to project net income can also be layered in. This means all of its expected interest expense, tax expense, and depreciation and amortization expense. We'll explain how these are calculated later when we discuss accretion and dilution.

Along with the projected income statements, a model should also include projected balance sheets, and cash flows. And of course, all of the inputs, assumptions, and calculations that are used to project these numbers should all be clearly presented in the model, so that anyone who needs to review them can see exactly what's been done.

For purposes of this book, we won't be going into all of the details on how a model should be built, or all of the types of assumptions and calculations that go into them. It would simply be too much to cover. Instead, we're going to assume that competent people with the right skills have been brought into a deal to run the model. This way, we can focus our attention on what's important from a higher level, so that as buyers we know how to get comfortable with a DCF when having to make decisions about price.

For readers that are interested though, in seeing the details of how models are built, and the types of calculations and assumptions that go into them, we have provided examples in the appendix of this book. This way, as topics are discussed, readers who are interested, can refer to the appendix to see how these things are done. With this being said, to see an example of what a typical model's projected income statements, balance sheets, and cash flows look like, refer to Appendix Seven.

The DCF Calculation

Once the income statements, balance sheets, and cash flows of a business have been projected, the DCF analysis can begin. What the DCF analysis does, is it takes the amount of future cash flows that a business is expected to generate, and it then discounts those future cash flows to arrive at a net present value for the business. There are sometimes different cash flow measures that are used for different purposes when doing a DCF, but in an M&A deal, when you're trying to calculate the enterprise value of a business, the measure you want to use is called the unlevered free cash flow.

The unlevered free cash flow is basically a term for the amount of cash that a business without any debt generates. In theory, it's the amount of cash that could either be used to pay off its debt, if it had any, or be taken out as dividends by its owners. Without going into too much detail on the calculations, it basically starts with a company's EBITDA, and then reduces that EBITDA for certain uses of cash that EBITDA doesn't include. Like the business' income taxes (on a cash basis), investments in working capital, capital expenditures, or any other reinvestments of cash that would need to be made back into the business. In other words, it's the cash that could be taken out of the business after it's covered all of its expenses, paid its taxes, and reinvested in itself.

Once the unlevered free cash flow has been calculated for all of the projected periods in a model, it's then discounted in order to calculate the net present value of the business based on those future cash flows. For this, there's basically four important pieces to the DCF calculation. First, there's the value of the cash flows that are generated during the projection period. Those need to be valued. Second, there's the value of cash flows that will be generated after the projection period, well

170

into the future. That needs to be valued. Third, depending on the deal, there could be tax benefits that last longer than the projection period, but don't last forever. Those need to be valued. And finally, there's the discount rate that's used to calculate the net present value of all those future cash flows.

For purposes of this book, we won't go all the details on how these calculations are done. Because unless you're a valuation or a finance person, it would be too much brain damage and simply too much to cover. So instead, we'll focus on the highlights of these calculations, so that we understand what drives them. And again, as we do this, we'll include examples in the appendix. With this being said, for an example of what a DCF calculation looks like, including how unlevered free cash flow is calculated, refer to Appendix Eight.

The Projection Period

The projection period of a model is nothing more than the number of years in which you run out your financial projections. If you're wondering how long this should be, there really is no one answer for all situations. The answer is that it depends. It depends on who's preparing the projections and how far out they think they need to go until the business would be in a fairly predictable or steady state. The time frame could be relatively short, or it could be relatively long. In fact, it's not unusual to see a model run out for as much as ten years in an early stage business. Although in reality it's hard to predict anything that far out.

This is why in most situations, at least in the middle market where many of the businesses you look at are already past their startup years, you see models that run out about five years or so. Because usually, at least with an established business, that's about enough time to bake in any changes that you'd expect to have. Besides, projecting anything farther than that, really just becomes a mathematical exercise and too hard to predict.

Let's say that we were using a model with a projection period of five years. During this five-year period, we would have very specific assumptions about how we think the business will perform. How sales will grow, how expenses will trend, and how the business will change over time. By the end of the five-year period, we would have a model that bakes in all of the changes we would expect to see, at least for now.

During the projection period, we also end-up having very discrete cash flow estimates for each year that we've projected. In order to calculate the present value of those discrete cash flows, we simply discount them using an appropriate discount rate, which we'll discuss later. To see how this is done, refer once again to Appendix Eight.

The Terminal or Residual Value

So, what happens at the end of a model's projection period? Does the business just stop existing? Sure hope not. The truth is, that unless you want to run projections out for as long as you think the business will continue to exist, and use that to value its future cash flows, then you need to make some assumptions about how much cash the business will continue to generate after the projection period has ended. This estimate is referred to as the terminal or residual value of cash flows.

The way this works with a DCF, is that at the end of a projection period in a model, you have some amount of free cash flow that the business is generating. Let's say this is happening in year five of the model. But, unless you want to continue running your projections out forever in order to estimate its remaining cash flows, you need to make some assumptions about how that amount of cash flow will continue to trend into the future. Which basically means, forever. For this, we use a perpetuity formula, one that allows us to make an assumption as to what we believe the long-term growth rate should be, or not, for the company's cash flows in a long-term steady state.

By applying this formula, we're able to put a value on the cash flows that the business will generate after the projection period. This value is called the terminal or residual value of cash flows, and it's then discounted to a present value by simply applying the same discount rate that was used when discounting the discrete cash flows.

The terminal value is by far one of the more sensitive parts of a DCF calculation. This is because it's basically calculating the value of all the future cash flows that a business will generate after a projection period has ended. Which again, means forever. And because forever is a long time, it's a lot of assumed cash flow. It's why the terminal value will often account for 60% or more of the value that a DCF will calculate for a business. We'll discuss more on this point in the next chapter when we explain how to sanity check the values of a DCF.

To see the perpetuity formula that's used in estimating the terminal value of a business, refer to Appendix Eleven, and to see how that terminal value is then discounted to a present value and included when calculating the enterprise value of a business, refer once again to Appendix Eight.

Valuing Tax Benefits

Remember earlier in the book when we said that for tax purposes, in an asset deal, buyers get to amortize and deduct the value of all the intangible assets and goodwill that are acquired? Well, in a DCF, if not valued correctly, this can cause an issue. You see, in an asset deal, the value of the intangible assets and goodwill that are acquired can be very significant, and the tax savings that come from being able to amortize and deduct those things, can also be significant. The issue is that these deductions only last fifteen years.

Because these tax deductions only last fifteen years, at the end of a model's projection period, when it's time to calculate the terminal value of cash flows, if a buyer were to base that terminal value on a cash flow number that included those tax deductions, then they would be over estimating the amount of cash flow that the business would generate into the future. This is because, the perpetuity formula that's used to calculate the terminal value, would automatically assume that those tax savings last forever when they don't. They expire. Once they expire, the business will pay higher taxes because they'll no longer have those deductions. Which means, they'll have less cash flow. The perpetuity formula doesn't account for this.

It's because these deductions expire after fifteen years that they need to be valued separately in a DCF. To model these correctly, we need to keep all the tax savings benefits that come from the amortization of intangible assets and goodwill, separate from the unlevered free cash flows that are calculated in the projection period and the terminal value. After these tax savings have been valued separately, they can then be added to the overall value of the business when calculating its enterprise value.

Later in the book, we'll explain how intangible assets and goodwill are valued. But for now, it's just important to keep in mind that the tax savings benefits that come from the amortization of the intangible assets and goodwill need to be valued separately in a DCF. To see an example of how these tax savings benefits are valued refer to Appendix Ten, and to see how they're then added to the overall value of a business in a DCF, refer once again to Appendix Eight.

By the way, if you followed all that, and you're wondering if any of this would apply in a stock deal, where a target company could have pre-existing intangible assets and goodwill that it's been deducting from prior acquisitions? Well, those wouldn't necessarily go away in a stock deal. Because in a stock deal, a company's pre-existing tax attributes, including these types of benefits, would tend to carry over. So, there could still be some remaining tax savings. If this was the case, you would still want to value these benefits separately, because of the timing in which you would get those deductions.

The Discount Rate

When an investment is considered to be more risky, it needs to be able produce a higher rate of return in order to be attractive enough for an investor to take on the risk. On the other hand, when an investment is considered to be less risky, it may not need to produce as high a rate of return, because it would be a safer investment. One of the ways these risks and returns are priced into a DCF, is through the discount rate.

In a DCF, the expected future cash flows of a business are discounted to a present value by applying a discount rate. When a business is considered to be more risky, a higher discount rate is used.

This means that the expected future cash flows of the business are discounted more heavily, resulting in a lower net present value for the business. Basically, pricing in the risk. When a business is considered less risky, a lower discount rate is used. In this case, the cash flows would not be as heavily discounted, and would result would in a higher net present value for the business since it would be a safer investment. One way to think about it, is that the discount rate represents the rate of return that a business needs to generate in order to make it worthwhile for an investor. The more risk, the higher the return needs to be. The less risk, the lower it needs to be.

The discount rate that should be used when calculating the enterprise value of a business in a DCF, is the weighted average cost of capital (or the "WACC") for that business. In its most simple terms, the WACC is basically an estimate of what a reasonable rate of return should be to the investors of a business.

It starts by taking the rate of return that an investor could earn from a relatively risk-free investment (like a U.S. Treasury), and it then increases that rate of return to reflect the additional risks of investing in that business. It considers the riskiness of investing in equities in general, the type of business, the size of business, and other factors. What it tries to do, is estimate a rate of return that would be reasonable for the level of risk involved.

The Weighted Average Cost of Capital

There's a formula that's used to calculate the WACC for a business. It relies on a combination of inputs and assumptions. For purposes of this book, we won't go into all the details on the formula, or where the inputs and assumptions come from, because unless you're a finance person who deals with it, it's just too much brain damage. Instead, we'll explain what the WACC is, and how it's developed from a high level. Then, we'll point out where there's subjectivity in it. Because sometimes, especially when it comes to estimating the WACC for a privately owned business, the assumptions can be very subjective, and they can have a very big impact on the value that a DCF will calculate for a business.

To put the WACC for a business in context, it's basically the rate of return that a business needs to generate in order to produce a reasonable enough level of returns for its stakeholders. Who are its stakeholders? Well basically, these would be a combination of its debt and equity holders. In other words, the WACC represents the rate of return that a business needs to generate in order to cover its debt and compensate its owners.

The formula calculates this in two parts. The first part calculates the returns that the business needs to provide to its debt holders, and the second part calculates the returns that the business needs to provide to its equity holders. The weighted average of these two amounts is its WACC. Once its calculated, what you end-up with is a percentage. It could be 10%, 15%, 20%, whatever. This percentage represents the overall expected rate of return that the business should generate based on the level of risk involved. If you're curious enough that you want to see the actual formula and its inputs, refer to Appendix Eleven.

Most of the inputs that are used to calculate a company's WACC, if you were to use the formula, are based on market data. They include things like the value of a company's debt, the value of its equity, and the types of returns that investors would reasonably expect on those things. This means, that if you wanted to calculate the WACC for a publicly traded company. The information to do it would already be available. You could go online, look up the data you need, plug it into the formula, and calculate its WACC. But when you're trying to calculate the WACC for a privately owned business, it's different. It's not publicly traded, so you can't go online and see how investors are already valuing its debt or its equity, or the returns they would expect from it. When it's a privately owned business, you basically need to decide this for yourself. What kind of returns would an investor expect? And, what kind of returns should you expect? This is where the subjectivity comes from.

Deciding the Discount Rate

In order to decide the discount rate that should be used for valuing a privately owned business, you basically have two options. You can either just assume one, which some buyers do based on their experience and maybe some benchmarks, or you can take a more detailed approach and build one up.

Now clearly, if you just assumed a discount rate, it would be totally subjective. It might be a rate that you decided to use in order to price the deal and achieve a certain rate of return, which we'll talk about later. Or, it might be a rate that was thought to be a reasonable one for the business. Either way, when buyers do this, it's fine for purposes of pricing the deal. Because after all, whatever price is finally agreed between a buyer and a seller, it's going to be a negotiated amount. But because it's such a subjective approach, if there ever came a time to do a formal valuation on the business, either for tax purposes, accounting purposes, or legal purposes, a valuation professional might take a different view. This is because, generally speaking, for a privately owned business, a valuation professional would probably do a buildup, so that they would have an analysis that supports the discount rate they used.

To build up a discount rate for a privately owned business, you basically use the same exact WACC formula that you would if you were calculating it for a publicly traded company. The difference though, is that because it's not publicly traded, you don't have market data on that specific company to use as inputs. Instead, you end-up using market data, in order to develop assumptions for inputs.

To do this, you look at publicly traded companies that are in the same industry as the target, and you pull certain bits of information from those companies. Without getting too technical, these would include things like debt and equity ratios, and betas (which help measure the riskiness of a business). And then from there, you would begin building up the formula in order to assume what a reasonable WACC would be for the business.

There's the risk-free rate of return, the types of premiums that investors expect from equities in general, the size of the business, and even the country that the business is in. But generally speaking, there's market data for all of these things. You'd eventually get to the point where you've calculated a WACC based on as much market data as you could find related to that business. So, let's say you did all that, and you calculated a WACC of 10%. The problem is that it's all based on market data, and it's not specific to the actual company itself.

Sure, it's related, and it's the best information you've got for what an investor might expect for that type of business. But unless the business you're trying to value fits the profile of what that market data represents, then there could be other, more specific risks that you're not capturing. Things that would be specific to that particular company. These are called company specific risks, and this is where a lot of the subjectivity comes from when building up a discount rate to use for a privately owned business. For an example of how market information can be used to build up a WACC, refer to Appendix Twelve.

Company Specific Risks

When market data is used to build up a WACC for a privately owned business, it's important to keep in mind that this data comes from publicly traded companies. As we discussed earlier, these are companies that are held to a high standard in order to be listed, and they're liquid investments. But a privately owned company may not be operating at that same level, and they're not liquid investments. When you're building up a WACC for a privately owned business, you need to adjust for these things.

Remember some of the differences between public companies and private companies, and why the multiples for them would be different? There were lots of reasons. Customer concentration could be a bigger issue, there could be a lack of diversification in its products and services, bigger competition risk, it could be more dependent on its management teams or certain suppliers. Their systems might not be up to standard, and of course, they're not liquid investments. All of these are risks that the market data may not be capturing, and there could be more.

It's because of these risks that you will usually increase the discount rate for a private company well above what you would calculate from market data alone. It's called the company specific risk premium, and it can easily increase the WACC you would calculate from market data alone by up to 30% or more, depending on the specific facts involved. In other words, a WACC that you might have calculated from market data of 10%, could be increased to 13%, 15%, or more depending on the circumstances.

The company specific risk premium is where the subjectivity is when developing a discount rate for a privately owned business, and it's basically what bridges the gap between what market data would suggest and what a buyer is actually willing to pay. It's totally subjective, there's no formula for it, and there's no empirical data to rely on for what an appropriate company specific risk premium should be. It's purely based on judgment, experience, and what a buyer is willing to pay.

In the end, a buyer may very well end-up coming to the same conclusion that they would have if they had just started out by assuming a discount rate. Because ultimately, what a buyer is trying to do is think through the risks that are involved in order to price the deal. After all, investors have choices, and so do sellers. If an investor can get a better return with less risk somewhere else, that's what they'll do. And if a seller doesn't get the price they want, they won't sell.

For an example of the types of issues that a buyer might consider in estimating a company specific risk premium and how it can affect the estimated WACC for a business, refer to Appendix Thirteen.

Chapter 21: Sanity Checking the DCF

While the DCF is one of the most widely accepted and commonly used valuation methods, it's still not perfect. This is because, just like other valuation methods, the DCF relies very heavily on assumptions. But, it's because of how a DCF works in particular, that certain assumptions can have a very big impact on the values that a DCF will calculate for a business. In fact, it's because of how sensitive a DCF can be to these assumptions, that some buyers don't put a lot of faith in them.

Even though a DCF may not be perfect, there are still very good reasons for using one when valuing a business. This is because, a DCF gives a buyer a framework for thinking about the fundamentals of a business. Mapping out where it earns its money and spends its cash. By doing this, a buyer can see how all the different pieces of a business and a deal come together to create value. Like what's driving its growth, the value of synergies, and the benefits of doing an asset deal. But this can only happen if a buyer can get comfortable with what their DCF is telling them.

In the last chapter, we covered the basics of how a DCF works. In this chapter, we'll to turn our attention to now focus on where a DCF tends to be sensitive to certain assumptions. Assumptions that can have a very big impact on the values that a DCF will calculate. As we do this, we'll explain ways that buyers can sanity check these values. Because when a buyer knows where a DCF tends to be sensitive, and they know how to sanity check its values, they can spend less time worrying about whether or not the numbers make sense, and more time thinking about the fundamentals of the business and where the value is being created. For this, we'll focus on the three main areas that a DCF usually needs to be sanity checked. These are the projection period, the terminal value, and of course the overall enterprise value that's being calculated for the business.

Assumptions

Before we go into the types of assumptions that tend to drive the values of a DCF, let's take a minute to talk about what assumptions really are. Assumptions, at least when it comes to valuing a business, are basically just ways of explaining through numbers what a person thinks about a business they're trying to value. For example, if someone were doing a comparable transactions analysis, they would look at the multiples that were paid for similar businesses and they would make assumptions about what they think a reasonable multiple might be for the business they were valuing.

With a buyer's DCF, it's the same idea, they're trying to form a view on what they think a business should be worth. The difference though, is that with a DCF, there are many more assumptions, and at a much more detailed level. So detailed in fact, that you end-up making assumptions on just about aspect of a business. Commercially, operationally, and financially. How much its sales will grow, which products or services will drive that growth, how stable its customers are, how much margin it will make, its costs, and how much profit it will generate. And then, after you've made all those assumptions about how the business will perform, you'll make more assumptions about how to value it.

The thing is, that when it comes to making assumptions, nobody has a crystal ball to predict the future or say exactly what the risks are in achieving the results. It's all subjective, and it's all based on estimates and judgement. The simple fact is that assumptions will never be perfect. You just want them to be reasonable, and hopefully supported by facts and logic.

With a DCF, there are sometimes so many assumptions that it can be very easy to get wrapped up in the details if you're not careful and end-up calculating a value for a business that just doesn't make any sense. This is because, sometimes, even if all the individual assumptions seem reasonable on their own, they can end-up calculating something crazy when it's all put together. This is why, with a DCF in particular, there are certain points where you need to take a step back and look at what's being calculated from a high level. To see if it makes sense. If it doesn't, it means you need to revisit the assumptions you made. Not only to see if those assumptions are reasonable on their own, but also to see that the values they're calculating are reasonable. This being said, let's talk about what those assumptions and values are.

The Projection Period

Generally speaking, the risk to a DCF that comes from the projection period, is that the projections just aren't realistic. It could be that the sales growth rates are too high, that the expense levels are too low, or that the real-world business risks of market forces, competition, and the operations of a business, just aren't realistically baked in. If any of these things were the case, it could mean that the expected future cash flows being projected also aren't realistic and might be too high.

When it comes to running out the projections of a business, you want these things to be as well-thought-out and as reasonable as they can be. It's a combination of looking at a business from a detailed level, in order to build the projections. But then also taking a step back, and looking at those projections from a high level to ask if they really make sense? Not just from a mathematical standpoint, but from a commonsense standpoint. Can a business really grow like this? Can it really generate these kinds of profits? What are all the things that could go wrong and reasons why these numbers might not be hit? Have all those things been thought through?

Remember when we said earlier in the book how important it was to involve the business team that would be responsible for running the business after the deal closed? Well, this is exactly why their involvement is so important. Because it should be the business team who knows the market, the customers, the competitors, the suppliers, the technology, and changes taking place in the business. It's the business team that should know where the opportunities are and where the risks are. It should be the business team that has the commercial and operational experience that's needed to plan these things out. They need to be the ones that get to call the shots on everything from sales, right down to EBITDA, and they need to be the ones who can say why the projections make sense.

Of course, this doesn't mean the business team should be working in a vacuum or on their own. In fact, it should be a broader team effort where the business team is supported by everyone, from the person that's running the model, right down to the due diligence teams that are working on the deal. But when all is said and done, it has to be the business team that's going to own the projections, because they need to be committed to achieving its results. And, when others like the finance team or the investment committee have questions or challenges to the projections, it needs to be the business team that can answer those questions and get the team comfortable that those projections are realistic. If they can't, or if the team isn't comfortable, it means the assumptions need to be revisited.

The Terminal Value

Remember what we said in the last chapter about the terminal, or residual value of cash flows in a DCF? It's the calculated value of all the future cash flows that a business will generate, after the projection period in a model. This basically means, it's the amount of cash flows that will be generated forever into the future, beyond the projection period. Because forever is a long time, it's a lot of assumed cash flow, and it's why the terminal value will often account for 60% or more of the value that a DCF will calculate for a business. This makes the terminal value by far one of the more sensitive parts of a DCF.

You see, the projection period cash flows are one thing. They get discounted to a present value. But then, the terminal value cash flows are another thing. They get valued in a big lump sum at the end of a projection period by using a perpetuity formula. To once again see this formula, refer to Appendix Eleven.

The perpetuity formula that's used to calculate the terminal value basically depends on three things. First, it depends on the level of cash flow that a business is expected to generate at the end of its projection period. Second, it depends on whatever assumptions are being made about how those cash flows will continue to grow, or not, into the future. And third, it depends on the discount rate that's being used, which we explained earlier, but we'll discuss once again in a minute.

So, let's assume that you've scrubbed your projections and you're comfortable that the expected level of cash flows at the end of the projection period are realistic. Check the box on that. Now you need to decide how much you think those cash flows will continue to grow into the future. Are you feeling bullish, bearish, or are you just not sure because it's five years from now and who knows what will happen after that? So how should you be thinking about a long-term growth rate?

You see, this particular growth rate is notorious for having a very big impact on the value that a DCF will calculate for a business. If the growth rate is too high, your valuation will be too high. If it's too low, your valuation will be too low. So how should you be thinking about this, and is there a way to sanity check it?

While there's no one answer for how it should always be done, there are some rules of thumb. For example, with a healthy, steady state business, at the end of a projection period, it wouldn't be unreasonable to see a long-term growth rate that's anywhere between the long-term expected rate of inflation (of say 2% to 3%) and the long-term expected rate of economic growth (of say 4% to 5%). You can think of these as floors and ceilings for what could be realistic. Although, it's probably most common to see a growth rate that reflects only a slight premium to the expected rate of inflation.

In any event, whatever growth rate is used, it needs to be thought through. Because if a growth rate is too high, even though it may only be a slight difference in the assumption, it can have a huge impact on the value that a DCF will calculate. Because again, the assumption is forever. So, if a growth rate can't really be justified, or it just doesn't seem logical based on the long-term rate of inflation or economic growth, then it probably needs to come down. And, for whatever growth rate is used, it needs to be sanity checked. For that, there's a simple way to do it.

When you calculate the terminal value at the end of a projection period, probably the most simple way to sanity check how reasonable the assumptions are, is to compare the terminal value that's being calculated at the end of that projection period with the level of EBITDA that the business is generating, also at the end of the projection period. If you divide the terminal value by that level of EBITDA, both at the end of the projection period, then it gives you an implied EBITDA multiple for the value of the business, also at the end of the projection period. If that multiple doesn't seem reasonable, either in terms of what you would pay today for the business, or what you think it would be worth at the end of the projection period, then you know something is off, and it's time to once again revisit some assumptions. Including the discount rate, which we'll discuss again, next. To see how these multiples are used in an actual model, refer to Appendix Eight.

The Enterprise Value

Once a buyer is comfortable that the projections and terminal value of their DCF make sense, it's time to sanity check the enterprise value that the DCF is calculating. To sanity check this, you basically compare the revenue and EBITDA multiples that the DCF is implying the business is worth, to whatever multiples you would have expected the business should be worth. In other words, by using multiples as the benchmark, you can gage how reasonable or not the DCF is.

To do this, you first need to calculate the DCF's implied revenue and EBITDA multiples. This is done by simply dividing the calculated enterprise value of the business, with its current levels of revenue and EBITDA. These multiples are called the 'implied' multiples because they're the multiples that the DCF is implying the business is worth. These multiples can simply be compared to other benchmarks. Like what others have paid in comparable transactions, or industry multiples, or simply whatever you would have expected the business should be worth.

You can then decide for yourself how close, or not, the DCF's implied multiples are to those other benchmarks. If the multiples look off, or the value that's being calculated just isn't what you would have expected, then it's time to once again revisit the assumptions.

That's basically it. But now that you're at the point, where you have a fully developed model, if it is time to revisit or even just review the models assumptions, you don't only want to do it for the projection period and terminal value in the ways we just discussed, you also want to do it for the discount rate.

So, let's revisit for a minute what the discount rate is, and the impact that it has on a valuation. If you remember from the last chapter, the discount rate is basically the rate of return that the business needs to generate in order to make it worthwhile for an investor. When there's more risk, the discount rate is higher, which results in a lower net present value for the business. And when there's less risk, the discount is lower, which results in a higher net present value for the business.

This assumption, about the discount rate, has a very direct and very significant impact on the value that a DCF will calculate for a business. This is because the calculated value in a DCF is basically just the added up present value sum of all the business' expected future cash flows. From the projection period, the terminal value, and any expected future tax benefits. But the thing is, all these cash flows are discounted using the same discount rate. Which means, the discount rate isn't just discounting the cash flows over the next two, three, or four years. It's discounting everything. All the cash flows that go out forever. It's because of the everything and forever factor that any slight change in the discount rate will usually have a very big impact on the value that a DCF will calculate for a business. It's a very sensitive and important assumption. And do you remember what we said earlier? It's also very subjective.

So, who gets to decide at the end of the day what the rate of return should be? Well, it's not the seller. Because after all, it's the buyer's money. And the buyer gets to decide what they are or are not willing to put their money into. If a buyer prices a deal too low because they want a high rate of return, there simply won't be a deal, because a seller won't sell. This is where the balance of risk and reward meets reality. And once again, why it comes down to what a buyer is willing to pay and what a seller is willing to accept. In the end, that's what's going to determine the buyer's rate of return.

Chapter 22: Measuring Returns

Buyers invest in businesses to make money. Which means, when they invest, they either want a business to generate cash, so they can take that cash out, or they want the business to grow, so their investment can become more valuable. In order to make good decisions though, about where to invest, buyers need ways of evaluating their potential investments. So that if they're looking at different opportunities, they can compare those opportunities and put their money where it's going to provide the best returns. Or, if something isn't going to provide a good enough return, they can choose not to invest. Two ways that buyers will evaluate potential investments in order to make these types of decisions are by estimating return on investment (or, "ROI") and the internal rate of return (or, the "IRR").

Let's say for example, that an investor was looking at two nearly identical investment opportunities. One of them was expected to generate a 7% return, while the other was expected to generate a 15% return. If the risk level from both these investments were exactly the same, and all other things were equal, wouldn't it make sense that the investor would choose the opportunity with the 15% return? Of course it would. Because making more money is always better than making less money, right?

When a buyer is looking at doing acquisitions, ROI and the IRR are used for these exact purposes, and they can help a buyer decide two very important things. First, they can be used to make comparisons between different investment opportunities, so that a buyer can allocate their capital to where it will get the best returns. And second, they can help a buyer decide if an acquisition will even generate enough of a return that it's worth the risk of investing.

There's a catch though. You see, there are no standard definitions for how buyers should be measuring ROI or the IRR in an acquisition.

In fact, there are different ways it can be done, and sure enough, different buyers will sometimes use different approaches, depending on what they prefer. Some buyers might prefer using a measure of GAAP earnings to calculate ROI, while others might prefer using a measure of cash flow. And some, may only use ROI, because calculating the IRR can be too confusing.

No matter how a buyer decides to measure returns though, all that really matters is that the approach they do decide to use makes sense for purposes of comparing the returns that different acquisitions will generate. This way, they're allocating their capital to where it will produce the best returns. And, they can make sure that any acquisitions they do decide to go forward with, meet whatever thresholds or hurdle rates the buyer wants to set.

In this chapter, we'll explain what ROI and the IRR calculations are, and how to calculate them. We'll also discuss ways that buyers can think about setting minimum returns thresholds, which are also known as hurdle rates, that their acquisitions would need to meet before they should consider investing. By having a good understanding of how to measure these types of returns, and how to use them in making investment decisions, buyers can make better informed decisions about the deals they should and should not be doing.

Return on Investment

Return on investment (or "ROI") is a metric that's used to measure how profitable an investment is over a certain amount of time. It's calculated by dividing the amount of gain or loss that an investment generates, by the cost of that investment. So for example, if a person invested $100, and one year later that investment grew to be worth $110, it would be a 10% ROI. Calculated by dividing the $10 increase in value, by the $100 investment.

ROI is really a very basic metric that represents a simple percentage gain or loss. It can be very useful when used for certain purposes. But, one of the drawbacks of calculating ROI, is that it doesn't take into consideration when there's more than one time period involved. In other words, a $10 gain on a $100 investment would be considered a

10% ROI whether it was a one, two, or a three-year time frame. You see, it doesn't calculate an annual rate of return. Just a total rate of return, for whatever time period is used.

Because ROI doesn't calculate an annual rate of return over more than one time period, it's not actually that useful for measuring the overall performance of something like an acquisition. Because in an acquisition, you usually have several years to measure, and different income streams to value. For that, there's a different metric which we'll discuss next, called the internal rate of return. But what ROI is useful for, at least when it comes to an acquisition, is measuring how an investment will perform during very specific time periods. Like the first few years of ownership.

For example, in a buyer's model, there are usually very specific estimates for how a business is expected to perform. There's EBITDA, operating income, net income, and cash flow. They're there for each year in a model's projection period. By simply dividing one of these performance measures, by the cost of investment for each year, a buyer is able to calculate ROI for each year in their model. For example, the first year might have a 10% ROI, the second year 15%, and the third year 20%. These ROIs can then be used to help make investment decisions.

To illustrate this point, let's assume that a buyer was acquiring 100% of a business, and that they decided to use cash flow as the measure of performance. By simply dividing the amount of cash flow the business is expected to generate each year, by the cost of investment, a buyer is able to calculate ROI for each year in their model. Let's say a buyer did this and calculated a 10% return for the first year, 15% for the second year, and 20% for the third year. If those returns were better than other investment opportunities being looked at, and they met whatever thresholds or hurdle rates the buyer wanted to set, then that buyer would be able to make a fairly confident decision about investing in that business, at least from a returns standpoint.

Of course, by no means would this be a perfect calculation of the total returns that the investment would generate, but it would help the buyer make a well-informed decision about its return on investment, at least during the first few years of ownership.

Now truth be told, this calculation can get quite complicated at times, for example when you start getting into details like how much of the business is being acquired, or how much debt it will carry. But generally speaking, this is all very manageable. In fact, if a buyer is using a template-based model, it's very likely that this functionality would already be built in. The question becomes though, how should a buyer calculate their ROI? In other words, what's a good measure?

This brings us back to a point we mentioned earlier about how there really is no standard definition for how ROI should be calculated in an acquisition. You see, some buyers might prefer using a measure of GAAP earnings, like operating income or net income, while others might prefer using cash flow or some other metric. It really comes down to what a buyer is comfortable with and how they want to look at their investments. This being said though, there are some differences that should be understood when deciding which measures to use when making these types of decisions, we'll explain.

Measuring ROI

For the most part, cash flow should be the preferred measure for gaging the performance of an acquisition. Why? Quite simply it's because any other measure of earnings that's used, whether it's EBITDA, operating income, or net income, is likely to either be missing real uses of cash that the business will have, like capital expenditures and debt payments. Or, it would be likely to include non-cash expenses like amortization.

This means that a buyer would either not be capturing the total economic picture of a business, because there are things that aren't being captured, or they would be overburdening it with expenses that don't really exist, like the amortization of intangibles which we'll discuss in the next chapter. It's very simply for these reasons that cash flow really ought to be the preferred measure of returns. Because cash flow, cuts right to the economics of a business and paints a more complete and accurate picture of the value that a business generates.

The question becomes, what measure of cash flow should be used? Unfortunately, the answer is that it depends. It depends on the structure of the deal and what investments a buyer is actually making in a business. For example, a buyer could just be investing in straight equity, or they could also be putting a loan on the business as part of a recapitalization where the business will make interest payments back to the buyer over time. Each of these scenarios would mean a different approach to calculating a buyer's ROI. But let's ignore all that for a minute, because honestly, it would be too complicated for what we're trying to accomplish in this book.

For purposes of this book, let's assume that a buyer was just investing in straight equity. Buying 100% of a business. The cash flow measure that the buyer would want to use, would be the free cash flow attributable to that buyer's equity. This basically means the amount of cash flow that would be available for that buyer to take out of the business. After all expenses have been paid, reinvestments have been made back into the business, and any debt payments that needed to be made were also paid.

It's called the free cash flow to equity because it represents the amount of cash flow that the owner of that equity could take out of the business if they wanted. By dividing the free cash flow to equity for each year in a model, by the cost of investment, it would provide a useful ROI metric for purposes of measuring the cash flow that investment would generate each year. For an example of what this looks like, refer to Appendix Fourteen.

Once again though, because ROI is really only useful for measuring returns over specific periods of time, and it can't calculate an annual rate of return over more than one time period, it's not something that can measure the overall returns that an acquisition will generate. For that, there's the IRR, which we'll discuss next.

Internal Rate of Return

When it comes to measuring the overall economic performance of an acquisition where there can be different streams of gains and losses over the course of many years, the internal rate of return (or, the

"IRR") is probably one of the best ways to do it. The IRR is a calculated amount. It represents the overall annual rate of return that is expected to be generated over the life of an investment. It's based on a formula that takes into consideration the cost of an investment, and by comparing that cost to the gains and losses that are expected to occur over time, it calculates the annual rate of return that would produce those results.

You see, where ROI is really only useful for measuring returns in specific time periods like the individual years of a model, the IRR can do this over many time periods, for all the years in a model. And when certain assumptions are used, a buyer can estimate an overall annual rate of return for their entire investment.

Here's how it works. The IRR is a formula driven exercise. It takes the cost of an investment, and the expected gains and losses that are expected to be generated by that investment over time. Through a process of trial and error, it calculates the annual rate of return that would result in that investment achieving those expected gains and losses.

It's called the internal rate of return because it doesn't need any outside inputs. Just the cost of the investment, the gains and losses that are expected to come from that investment, and the time periods over which those gains, and losses will occur. By using only these inputs, it solves for the annual rate of return that would achieve those results.

To calculate the IRR, you don't actually need to know a formula. In fact, the formula would depend on the amount of time periods involved anyway. Instead, to calculate the IRR, a buyer would simply use the IRR function in their model to solve for it. For example, if a buyer's model was built using Microsoft Excel, then there's already a function that will do this. So long as the buyer uses the right inputs for doing the calculations, and the appropriate function, the model will do all the work and calculate the IRR. That being said, let's discuss the inputs that a buyer would use, because this is where it can get a little complicated and why some buyers simply don't do it.

So, what inputs should a buyer use to calculate the IRR? Once again, the answer is that it depends. It depends on the structure of the deal and what types of investments the buyer is making. For example, if the buyer was just investing in straight equity, or if they were also putting a loan on the business. But, once again, for purposes of this book, let's keep it simple and assume that a buyer is just investing in straight equity and buying 100% of a business.

Basically, there are two measures that a buyer will want to capture for calculating the IRR. First, there's the cash flow that the buyer will earn during the model's projection period, and then, there's the value of that buyer's equity at the end of the projection period.

To capture the first part, in other words, the cash flow that the buyer will earn during the model's projection period. The cash flow measure to use is the same free cash flow to equity measure that was used in calculating ROI. Because after all, that's the amount of cash that the buyer could take out of the business if they wanted.

To capture the second part, in other words, the value of that buyer's equity at the end of the projection period. The buyer would take the terminal value that they've already calculated as part of their DCF at the end of the projection period. Plus the value of any remaining tax benefits, also at the end of the projection period. So that together, these two amounts would represent the projected enterprise value of the business at the end of the projection period. They would then deduct whatever debt still exists on the business at that time. And this, would estimate the value of that buyer's equity at the end of the projection period. In other words, the expected enterprise value of the business, minus the expected value of debt, would equal the expected value of equity.

To a non-finance person this may sound complicated, but it really isn't that bad. Especially if you're using a model where the functionality may already be built in. In any event, it's a combination of these two pieces. The free cash flow to equity during the projection period, and the value of the buyer's equity at the end of the projection period. This represents the total future value of that buyer's investment. Which can then be compared to the current amount being invested in order to calculate the IRR.

In the same way that buyers can use ROIs to make investment decisions, they can also use the IRR. But, one of biggest benefits of using the IRR, which ROIs cannot do, is that the IRR can give a buyer a sense of the overall rate of return that their entire investment will generate. Not just one year, or a few years, but the whole thing. And it puts it in very simple percentage terms. To see an example of what an IRR calculation looks like, refer once again to Appendix Fourteen.

The Difference Between the IRR and the WACC

You might be wondering, if a buyer's IRR would be equal to the discount rate that they used to calculate the enterprise value of the business in their DCF. If you were, it's a very intelligent and complicated question. The answer, once again, is that it depends. It depends because the buyer may not be buying 100% of the business. It could be for something less than that. And, the buyer may want to use debt to finance part of the deal.

These things mean, that the investment a buyer ends up making into a business, could be very different than the enterprise value. Also, the amount of cash flow that the buyer may be entitled to going forward, could be very different than the unlevered free cash flow that was used to value the business in a DCF. Because both these things could be different, the buyer's IRR may not be the same as the discount rate that was used to value the business.

Also, there's one more thing we didn't really talk about yet in all of this, and that's deal costs. In other words, the cost of hiring lawyers, accountants, and other advisors to do the deal. With these, a buyer will usually not include them when valuing a business in a DCF, because they're not part of the business itself. But, when calculating the IRR, some buyers will include them, because it's a cost of doing the deal. This way, they're getting a complete picture of the total costs of their investment compared to the total benefits that they'll get out of it. On the other hand, some buyers consider these to be sunk costs and don't like to include them when calculating the IRR.

Using ROI and the IRR Together

When ROI and the IRR are used together, they can actually help complement each other very well in making investment decisions. Why? Because basically, ROI is a good measure of short-term returns. In other words, the first one, two, or three years of an acquisition. If you think about it, this is an important period of time because most buyers will want to see some sort of a return on their investment as quickly as possible. Unless it's a startup, where the payoff may not be for several years down the road.

But setting this aside, a buyer will also want to know what their overall returns will be, which ROI cannot do, but the IRR can. By using these two metrics together, a buyer simply gets a better view of both the short and long-term performance of an investment.

Once these returns have been calculated, the buyer can use them, to make comparisons between different potential acquisitions. This way, they can choose where to allocate their capital in order to produce the best returns. Also, a buyer can use these metrics to decide if an acquisition is even worth doing based on the risk of investing. In other words, does it meet the buyer's hurdle rates? Which, we discuss next.

Hurdle Rates

A hurdle rate is a minimum level of return, or a threshold, that an investment needs to meet, before it's considered acceptable. With acquisitions, buyers will often set hurdle rates in order to establish a minimum level of returns that each deal needs to meet before that buyer will do it. For example, a buyer might set hurdle rates where all deals need to meet a 10% ROI in the first year, followed by a 13% ROI in the second year, and a 16% ROI in the third year. They could also set an overall IRR threshold that would need to be met. If an acquisition couldn't meet these thresholds, the buyer simply wouldn't do it.

Some buyers set a minimum rate of return that all acquisitions need to meet. Sort of like having a floor for all deals. This type of a threshold is usually based on a buyers WACC, plus an additional amount of cushion that's meant to reflect the added level of risk that's associated with doing most acquisitions. That, and the need to create some level of returns that are above its own cost of capital for its shareholders.

This method of using the buyer's WACC, plus a cushion, is based on the theory that if an acquisition can't meet this threshold, then the buyer would be better off either using that capital to pay down debt, or returning that capital to its shareholders through a buyback of their own shares. For purposes of this book, we won't go into details on this. But the point is, a corporate buyer has an obligation to be allocating its capital to where it will generate the best returns for its shareholders. If an acquisition can't generate an acceptable level of returns for those shareholders, then the buyer probably shouldn't be doing that deal.

Sometimes, buyers will also use floating hurdle rates. This means that the threshold each acquisition needs to meet will float based on the specific business being acquired. For example, let's say that a buyer's WACC was 10%, and they decided that all acquisitions needed to meet a minimum IRR threshold of 15%. Now let's say, this buyer was looking at a business in China, and based on an analysis, the target business had an estimated WACC of 20%. Here, the buyer's hurdle rate should be at least 20%, if not more. Otherwise, the buyer would be overpaying, because they would be earning less than what an ordinary investor would expect to earn on that target business.

You see, hurdle rates can be set in two parts. Part one, is a floor based on the buyer's WACC, plus some level of cushion. And part two, is the target's WACC, because this should reflect the actual level of risk associated with the target business. Generally speaking, a hurdle rate should never fall below the higher of these two amounts. If it did, it would beg the question as to why the buyer would even be doing the deal.

Chapter 23: Accretion and Dilution

Using returns as part of making investment decisions is very important. But because returns are basically just calculated percentages, they don't consider the bottom-line impact that an acquisition will have for a buyer. In other words, a small acquisition can still generate a good return, but because it's small, it may not generate enough of a profit for a buyer to even be noticed. If that were the case, it may not be worth the time, effort, or cost of even doing a deal. The fact is, that if returns were the only deciding factor, a lot of resources could be spent on doing lots of small deals that never really move the needle.

For example, let's say that a buyer was looking at two different deals. Both of them were expected to generate ROIs of 10% in the first year, 12% in the second year, and 16% in the third year. Now let's say that the first deal was a $5 million investment, and the second deal was a $50 million investment. Based on the first year's ROI, the $5 million investment would produce a net cash flow of $500,000. While the $50 million investment would produce a net cash flow of $5 million. Clearly, the $50 million investment would have a much bigger bottom-line impact. In fact, the buyer would need to do ten of those smaller deals just to have the same bottom-line impact that the one larger deal would.

If both those deals required the same amount of time and effort to do, and having the capital to do either one of them wasn't an issue, then which one would make more sense to focus on first? You see, decision makers need to be thinking about these sorts of things. And, they need to be allocating their resources to where those resources will create the most value for their own shareholders. Not only generating returns, but also maximizing the bottom-line impact. One of the ways this value is measured is with accretion and dilution.

Accretion and Dilution

Accretion and dilution are two terms that refer to the impact that an acquisition will have on a buyer's earnings per share (or, "EPS"). What is EPS? EPS is the amount of earnings that a company generates per share of common stock that's owned by its shareholders. It's calculated by taking the amount of net income that a company generates (minus any preferred dividends) and dividing that amount by the number of common shares that a company has outstanding. Hence the term, earnings per share.

For example, let's say that a company, before looking at any acquisitions, earned $100 million of net income in the last twelve months. And let's say that same company had 50 million shares of its own common stock outstanding. That company's EPS would be calculated by dividing the $100 million of net income, by its 50 million shares of common stock. The result is $2.00 of EPS.

A trailing EPS is when this calculation is done on the most recent trailing twelve-month period, whereas a forward EPS would use an estimate of the earnings that are expected to be generated over the next twelve months.

When an acquisition is accretive, it means that it's expected to help increase a company's EPS. When an acquisition is dilutive, it means that it's expected decrease a company's EPS. The amount of accretion or dilution that's created by an acquisition, is basically measured by the amount of net income or loss that acquisition is expected to generate each year, divided by the number of common shares that the buyer will have outstanding. We'll discuss more on this in a minute, but generally speaking, acquisitions that bring with them more net income, create more accretion.

Accretion is a Big Deal

For corporate buyers that are themselves publicly traded companies, accretion is a big deal. This is because, over the long run, a company's ability to grow its EPS has a direct impact on its stock price. In fact, it might be one of the most important drivers of a company's stock price. This is because EPS represents the profitability of a company on a per share basis. The more profitable it is, or is expected to be in the future, the higher it will be valued in the eyes of investors.

Technically, one of the ways that investors value a company's stock, is by comparing its EPS to the price that its stock is trading at. It's called the price earnings ratio (or P/E ratio). It's calculated by dividing the price of a company's stock by its EPS. This is also called the P/E multiple because it represents the multiple that a company's stock will trade at over its EPS. For example, let's say that a company's stock was trading at $45.00 per share, and that it had an EPS of $3.00. Here, the company's stock would be trading at fifteen times EPS.

P/E multiples can be calculated on a trailing EPS basis, or a forward EPS basis. In either case, they're used to help gage how expensive, or not, a company's stock price is compared to the level of earnings that it generates or is expected to generate. And while these multiples do tend to increase and decrease over time with cycles and trends, for the most part, they're driven by expectations about a company's future performance. The higher the expectations are about that performance, the higher its multiple is likely to be. And if that company can grow its EPS, the higher its stock price will go.

Generally speaking, the more consistent a company is in maintaining and growing its EPS, the more valuable its stock will be in the eyes of investors. It's one of the main reasons that management incentives are often tied, at least in-part, to growth in EPS. Because it's an important ingredient in creating value for shareholders.

The Impact That Acquisitions Can Have on EPS

When a newly acquired business brings a new stream of earnings or losses to a buyer, that acquisition could have an accretive or dilutive impact to its EPS. Accretive means that the acquisition will make EPS go up, and dilutive means that the acquisition will make EPS go down.

The amount of accretion or dilution that's created by an acquisition is basically measured by taking the expected amount of net income or loss that an acquisition will generate and dividing it by the number of common shares that the buyer will have outstanding. If a deal is being done in cash, meaning that a buyer won't be issuing any new shares in order to do the deal, then this would simply be the buyers' current number of shares outstanding. The result is the amount of accretion or dilution that will occur on a per share basis, which can be calculated for each year in a buyer's model.

For example, let's say that a buyer was acquiring a business that was expected to generate $5 million of net income in the first year, and $8 million of net income in the second year. Let's also say, that the buyer was acquiring the business in cash and had 50 million shares of its own common stock outstanding. To calculate the impact that the acquisition would have on that buyer's EPS, the buyer would simply divide the $5 million of net income expected in the first year, and the $8 million of net income expected in the second year, by its 50 million shares of common stock outstanding. The result would be a ten-cent increase to EPS in the first year and a sixteen-cent increase to EPS in the second year. In other words, the deal would be accretive to EPS by ten cents in the first year and sixteen cents in the second year.

Deals aren't always accretive. Sometimes they can be dilutive, especially if a buyer plans on making a lot of changes to a business. When this happens, it will usually affect the first year or so while those changes are taking place. That's because, during this time, there can be a lot of additional costs and write-offs that occur as part of transitioning a business. These costs can sometimes create losses that will dilute a buyer's EPS, at least initially. Which is sometimes why, when deals are announced, they can be dilutive in the first year, and accretive after that. But setting this aside, for the most part, buyers want to do deals that are accretive to EPS, so that in the long run they are growing EPS and increasing value for their shareholders.

Estimating Accretion and Dilution

In order to estimate the amount of accretion or dilution that an acquisition will have on a buyer's EPS, that buyer needs to estimate the amount of net income the acquisition will generate. Afterall, that's what gets divided by the number of shares the buyer has outstanding in order to calculate accretion and dilution. With this being said, let's talk about what goes into estimating net income for a newly acquired business, because it's not the same as what it used to be, before the acquisition took place.

When we covered purchase price multiples, DCFs, and returns, for the most part, were talking about either EBITDA or cash flow. But net income is different. Because net income, is based on generally accepted accounting principles (or "GAAP"). And net income according to GAAP, is not the same as EBITDA or cash flow.

If you recall, when we discussed purchase price multiples and EBITDA, we said that EBITDA intentionally leaves certain things out so that a buyer can measure how profitable a business is compared to other companies. But net income according to GAAP is different because it has to include those things.

Then, when we discussed how businesses are valued using a DCF and we wanted to calculate cash flow, we basically started with EBITDA, but then we reduced it for certain uses of cash that EBITDA left out. Like income taxes and reinvestments. But net income according to GAAP, isn't based on cash flow.

With this being said, let's use EBITDA as the starting point, and from there, we'll discuss each of the items that need to be included in order to estimate net income for a newly acquired business. Which is interest expense, income tax, depreciation, and amortization.

Interest Expense

This one's actually pretty easy, because when a buyer is doing a deal, they should know the amount of debt, if any, that they'll be taking on as a result of the acquisition. This means, the buyer should know how much they'll borrow, the financing fees they'll pay, and the amount of interest expense that they'll have going forward. Of course, a buyer will also need to be careful about whatever covenants might be associated with any loans, but assuming that's being looked at and baked into the model by the right people, let's check the box on interest expense.

Income Taxes

Here's where it begins to get a little tricky. Because when a buyer values a business using a DCF, or when they want to measure returns, they'll generally use cash flow. When cash flow is the measure, income tax is calculated on a cash basis. In other words, it's the amount of tax that the buyer will actually have to pay in 'cash' each year. But, when a buyer wants to calculate net income, for purposes of measuring accretion and dilution, they can't do it on a cash basis. They have to follow the rules of GAAP. It's because of this, that the amount of tax that's calculated for purposes of net income, will often be very different than what was used to measure cash flow.

The amount of income tax expense that a company records under GAAP, for purposes of calculating net income, is often referred to as its 'book' tax expense. Because, that's what you see on its books. Or more specifically, it's what you see on its income statement. This is sometimes very different than the actual amount of tax that a company will pay in cash each year, which is often referred to as its 'cash' tax expense. Why are the two different? Because book tax is calculated according to GAAP, and cash tax is calculated according to whatever tax rules apply. These are two very different sets of rules. One is for financial reporting purposes, and the other is for paying taxes, and it's why the two numbers are often very different.

For purposes of this book, we won't go into details on all the differences between book and cash taxes. It's just too complicated for what the average person needs to know, and in reality, it ought to be left to the accounting and tax folks anyway. But what we will do, is explain why the two different sets of rules exist, and we'll explain one of the biggest and most common reasons that book tax and cash tax are often different after an acquisition. Which is, depreciation and amortization.

GAAP Rules Versus Tax Rules

So, why are there two different sets rules, and what's the difference? Well basically, a good way to think about it, is that the GAAP rules try to reflect the long-term economics of a business, for investors. They try to recognize revenues when they're earned and reflect the expenses that are associated with those revenues at the same time. This way, there's a matching of revenues and expenses as a business generates its earnings. When there are things that are used, or occur, over a long period of time, the GAAP rules try to spread them out. For example, when there are revenues that are earned or assets that are used over a number of years.

The result of the GAAP rules is that a business' earnings tend to be much smoother from year to year than they would be if they were done on a cash basis where the actual timing of collections and payments for things can be very lumpy. You see, the GAAP rules are created by accountants who put a lot of thought into how the financials statements of a business should be presented in order to reflect the economics of a business, for investors.

The tax rules though, aren't concerned with painting a picture for investors. They're created by legislation and driven by things like public policy and politics. They aren't trying to reflect the economics of a business, they're trying to either create incentives for businesses by allowing them to take certain deductions for things, or they're trying to collect revenues for the government by not allowing deductions for other things.

The point is, that the two different sets of rules have two very different purposes. The GAAP rules are trying to reflect the long-term economics of a business, while the tax rules are trying to calculate the taxes that are owed. The result is that book and cash tax expense will often be very different in any given year. It's purely a result of the two different sets of rules. Some of these differences are temporary, for example when the timing of an expense is different under GAAP than it is under the tax rules. And some of these differences are permanent, for example where something is treated like an expense under GAAP, but not allowed as a deduction under the tax rules.

Again, in this book we won't go into details on all the differences between the GAAP rules and the tax rules. But what we will say, is that buyers should be calculating both in their models. Book tax for purposes of calculating net income, and a cash tax for purposes of calculating cash flow. With that being said, we're going focus on the one area that tends to create the biggest difference in book and cash tax expense after an acquisition, and that is, depreciation and amortization.

Next, we'll explain what gives rise to depreciation and amortization after an acquisition, and then, we'll revisit the tax discussion once again so that we can highlight how depreciation and amortization create differences between book and cash taxes.

Depreciation and Amortization

In accounting, when a company buys a long-term asset, meaning one that's going to be used over a long period of time, that asset doesn't get expensed right away. It gets capitalized. This means that the asset is recorded on the company's balance sheet, where it's then written-off over time by expensing it to the income statement through either depreciation or amortization expense.

Depreciation refers to when you do this for physical assets like property and equipment, and amortization refers to when you do this for intangible assets like intellectual property. For the most part, these assets get written off, or expensed, over their economic lives. A little bit every year, until they're fully depreciated or fully amortized.

In an acquisition, whether it's a stock deal or an asset deal, once a buyer obtains control of another business, the accounting for that business changes. It's called purchase accounting. Under GAAP, the purchase accounting rules say that a buyer needs to identify, value, and record all of the assets and liabilities that are acquired as part of that deal, at their fair market values. This includes both the physical and intangible assets.

Basically, all of the physical assets of the business are either written up or down (although it's usually up) to their fair market values, and all of the intangible assets are recorded, sometimes for the first time, at their fair market values. If any intangible assets were already on the books, they get replaced with new values. All of these assets are recorded at their fair market values on what's called the opening balance sheet. They're then depreciated or amortized based on these new values.

The end result of all this, is that a business usually ends up with a higher value of assets on its balance sheet than it used to have, before it was acquired, because of all the revalued and sometimes newly recorded assets. And because the value of these assets are higher than they used to be, the business usually ends up having a lot more depreciation and amortization expense than it used to have. All of this new depreciation and amortization expense reduces the amount of net income that a business will report after an acquisition, which affects the amount of accretion and dilution that a buyer will get out of a deal. It's all because of the purchase accounting.

For GAAP purposes, it doesn't matter if it's a stock deal or an asset deal. The purchase accounting is the same. The assets get adjusted to fair value, which usually results in more depreciation and amortization expense going forward. This makes identifying and estimating the value of those assets a very important exercise, because it directly affects the amount of accretion and dilution that a buyer will get. It also means that the buyer's model needs to capture the value of those assets and estimate the amount of depreciation and amortization expense that they'll create going forward. Otherwise, the buyer's estimate of the impact that the deal will have on its EPS won't be right.

Later in the book, we'll explain how physical and intangible assets are identified and valued. But for now, let's revisit the impact that depreciation and amortization expense has on taxes. Because again, it's one of the biggest and most common reasons that there are differences between book and cash taxes after an acquisition.

Deferred Taxes

Under the GAAP rules, once a buyer obtains control of another business, it has to record all of the newly acquired assets on the opening balance sheet at their fair market values. This includes the value of the intangible assets and any goodwill that's acquired. Once recorded, the intangible assets are amortized over their economic lives, while the goodwill basically just sits there on the balance sheet, unless there's a reason to write it down at some point. Under these rules, a buyer will end-up recognizing amortization expense on the intangibles, but not the goodwill. And under GAAP, the book tax expense that's calculated reflects this. In other words, there's no book tax deduction for goodwill. But for cash tax purposes, the treatment of these items is different.

For cash tax purposes, if it's an asset deal, the intangible assets and goodwill are both still recorded, but instead of only amortizing the intangible assets and not the goodwill like the GAAP does, they're both amortized and deducted over a period of fifteen years. This means that over the long run, in an asset deal, a buyer will get more real tax deductions for cash tax purposes than they'll show for book tax purposes. Which again, is because of the goodwill deductions that are allowed for cash, but not for book.

In a buyer's model, these differences between book and cash taxes need to be accounted for so that the projected income statements (which reflect book tax), reconcile with the projected cash flows (which reflect cash tax). These differences are accounted for through the use of deferred tax assets and liabilities on the projected balance sheets, and they represent nothing more than the differences that are expected to occur between book and cash taxes each year.

Stock deals are a little different. With these, generally speaking, a buyer doesn't get to record any new intangible assets or goodwill for cash tax purposes. Which means, that a buyer will usually show more amortization expense under GAAP for the amortization of the intangibles, than what they're actually able to deduct for cash tax purposes. Here, over the long run, they'll usually show less book tax expense than they'll actually pay in cash tax. When this is the case, the buyer records a deferred tax liability on the opening balance sheet, which is then used over time to offset this difference between book and cash taxes. It's not actually a liability that's owed to anyone, instead it's something that's created because of the differences that exist between the GAAP rules and the tax rules.

For purposes of this book, we won't go into any more details on deferred tax assets and liabilities, because it's simply too complicated and not where we want to spend our time. But what we will say, is that from an M&A standpoint, buyers need to model book tax for accretion and dilution purposes, and cash tax for DCF and return measuring purposes. They also need to use deferred tax assets and liabilities in their models as a way to reconcile the differences that exist between the two different sets of rules.

Pro Forma Capital Charges

After a buyer has estimated interest, tax, depreciation, and amortization, and calculated the amount of net income that an acquisition is expected to generate, they can then estimate how accretive or dilutive the deal will be to their EPS. Again, this is simply done by taking the expected amount of net income or loss that the acquisition is expected to generate and dividing it by the number of common shares that the buyer will have outstanding.

Sometimes though, buyers don't see this as the actual impact to their EPS. For example, let's say that a buyer was doing a deal in cash, and that previously they had that cash sitting in a relatively safe short-term investment earning some amount of interest. Once the buyer spends that cash to do the deal, they'll no longer be earning interest. This is referred to as a lost opportunity cost.

Almost all buyers will include some assumptions in their models that reflect the impact of lost opportunity costs when measuring how accretive or dilutive an acquisition will actually be to their EPS. In the example we just used, where the buyer used cash on hand to do the deal, this would be the lost interest income that they'll no longer be earning on that cash. Some buyers, who carry debt, will sometimes make an assumption that the cash they use to do the deal could have been used to pay down debt instead.

These assumptions are often baked into a buyer's model by assuming some level of cost, or some sort of an interest charge, on the amount of cash that's actually used to do the deal. This assumed interest expense (net of tax), is then charged against the amount of net income that the acquisition is expected to generate in order to estimate the total pro forma impact that the entire deal would have on EPS.

Of course, when it comes to these types of lost opportunity costs, it's always very subjective about what the right interest charge ought to be on the cash that's used to do the deal. So, when buyers are looking at an acquisition and the impact that acquisition will have on its EPS, they may want to look at it both ways. First without a charge for lost opportunity costs, and then with a charge for lost opportunity costs. This way, if a buyer believes those lost opportunity costs are real, then they'll at least have a fully informed view of the pro forma impact that the deal will have. To see an example of how pro forma capital charges can be applied against net income in a model, refer to Appendix Seven, and to see how accretion and dilution can be looked at both before and after opportunity costs, refer to Appendix Six.

Chapter 24: Deciding the Price

By now, you could probably decide for yourself how you'd use the valuation methods we discussed in this book to decide the price you'd be willing to pay for a business. But before we end the valuation discussion, let's take a minute to recap everything we've covered so far in this book. Because whether you realize it or not, the entire book has been leading up to this point, where a buyer can confidently decide the price that they'd be willing to pay for a deal.

In part one of the book, we discussed how important it is that buyers have a process for bringing the right people into a deal. In other words, not just having a small group of people negotiating a deal behind closed doors. But instead, involving the business team that will be responsible for running the business, and the functional teams that are all needed to perform the due diligence. All of them, working together, supporting the deal team leader and the investment committee.

This team effort means that the business and functional teams all have the opportunity to provide input on the buyer's model. Afterall, the model is what's being used to evaluate the business, project it's performance, and place a value on it. Without a process that brings these different skillsets together, a buyer may not be considering all the facts that they should. But by having a fully baked view of the business, one that includes the opinions of the business team, the results of due diligence, and is realistic in terms of what's achievable going forward, a buyer is simply in a much better position to make a well-informed and confident decision.

If the business team that's going to be responsible for running the business isn't involved, then who will be committed to achieving the results of the model? If the proper amount of due diligence hasn't been done, then who's to say there aren't timebombs waiting to go off? Or, if the right technical people weren't involved in building the model and valuing the business, then how would a buyer know if they're paying a good price? You see, M&A is a team effort. Which means, having the right people involved is the only way that a buyer can know that they've considered all the risks, that they're not overcommitting, and that they're not overpaying.

In part two of the book, we explained the differences between asset deals and stock deals, including how asset deals can create additional tax benefits for buyers. We also explained how working capital and net debt adjustments work. Without having an understanding of how the tax structure of a deal can add value, or how a buyer can structure a deal to keep the economics fair, or to leave behind unwanted liabilities, there would have been unanswered questions as to what value the buyer was actually getting from the deal, and the amount of risk they're taking on. Without having this knowledge of how deals are structured, making a decision on price would have been incomplete, and left unanswered questions.

As we said earlier, without price there's no deal. But now that we're here, and we understand the process, how deals are structured, and the different ways that businesses are valued, we're in a much better position to be looking at each deal holistically, before deciding the price.

Triangulating the Price

Earlier in the book, we said that buyers will often use a combination of different valuation methods to triangulate a value when deciding the price of a deal. What did we mean by that? Well, now that we've covered each of the different valuation methods, we can hopefully appreciate that each method, on its own, has flaws. For example, with comparable transactions, the comps might not really be that comparable. Or with a DCF, the assumptions, even if they're reasonable on their own, could be calculating a value for the business that just doesn't make sense. But, when these methods are used together, along with using returns and accretion estimates, they can be looked at holistically.

In other words, do the DCF's implied multiples seem reasonable compared to other transactions or industry multiples? Do the returns meet the buyer's hurdle rates? Is there enough accretion that it's worthwhile to do the deal? The fact of the matter is that a buyer needs to have a view on all of these things in order to make a well-informed decision. Not just on what a fair price should be for the business, but whether or not it even makes sense to do the deal.

At the end of the day, if a buyer is comfortable that they're paying a fair price, and that the returns and accretion they'll get from the deal are good, then the question about whether or not to move forward isn't about price. It's about strategic fit, cultural alignment, the ability to execute, and whether or not investing in that business will ultimately help the buyer advance their strategy and achieve their goals.

To see an example of the summarized results of a buyer's model, including all the key valuation metrics that can be used to help decide price and evaluate the overall financial impact of a deal, refer once again to Appendix Six.

The Value of Synergies

One topic that comes up quite a bit for corporate buyers is whether or not they should be pricing the value of synergies into their deals. Especially when a seller makes the argument that a buyer should be willing to pay more for a business, because of the value that synergies bring. Which sometimes, is a view that's driven by their advisors.

They'll make the argument that the buyer already has an overhead structure in place and that they bring scale and operating efficiencies to a business, so that once the two are combined, the buyer will be able to reduce costs and realize those efficiencies. They'll make the argument that the buyer 'should' be willing to pay more because of this.

The problem with this kind of logic, is that it's basically the same thing as telling someone that they should be willing to pay more, because they can. When in reality, that shouldn't matter. The only thing that should matter is whether or not the buyer is paying a fair and competitive price, regardless of how they got there.

When a seller makes assumptions about the amount of synergies that a buyer brings, it's usually a one-sided view. This is because they probably don't not know the buyer's business all that well, and they're probably making assumptions about the amount of synergies that actually exist. You see, sometimes synergies don't exist. In fact, sometimes there are negative synergies, where costs will actually need to be added to a business in order to bring it up to a buyer's standards. Especially in the middle market. And even when there are synergies, there's risk to them, because they don't always work out.

If a buyer wants to increase their price by including some amount of synergies that they bring, that's one thing. But it's up to the buyer to decide on how they want to get there and whether or not they want to include synergies in their price. Some buyers are OK with it, but some are not because there are so many other factors that are involved in pricing a deal. Like how the business will perform, and the risks of executing.

For buyers who tend to go back and forth on what to do with synergies, who are looking for an objective way to think about them, here's an idea. There's a subtle difference in the types of synergies that just about any buyer would probably have, and the types of synergies that might be special or unique to only one specific buyer.

For example, a buyer's model will usually include all of their assumptions about synergies. Like synergies from the ability to scale products and services, or cost synergies. But with these synergies, there are some that just about any corporate buyer in a space would probably have. Like redundant corporate overhead costs, or maybe some back-office functions that could be leveraged. But there could be things that are unique to a buyer. Things that others just wouldn't have. Things that were created through that buyer's own efforts that have created a competitive advantage for that buyer through either scale, efficiency, or some sort of technology that they've developed over time.

When it comes to pricing a deal, a buyer may want to include some assumptions about the level of synergies that other buyers would bring to the table and possibly include those in their price. But the things that are unique, that no one else has? Those are different. Because nobody else has them.

When a buyer separates these things in their model, they can value them as part of their DCF, so that they're quantifying the value that only they can bring to the table. This way, that buyer can decide very objectively whether or not they want to include the value of those synergies into their price. To see an example of how synergies are valued, refer to Appendix Nine. And to see how the value of those synergies can be included in a buyer's DCF when calculating the enterprise value of a business, refer once again to Appendix Eight.

When it comes to whether or not a buyer should be willing to pay more for synergies, it should come right back to the real question of whether or not the buyer is paying a fair and competitive price. If a seller would be likely to get an offer from someone else that includes a certain amount of synergies that just about any other buyer might have and be willing to pay, then a buyer may want to include them. But, if there are synergies that are truly something that no one else has, then that buyer might not want to include them, and instead keep those synergies for the house.

Part 4:
Advanced Topics

*'A buyer needs to do their due diligence, develop a plan…
and make sure that the future cost structure of that business
is reflected in their model.'*

214

Chapter 25: Quality of Earnings

Did you happen to notice, that when we explained the different valuation methods, EBITDA kept coming up? With purchase price multiples, it was one of the key measures used for estimating the value of a business. With DCF and return calculations, it was the starting point for estimating a business' cash flow. And with accretion and dilution, it was also the starting point, for estimating net income. It's why we said earlier that EBITDA is probably one of the most important financial measures in M&A, because a lot of things depend on it.

So, what would happen if the amount of EBITDA that a buyer used to value a business and make projections about its future wasn't right? What if it included things that it shouldn't, or that won't be there in the future? What if it was overstated and too high? You see, if it turned out after a deal that the amount of EBITDA a buyer used to value a business was too high, then that buyer's valuation and estimates for returns and accretion could all be wrong. The question would be, how wrong was it?

This is where financial due diligence plays a key role in a buyer's valuation of a business. Because one of the main focus areas of financial due diligence is the amount of EBITDA that a company generates, and how normal and sustainable that number really is.

What is Financial Due Diligence?

Financial due diligence is a process that a buyer goes through in order to get comfortable with a business from a financial perspective. It involves looking at the books and records of a target company, doing analysis, and asking questions on both the numbers and the business in order to decide if the numbers are not only correct, but if they fairly represent the performance of that business. It will also try to identify if there any financial risks or exposures that a buyer would need to know before doing a deal.

Financial due diligence is usually performed by CPAs who specialize in M&A. They're a little different than your typical accountants, because they don't only need to know accounting, they also need to know M&A. They need to know how the deal process works, how deals are structured, and how businesses are valued. In other words, they need to know what's important from a deal perspective. It's a combination of both accounting knowledge and M&A expertise. A typical CPA who does accounting or audit work wouldn't necessarily be familiar with these things.

Also, financial due diligence is very different than an audit. You see, when accountants do audits, they look at the books and records of a company to decide if the accounting is correct or not, according to GAAP. They do this by following checklists, testing things, and confirming things. And after a few weeks, or even a few months, they'll give an opinion if a company's financial statements are 'materially' correct or not. But when a deal is happening, especially if it's a competitive process that needs to move fast, nobody has the time to wait weeks or months for an audit. And even if a company's accounting was technically correct from a GAAP perspective, which is what an audit would tell you, there could still be lots of reasons why the financial statements of that business could be very misleading to an investor.

You might be surprised, but the accounting rules actually allow for a lot of things that an investor would look at very differently for purposes of valuing a business and structuring a deal to buy it. We'll cover more on that in a minute. The point is, that while financial due diligence still does have to look at a company's accounting, it needs to be done much faster than audit, and it needs to identify what's important to an investor.

To accomplish these things, financial due diligence is for the most part based on analysis and interviews. It involves analyzing a company's financial statements, looking at what supports those financial statements, and digging into the business' trends and operating metrics in order to get a feel, not only for whether or not the accounting is correct, but also for how the business is performing. Understanding its different sources of revenue and what drives those revenues, what makes up its operating expenses, and how they're trending. It also digs into a company's balance sheets. The end result is usually a very detailed view of the business and the numbers behind it. Including the things that would be important for an investor to know, which can usually be put into one of three different buckets.

First, there may have been things that have affected the earnings of the business or will affect its earnings that, if left alone, could be misleading. This is referred to as the quality of earnings, which basically refers to whether or not the earnings are of a good enough quality that an investor can rely on them. The second has to do with working capital, and the third has to do with debt, both of which we discussed earlier in the book. These three areas, the quality of earnings, working capital, and debt are important in just about every deal. The quality of earnings helps a buyer value the business, while having a good understanding of its working capital and debt helps the buyer structure a deal.

In this chapter, we're going to focus our attention on the quality of earnings. We'll explain what it is and some of the more common things that can cause quality of earnings issues. This way, buyers can have a sense of what to watch out for. Then, we'll explain why it's important that buyers reflect the findings of a quality of earnings in their model before they finalize the price of a deal.

What is a Quality of Earnings?

A quality of earnings is one of the main outputs of financial due diligence. Its purpose is to present the amount of EBITDA that a company generates in a way that it fairly represents the economic performance of that business in the eyes of an investor. What does this mean? To put it in context, let's take a step back and think about what EBITDA represents and what it's used for in a deal.

In its simplest form, EBITDA represents a company's sales, minus its operating expenses, excluding the things that don't necessarily relate to its operations, like interest, tax, depreciation, and amortization. In most deals, when a buyer builds the projections of their model, they're using that business' current level of sales and operating expenses, which make up its EBITDA, as the starting point for those projections. In other words, it's the numbers that make up EBITDA that are used as the baseline from which projections are then made on how the business will perform in the future. For sales, operating expenses, cash flows, everything. To once again see an example of a buyer's projections, refer to Appendix Seven.

So, what would happen if the starting point that was used to project sales in a model was too high, or if the starting point that was used to project operating expenses were too low? Well, if either of those things were the case, the buyer's projections would be wrong. Why? Because the baseline that was used to build those projections was wrong. Sales would be starting from too high a starting point, or expenses would be starting from too low a starting point. So how can a buyer prevent this from happening? How can they make sure that they have a clean baseline with reliable numbers to make their projections? And, what is it that financial due diligence can do to help? The answer is in the quality of earnings.

The main goal of a quality of earnings is to present the current level of a company's sales and operating expenses, which make up its EBITDA, on a normal and sustainable basis. What does this mean? It means that there shouldn't be any unusual things skewing it, or things that would make it misleading to an investor. If there were reasons that a company's current level of EBITDA wasn't normal, because there were unusual, one-time, or non-recurring things in it, then these would be called out in a quality of earnings. Or, if there were things that were happening in a business that would cause EBITDA to be misleading to an investor, because it wouldn't be sustainable for some reason, then these would also be called out. Once a buyer has a view as to what a normal and sustainable level of EBITDA is for a business, they can be more confident with the projections they're making about that business.

When a quality of earnings is done, its focus is usually on the most recent trailing twelve-month performance (or "TTM" results) of a business. It tries to present that company's TTM EBITDA on a normal and sustainable basis. Is it ever perfect? No. A buyer never has perfect information. But, it's usually one of the best sources of information that a buyer can get for purposes of measuring a company's performance and having a good baseline for projections.

Quality of Earnings Adjustments

When a quality of earnings is prepared, it's usually best summarized in a schedule. One that shows the amount of EBITDA that a target company initially reported, which is then adjusted to reflect the financial impact of issues that were identified in due diligence. In other words, by using a company's reported EBITDA as the starting point, each issue that's identified can then be quantified in terms of the financial impact that it would have on EBITDA. The issues can either be presented as increases or decreases to that EBITDA in order to arrive at a 'normalized' amount. To see an example of what a typical quality of earnings schedule looks like, refer to Appendix Fifteen.

For the most part, there's no specific rule for how normalized EBITDA should be calculated. Which means, there's a certain amount of subjectivity in it. And while sometimes it's pretty clear when something is misleading and should be shown in a different way for an investor, sometimes it's not, and it can involve a bit of judgement. This is where having the right mindset to thinking about what should and shouldn't be an adjustment becomes very important.

If you take the view that a business' current level of EBITDA needs to be representative of what a buyer should be able to expect going forward in a business, then it's usually pretty clear when something is misleading and should be adjusted. Except, sometimes it can be a little more technical than that. So next, we'll explain some of the different issues that can cause quality of earnings adjustments.

Corrections to the Accounting

When financial due diligence is performed on a business, that business' accounting needs to be looked at to make sure that it's following GAAP. Why? Two reasons. For one, if you're a corporate buyer, then after the deal closes, that's what the business will to have to follow anyway. And two, if a company isn't following the proper accounting rules, then who's to say that the numbers are any good or that the buyer can rely on them? This means, the financial due diligence team needs to look at how the business is accounting for things so they can be sure for themselves that the business is recognizing revenue, accounting for expenses, and recording things on its balance sheet the way it should. If it's not, any issues that are identified where the company isn't following the proper accounting rules should be called out and reflected in the quality of earnings.

If a company is audited, then it's usually a good sign and a good starting point. This is because, a company's auditors would have already had to look at the business and the way it accounts for things in order to give an opinion on its financial statements. Here, the financial due diligence team can usually leverage a lot of the work that was already done by a company's auditors, by looking at their workpapers and interviewing them. It doesn't mean that the financial due diligence team will always agree with the auditors, but it's a good place to start.

Sometimes though, especially in the middle market, a lot of the businesses you look at are not audited. When a company is not audited, it means that nobody has really looked at the business before to give an opinion if it's accounting for things correctly or not. When this is the case, it's usually not a surprise when they're not doing everything correctly. This is because, a lot of businesses in the middle market don't need audits. So instead of following the GAAP rules, they'll usually just follow the tax rules so that they can file their tax returns. Except, the tax rules are not the same as the GAAP rules.

In these types of situations, financial due diligence won't necessarily be able to replace the work that an audit would have done. But what it can do, is ask the right questions, so that a buyer can get a sense for where a company might not be accounting for things correctly and where things may need to be fixed going forward. If there's enough information to quantify the issues, the impact can usually be estimated, at least for the quality of earnings.

For example, if a software business wasn't accounting for its revenue correctly. As long that company had good data to quantify the issues, the impact of what revenues would have looked like if they did account for it correctly can usually be estimated.

Sometimes though, the information to make these sorts of estimates isn't available, or the data that is available just isn't reliable. In these types of situations, a buyer and seller can often just spin wheels trying to figure things out and never really make any progress. If it's a small issue, a buyer could just decide to make an assumption about it and move on. But if it's a big issue, it could mean that the deal might need to be put on hold while the seller takes some time to figure it out. In a situation like this, again if it's a big enough issue, it's probably a good idea that once the seller thinks they've got it figured out, and if it looks like there is still a deal happening, then they should probably get an audit done before the buyer comes back in, just to make sure they don't run into the same issues again.

In any event, if there are any areas where a company isn't following GAAP, these need to be called out in a quality of earnings with some sort of estimates as to what the EBITDA of the company would have looked like if it was following GAAP. This way, the buyer will have a better sense of what to expect going forward.

One-Time and Non-Recurring Items

Sometimes, even if a company is technically following GAAP, there can still be one-time and non-recurring items running through its EBITDA. If they're big enough, they can cause EBITDA to be misleading. These are usually things that a company has experienced, but because they're so unusual, they're not really expected to happen again, at least not any time soon. These can include things like settlements from lawsuits, severance charges from a one-time downsizing, moving costs from relocating a warehouse or an office, or even gains and losses from asset sales and write-offs.

When there are things like these that are flowing through a company's EBITDA, but they're not really part of a business' normal operations, they usually need to be pulled out. This way, the buyer can have a better sense of the true underlying run-rate of the business.

In order to justify removing these things from EBITDA though, they really do need to be one-time and non-recurring. Which means, they can't be normal business expenses that you would expect to always be there. For example, a consultant performing website improvements, or technology enhancements. Those aren't one-time, and you could definitely expect to have those costs again. Same goes for the cost of tradeshows, promotional events, and R&D activities. If it's an item that you'd expect a business to have, then it should be part of that business' operations and considered in a buyer's projections. It's only when an item is truly considered to be one-time and not really expected to happen again that it's excluded from EBITDA.

Seller Add-backs

When preparing to sell a business, a seller will often make the first attempt at normalizing a target company's EBITDA. Usually when they do this, it's well-thought-out, well prepared, and fair. In fact, sometimes a seller will even hire a third-party financial advisor to prepare a sell-side financial due diligence report that includes a quality of earnings analysis. These are known as vendor due diligence reports, or "VDD" reports.

Sometimes though, when a seller prepares a normalized EBITDA schedule for a buyer, it can be a little less than fair. Maybe even a little one-sided, where there's maybe a little bit of window dressing going on to try and make a business look more profitable. You see, there are different ways that a seller can window dress a business. One way is by dialing back on discretionary expenses where they spend a little less here and a little less there in order to try and beef up the profits of the business as it gets closer to a sale. We'll talk about that a little later. But the other way, is through add-backs. Where they can sometimes be a little selective, and maybe even aspirational, in how they decide to present a normalized level of EBITDA.

What's an add-back? An add-back is basically an expense that a business had but for one reason or another the seller wants to make the argument that it was either one-time and non-recurring or that it wasn't a normal business expense. The seller will want to 'add them back' to EBITDA, as if they never happened. For example, when there were personal expenses that may have run through a family owned business.

What do we mean when we say that a seller can be selective in their adjustments? Well, we basically mean that when a seller presents their version of normalized EBITDA, it only includes the positive adjustments. In other words, just the things that increase EBITDA, and nothing negative. Now whether it's true or not, it often begs the question if it's a fair view of what's really going on in the business when all you see are add-backs that say EBITDA should have been higher. It doesn't necessarily mean anything is wrong. It's just convenient how it works out that way.

What do we mean when we say that sometimes add-backs can be aspirational? Well put it this way, sometimes a seller will include just about every single add-back they can think of, just to try and increase EBITDA as much as they can. Sometimes including dozens of add-backs for all kinds of things.

Now at some point, a buyer will do their own financial due diligence. When they do, they'll usually find out whether or not the seller was being selective in their add-backs, and if there should have been other adjustments giving the business a more fair and balanced view. And as far as a seller coming up with dozens of add-backs? If they're truly valid add-backs, that's one thing. But unfortunately, sometimes a seller will prepare a big list of add-backs, and they won't have any support that would allow a buyer's team to validate those add-backs. In other words, no copies of invoices to prove what those expenses really were or that they were even paid by the business.

For buyers that have experienced this firsthand, it's difficult not to have an allergic reaction when you see it again. But if or when it happens, a buyer needs to remember that it's probably caused by a seller getting bad advice. So, rather than spinning wheels and debating dozens of add-backs that don't have any support, a buyer should simply ask who prepared the list, the logic they used to prepare it, and what support they have to validate those add-backs.

Sometimes it comes down to a buyer educating a seller, and sometimes their advisors, on what an appropriate add-back is and why it's important that the buyer can validate those add-backs as either being one-time and non-recurring or truly non-business-related expenses. This way, without spending any time debating, the seller or their advisor can go right back to the drawing board and come back if or when they have something that's supportable for the buyer to look at.

Future Improvements

Businesses will often make changes to the way they do things in order to try and increase sales or cut costs. It's just part of doing business. They'll change marketing programs, or suppliers, or maybe even decide to outsource something that they used to do themselves. Because after all, in business, change is constant.

Occasionally, when changes are taking place, a seller will try and estimate the financial impact that those changes will have on the business. Either by estimating an increase in sales and margins, or by estimating a reduction in costs. It's all well and good. But what's not well and good, is when recent changes to a business haven't proved themselves out yet and a seller wants to include them as add-backs to EBITDA as if they had already happened.

The truth is, that when it comes to recent changes in a business, nobody knows for sure the full impact that those changes will have until they've worked their way through the system. For example, a new sales and marketing program that's expected to increase sales, might not actually hit its targets. A change in suppliers that's expected to reduce costs, could have unexpected problems. And a decision to outsource something in order to reduce expenses, may not go according to plan.

When it comes to estimating the effects that new changes will have in a business, it's fine to estimate them and bake them into projections at whatever level a buyer and seller think is realistic. But in terms of normalizing a company's current level of EBITDA to reflect those changes as if they had already happened, it's not recommended.

Because unless it's already worked its way through the system without issues, you don't really know for sure how those things are going to pan-out.

Reserve Reversals

Under GAAP, a business is allowed to build reserves on its balance sheets. Without getting too technical, a reserve is basically a credit that sits on a company's balance sheet to cover the costs of a future event, like a write-off, or a liability that will need to be paid at some point.

The way it works, is that a company will record an expense on its income statement. That expense gets offset by a credit that goes onto the balance sheet in order to create the reserve. Sometimes these reserves will show up as liabilities that you can see, but sometimes you won't see them because they can be buried within certain accounts.

For example, a company will usually build up a bad debt reserve as part of its accounts receivable, so that at some point if a customer can't pay, the receivable can be written off against the reserve. The way this works, is that over time the company will record bad debt expense on its income statement. This bad debt expense is offset by a credit that goes onto the balance sheet to create the reserve. You wouldn't necessarily see this reserve, because it would be included as part of the company's overall accounts receivable. At some point, if a receivable can't be collected and it needs to be written off, it doesn't show up again as an expense because the expense was already recorded. Instead, the bad receivable gets written off against the reserve.

A company will do the same thing with its inventory, building up a reserve over time, so that if inventory goes bad, that inventory can be written off against its reserve. Accruals for liabilities work the same way, where an expense gets recorded in one period to create the liability, and then later, it comes off the balance sheet when its paid.

A typical reserve will be built up by a company over time by expensing a little bit each year in order to build it up. Companies will usually have some sort of a methodology that they use to do this which tells them how much of a reserve they should have on their balance sheet at any point in time. Over a long enough period, the expense can tend to go unnoticed, because a company will usually only have to record enough expense each year to maintain the reserve that's already there. But what happens is, if those reserves or accruals aren't used, and at some point, the company decides that they're no longer needed, that company can write those reserves down, or take them off the balance sheet.

The problem is that because these things are accounted for as credits on a balance sheet, when a reserve or an accrual is written down, it has the opposite effect of when it was created. In other words, instead of showing up as an expense on an income statement, like when it was created, it now shows up as income when its being written down. And, it's completely normal under GAAP.

What ends up happening, is an expense goes relatively unnoticed as a company maintains its reserves or accruals. But then, once a reserve or an accrual is no longer needed and it's written down, it gets reversed back to the income statement. Where it then creates a fictitious source of temporary income that's not part of a business' normal operations. It's more of a byproduct of the accounting. And sometimes when these things are reversed, they can happen in big amounts. Which means, EBITDA could artificially be too high and not sustainable because of the fictitious income that was created.

Reserve reversals are actually quite common to see when a seller is preparing a business for sale. They may try and justify it as cleaning up their balance sheets, but in reality, it's usually just part of the window dressing that takes place in order to make a company look more profitable. When financial due diligence is performed, this is something that's just about always looked for, and if it happened, those credits that caused EBITDA to be too high are removed in the quality of earnings so that EBITDA more closely represents the underlying operations of the business, without the accounting noise.

Changes in Reserve Methodologies

When a company changes the way it accounts for reserves, this can also affect EBITDA. Let's use bad debt reserves as an example, which are the reserves that a company maintains in case a customer can't pay.

Let's say that in the past, a company had always calculated the amount of this reserve that it needed to keep on its balance sheet by using a certain method. But recently, the company decided to change the method they used to calculate this reserve. If it turned out, that under the new method, the new reserve was either higher or lower than what the old reserve would have been, then it will have a temporary effect on EBITDA. Why? Because the company will either need to record more expense than it used to, in order to make the reserve bigger, or less expense than it used to, in order to let it come down.

In other words, because of a change in the reserve methodology, the run-rate in expense related to that reserve will be affected. The question is, by how much? Usually, the effect of these changes are only temporary, because once the reserve gets to where it needs to be under the new method, the run-rate of that expense will go back to normal.

These same principles apply whether you're talking about bad debt reserves, inventory reserves, or any kind of reserves. If there's a change in the methodology that was being used to calculated it, then EBITDA can be affected. The effect could be positive or negative. And more often than not, the expenses related to those reserves need to be normalized as if the company had always been using a consistent methodology. This way, EBITDA can reflect a normal run-rate of expense.

Related Party Transactions

Occasionally, a target company will have related party transactions. This is where it's doing business in some way with an owner, a family member of an owner, a board member, an affiliated company, or some other party who either has a personal relationship with, or some sort of a financial interest in, the target company. There's nothing wrong with these types of transactions, but sometimes they're not being done on what's called an arms-length basis. Or in other words, they're not being done on market terms because of the influence that those other relationships have. Usually, once a business is sold and those other relationships change, there's a pretty good chance that the pricing and terms for those related party transactions will also change.

For example, let's say that a seller of a target company was also the personal owner of a building that the target company rented. If a buyer was acquiring that business, but not the building, the question would be whether or not the target company was paying a market rate for its rent? Or, if it was even on the same terms that the seller would want in the future as the landlord of that building?

You see, if it turned out that the target's rent was below market, because the owner of that business was also the landlord of the building, then it's possible that after the business is sold, the seller will want to raise the rent in order to get a market rate. It could mean higher rent for the target and less profit for the buyer. And not to over complicate things, but in a situation like this, the purchase accounting rules would probably make the buyer recognize rent at market rates anyway. This is an example of where a related party transaction could result in a quality of earnings adjustment, to reflected to the market rate for rent that the buyer should probably expect to pay going forward.

The same can be said for the salary that an owner might have been taking from a business. Let's say for example, that in the past, an owner, who was also the day-to-day manager of that business, was taking a salary that was below market because they were also taking dividends out of the business. In the future, after they've sold the business and they're no longer an owner, they won't be taking dividends. Instead, if the seller is staying on to manage the business, they might want a higher salary than they used to take. Something that's more in-line with the market. If that's the case, and the seller stays on as a manager with a higher salary, then this would also be a quality of earnings adjustment, to reflect the salary expense that the buyer should expect to pay going forward.

Related party transactions aren't just limited to activities with individuals. They can also be related to commercial activities with other businesses. For example, when a target company sources products from another business that's also owned by the same owner, or same group of owners. Here, if a target company is getting products or services at below market prices because a supplier is also a related party. Then there's a good chance that once those businesses are no longer related, that the other business will start charging market prices. That would mean a change in the target's costs going forward. The question would be, by how much? Once again, something like this would be a quality of earnings adjustment, to reflect the pricing and terms that the buyer should probably expect to pay going forward.

Related party transactions can happen with customers, suppliers, landlords, employees, board members, and even contractors. Basically, anywhere that there's a person or an affiliate who has more than just a business relationship with a company. When it comes to these types of transactions, a buyer should always want to understand them in terms of what they are, their pricing, and terms. And it's a good idea, that whether there were contracts in place or not for those things, that the buyer get new contracts for them. Contracts that very clearly spell-out the pricing and terms that both parties should expect going forward.

Once a related party no longer has a financial or a personal interest in a target, things can change. So, it's in both parties' best interests to set those expectations up front, and of course, any changes that are expected, should be reflected in the buyer's quality of earnings.

Pro Forma Adjustments

The term pro forma is often used in a quality of earnings to reflect the financial impact of things that a buyer should be thinking about in their projections. Not only in terms of how the business is currently performing, but also for how the business should be expected to perform in the future.

For example, we mentioned earlier that when a business is getting closer to a sale, it's possible that its owners could have decided to dial back on discretionary expenses in order to beef up profits. Things like this can include reducing sales and marking spend, cutting back on R&D, even putting off capital expenditures to save on cash. But, when these things happen, they can have an effect on the future profits of a business. Why? Because, a pull pack in sales and marketing spend, can affect future sales. A cutback in R&D, can affect a company's pipeline.

And putting off capital expenditures, can just be kicking a can down the road for a buyer to pick up. When it comes to these types of things, and it looks like the run-rate of expenses or spending in a business has come down, it may not be sustainable if the business wants to maintain its growth. If that's the case, then a buyer needs to be aware of it, so that they can adjust their model for what those things should probably look like in the future.

Pro forma adjustments can also relate to things that a company needs to fix. For example, when due diligence is performed it's pretty normal for different functional teams to identify certain things that the company either wasn't doing well or should have been doing differently in the past. Here, a buyer may need to make changes in order to fix things or bring them up to a higher standard going forward.

For example, the HR team may have identified employment related issues, where the company wasn't paying the right amount of employment tax for contractors that 'technically' should have been treated like employees. Or, the IT team may have decided that the company's IT system isn't up to standard and that it needs to be upgraded. Or, the tax team learned that the company hasn't been paying the right amount of sales tax that it should have been. You see, there could be any number of issues where a company either isn't compliant with something or it just isn't up to a buyer's standards, and it needs to be fixed. Usually, there's a cost to these things that a buyer should be baking into their projections.

Pro forma adjustments can also be used to try and quantify the financial impact of changes that are taking place in a business. For example, the commercial terms that a target has with a major customer or a major supplier could be changing. Either for the better, or for the worse. If for some reason those changes were about to have a financial impact on the business, then the buyer should want to quantify them and reflect them in their projections.

For the most part, pro forma adjustments like these are intended to highlight and quantify the financial impact of things that a buyer needs to be aware of and thinking about. Because if there's something that will cause EBITDA to be either higher or lower in the future than it is today, then that buyer should be baking it into their model and their valuation.

Channel Stuffing

Channel stuffing is a situation where a company offers its customers promotions, incentives, or special payment terms in order to motivate them to buy now, so that the company can increase its current level of sales. For example, when customers are offered a special one-time only pricing promotion or a temporary window of special payment terms, that incentivizes them to stock up on inventory before there's a price increase. Or, before those terms are no longer available. It means that a company might be able to pull sales forward so that they can get those sales today. But in the next quarter or two, it's likely that the company won't be selling as much because those customers will need to work down what they already bought.

When this happens, it can have the effect of pulling a company's sales forward from future periods and overstating its EBITDA. That's because the profits that would have been earned in the future were pulled forward temporarily. If EBITDA isn't adjusted to smooth out the timing of when those sales probably should have happened under normal conditions, then it could be too high and misleading.

Some of the typical red flags that help identify things like this include an unusually high level of sales at the end of a period, or an increase in the amount of promotional activities, or extensions of credit terms with customers. If any of these things created a big enough impact that they can be seen affecting sales and EBITDA, then they should probably be looked at a little closer to see if sales and profits were pulled forward and need to be adjusted.

Changes in Accounting

When a company changes the way it accounts for things, this can cause EBITDA to temporarily be either higher or lower than it would normally be, simply because of the changes that were made. This can be the case whether it's a change in accounting for revenues or expenses.

Let's take revenues for example and say that in the past, a company sold products to customers where it allowed those customers to pay on 30-day terms. Meaning, that its customers had up to 30-days after they made purchases to pay the company what was owed. And let's say that the company used to recognize revenue from those sales when the customers paid. In other words, at the end of the 30-days. Now though, only recently, the company decided to begin recognizing its revenues earlier. So instead of waiting until they got paid at the end of 30-days, they would now begin recognizing revenues at the time that its customers actually made their purchases. In other words, recognizing revenue at the time of sale and no longer waiting until cash was collected.

This change in the company's accounting for revenue, would cause its revenue to be overstated for a short period time while the accounting change took place. At the sake of oversimplifying things, this would basically be because the company began recording new sales under the new method (by recording receivables for the first time), while it was still recognizing old sales under the old method (when cash was collected). The actual level of activity in the business may not have changed, but because the accounting changed, twice the amount of revenue would get booked for a short period of time as the change took place. Once this change was done though, those revenues would go back to a normal run-rate. You see, this is an example of what's called a cash to accrual change in accounting, and it can have a temporary impact on the level of profitably in a business.

Similar issues can happen when there's a change in accounting for expenses. Let's say for example that in the past, a company expensed all of the equipment that it bought. But recently, the company decided it would now start capitalizing its equipment. Here, you would have some level of expense on the company's income statements for equipment purchases that were made in the past, but those expenses would stop once the company decided to start capitalizing those things onto its balance sheets. Eventually, at some point, depreciation expense would begin building up on the income statements from the depreciation of that equipment. Although it would probably take time to come up to a normal run-rate. But again, it's an example of how a change in accounting can affect the run-rates of a business. And because these things are usually only temporary, a buyer needs to be aware of them when they happen, so that they can be thinking about how it should be treated in the quality of earnings, and how it might affect their projections.

Putting the Pieces Together

Once the financial due diligence team has prepared its quality of earnings, it's a good idea that they walk the buyer through each of the adjustments they've identified. This way, the buyer can decide for themselves what impact, if any, each of those items should have on their model and the price they're willing to pay for the business.

Why would price change? Because, if a buyer had certain expectations about the level of earnings a business was generating, that after due diligence turned out to not be the case. Then it's only fair that the buyer's view of price may have changed. Why? Because if a quality of earnings causes a buyer to change their model, then it's possible that their DCF may change. Their view of the multiple they were willing to pay may change, and the returns and accretion that they thought were going to get may also change.

Of course, if it's all small changes, then it's not likely that anyone will want to reopen pricing discussions. But if there are real issues that have now caused the buyer to rethink what the business is worth, then it's only fair that the buyer re-open those discussions and renegotiate a price that they're comfortable with before moving forward.

Chapter 26: Carve-Out Transactions

A carve-out transaction is where a parent company 'carves-out' and sells a business from within a larger group of businesses that it owns. A carve-out can be a business segment, a division, or just a group of products and services that happen to make up a business. Sometimes a carve-out will be housed within its own legal entity, or a group of legal entities. But sometimes it won't, and it could just be something that exists within an entity that also owns other businesses.

Sometimes, a carve-out will operate independently, where it doesn't really get any support from its parent or affiliates. When this is the case, a deal to buy it can usually be pretty straight forward and a lot like buying a regular stand-alone business. But a lot of the time, this isn't the case with carve-outs. That's because, carve-outs will usually have some sort of commercial relationships with their parents, or affiliates that are also owned by their parents. And they'll also get some sort of support from their parents.

When a carve-out business is being separated from its parent and transitioned to a new buyer, these things need to be looked at. Because if a carve-out had any commercial relationships with its parent or affiliates, then it's pretty likely that those relationships are going to change once the business is no longer part of that parent's group. And, if a carve-out was getting any financial or operational support from that parent, then that support is also likely to end once the business is sold.

Issues like these can create challenges for buyers when acquiring a carve-out business. Challenges that can relate to not only separating the business from its former owner, but then also re-establishing it, either as a stand-alone entity, or as part of a new buyer's portfolio of businesses.

Separating a business, transitioning it, and then re-establishing it, means a lot of change. Change that can affect how the business operates and its profitability. From a buyer's perspective, this means risk, and it's why all of the changes that are about to happen need to be understood, thought through, and planned out. From separating the business and transitioning it, to what it's all going to look like once it's been re-established somewhere else.

It probably goes without saying, but a carve-out transaction can be much more complicated and risky for a buyer than when buying an existing stand-alone business. In this chapter, we'll explain why this is the case. We'll also explain ways that buyers can prepare themselves ahead of time for the types of issues that they should expect to see in a carve-out situation. This way, they can quickly get their arms around the issues that matter and have a well-thought-out plan for how they're going to transition the business and operate it in the future.

Structuring a Carve-Out

Just like other types of transactions, a carve-out can be structured as either an asset deal or a stock deal. Let's say for example that there was a situation where a carve-out business was basically a division that sat within a seller's larger legal entity. An entity, that also owned other businesses. Here, an asset deal might make the most sense. Because with an asset deal, the individual assets and liabilities like the customers, intellectual property, and employees that make up the business, can simply be packaged up and sold to a new buyer. This way, the buyer can acquire the carve-out business' assets and liabilities and leave the legal entity with all its other businesses behind. On the other hand, if a carve-out was already housed within its own legal entity, or combination of legal entities, then it's possible that a stock deal might make more sense. It really just depends on the situation.

For the most part, the criteria that a buyer and seller would go through to decide between doing an asset deal or a stock deal would be exactly the same as what we discussed in part two of the book. And once they've decided which type of deal they want to do, most of the same mechanics would also still apply. In other words, the buyer will still want a working capital adjustment, a net debt adjustment, indemnities, and all the other protections that they would normally get.

But, because it's a carve-out, sometimes things don't apply, because of the situation. Or, when they do, they need to be tailored to fit the situation. For the most part though, when it comes to structuring a carve-out, a buyer should go-in wanting to follow all of the same principles, rules, and mechanics that they normally would, unless or until the circumstances don't allow for something. In which case, the deal would then need to be tailored to fit the situation.

Transition Services Agreements

It's usually pretty common that a buyer will need time and help from a seller in order to successfully transition a carve-out business. This is especially the case if in the past the carve-out got a lot of support from its parent. Why? Because if a business got a lot of support, and then all of the sudden, as soon as the deal closed, that support was to stop, the business could have problems. Especially if the buyer wasn't ready to take it over yet.

For example, let's say that a carve-out business was located inside a parent's headquarters where the parent provided IT, HR, and accounting support to that business. Let's also say that the carve-out business had some sort of a unique customer-facing software tool that it used on a daily basis to interact and transact with its customers. But, that software and all of its customer data sat on its parent's servers, where it was maintained and supported by the parent's IT staff.

Once a deal closes, if the parent just cuts-off all support to that carve-out business, it could disrupt the business' operations. For example, the carve-out's employees might not be allowed back into their old offices, because those offices were in the parent's headquarters. Their abilities to interact and transact with customers through the software tool they once used could be cut-off, because that software was on the parent's servers. Their websites, phones, email addresses, all of it gone, because the parent provided all of their IT support. You see, without that former parent continuing to provide support, until the buyer was ready to take over the business, then that business could be disrupted, and a lot of the value that a buyer thought they were going to get could be lost.

A carve-out business will often need time to transition itself away from an old parent, so that it can establish itself somewhere else. In the example we just used, the business would probably need to move its employees into a new office, buy them new laptops, move its websites to a new host, get new email addresses, new phones, new office equipment. It would need to transition its HR and accounting. And not to mention, it's customer-facing software tools and data would all need to be migrated off the old parent's servers and reestablished somewhere else. You see, if the old parent just shut everything down before the buyer was ready, there could be problems. So, to prevent these types of things from happening, a buyer and seller will usually enter into a transition services agreement (known as a "TSA") as part of a carve-out transaction.

A TSA is a contract between a buyer and a seller, where a seller agrees to provide a certain level of support and service to a carve-out business while the buyer has time to transition it. The typical TSA will include support for things like IT, accounting, HR, and other back-office functions. But it can also include operational support for things like R&D, customer service, manufacturing, warehousing, and distribution. It all depends on the specific situation and where the carve-out business relied on its parent or affiliates in the past.

In most TSA situations, once a parent has sold a carve-out business, they don't want to provide support to that business for any longer than they have to. After all, they don't own it anymore and they want the buyer to take responsibility for it. This is why, a seller will usually want to limit the amount of time they're willing to provide support under a TSA. It's a way of putting a buyer on notice that they'd better get moving on transitioning that business, because the support they're getting is not going to last forever. Also, if there's a cost to the support that a seller is providing, they're going to want to get paid for it. These are all reasons why buyers need to know what support a carve-out business gets and how long it's going to need that support while the business is being transitioned.

Identifying Carve-Out Issues

From a buyer's perspective, it's important to know what kind of support a carve-out got in the past from its parent. Not only for the things that the TSA will need to cover, but also so that the buyer can plan for how to transition those things and estimate the cost of replacing them in the future. In other words, a buyer needs to do their due diligence, develop a plan, make sure the TSA aligns with that plan, and make sure that the future cost structure of the business is reflected in their model.

Sometimes, as part of preparing a carve-out for sale, a seller will try to identify and quantify all the different kinds of support that it provided in the past to the carve-out. But sometimes they won't, or they won't capture everything, and it can become a learning process for both the buyer and the seller as they go through the due diligence. But this is why a buyer's due diligence is so important in a carve-out. Because whether a seller identified it or not, once that seller has cut the business off, the buyer is going to have to run it. Which means, if there's support the business needs, the buyer is going to have to provide it.

It should go without saying, but a buyer really needs to have a good understanding of what it takes to run a carve-out business. Everything from operations to back office functions. And if it turns out that something's going to change in the business, because of having to separate it and re-establish it somewhere else, then those changes need to be thought through in terms of both operations and profits.

Generally speaking, there are three main categories that these types of changes can be put into. First, there may have been commercial relationships that are about to change. Second, there may have been shared costs. And third, there may have been shared services. We'll discuss each of these categories next.

Commercial Relationships

A carve-out business will often have commercial relationships with either its parent, or affiliates that are also owned by its parent. It can be the case for both buying products and services and selling products and services.

For example, a carve-out business could be buying products that an affiliate manufactures, and it could be getting special pricing on those products because it's part of the parent's affiliated group. But once the carve-out is sold, and it's no longer part of that affiliated group, it's costs could go up. Why? Because the seller may want to start charging the same market prices to the carve-out that they also charge to their other customers.

The same thing can happen when a carve-out business is buying products or services through special pricing that its parent gets from a third-party. For example, a parent could have a contract that gives their entire portfolio of businesses special pricing from an outside vendor because of the volume they're able to buy. But once the carve-out business is no longer part of that parent's group, it will no longer have access to that pricing. So again, its costs could go up.

On the sales side of things, a carve-out business could be selling its products or services directly to a parent or an affiliate. Or, they could be selling indirectly to customers that are shared with a parent or an affiliate. In the case of selling directly to the parent or affiliate, if that parent or affiliate decide to buy similar products or services from somewhere else after the carve-out was sold, then those sales could just go away. And in the case of selling indirectly to customers that are shared with a parent or an affiliate, if it's the parent or affiliate that own those customer relationships, and again, they decide to replace the carve-out's products or services with something else, from someone else, then those sales could also be at risk.

You see, whenever there are commercial relationships between a carve-out business and its parent or affiliates, those relationships need to be understood. If those relationships are going to change in the future because the carve-out is no longer going to be part of that parent's group, then the buyer needs to know it, do their due diligence on it, and plan for what could happen. And, it's a good idea for the buyer to get those relationships in writing under new commercial contracts as part of any deal. This way, they can set-out the pricing and terms that both parties should be expecting going forward. And if the new terms are going to be different than the old terms, then at least the buyer will know what to expect, and what to bake into their model.

Shared Costs

A carve-out business will usually have a different cost structure than a stand-alone business. This is because a carve-out will usually share costs with its parent and affiliates in order to realize efficiencies. Things like this can include insurance, professional and consulting services, IT expenses, communications costs. Basically any product or service that a business uses, but rather than something that's specific to only the carve-out, it's shared.

For example, a carve-out's parent could be sourcing and managing all of the insurance products for its entire portfolio of businesses. Things like general liability insurance, product liability insurance, even its employees' health insurance. By managing all of its insurance needs as a group, a parent can often get better rates. But in a situation like this, when a carve-out's insurance has been covered under a parent's group policies, those policies don't transfer with the carve-out business, because they belong to the parent. This means, that a buyer will need to get their own insurance going forward. And by the way, they may not get the same rates.

Let's use another example, like audit fees. Public companies need to have audits, and usually the relationships they have with their auditors, and the fees they pay to their auditors, are all managed at a corporate level. Once a carve-out is sold, if a buyer is going to need audits on that carve-out going forward, then they'll have to do it through their own audit relationships.

Carve-outs can have shared costs for just about anything they use. And they may not only be coming from a corporate level for administrative things like insurance and audits, they can be operational too. For example, technology licenses, technology infrastructure costs, shared facilities, there could even be shared marketing and advertising expenses. And what makes these things challenging, is that sometimes they'll be pushed-down or allocated into a carve-out's financial statements where the buyer can see them, but sometimes they won't.

When things like insurance, or technology costs, or anything else that a carve-out business needs has been shared with either a parent or an affiliate, or it's been provided under a contract that isn't going to transfer with the carve-out business, then those things are going to change after a deal. Which could mean, different costs for the buyer going forward. What's worse, is if those costs weren't even pushed-down into the carve-out's financial statements and the buyer didn't see them or know about them. Then, those things wouldn't just go away. Because at some point, when the buyer is running that business, they're going to realize they need it. And if it wasn't built into the buyer's projections, it means that they're going to have costs they didn't expect.

When it comes to carve-outs, it's important that a buyer does their due diligence to identify as best they can all of the shared costs that a carve-out business had at both the corporate and operating levels. Whether those costs were included in the carve-out's financial statements, or not. This way, the buyer can plan for how to transition those things and what their costs will be going forward.

Shared Services

Shared services are similar to shared costs, but instead of being a cost for something that's used by the business, it's the cost of internal people's time for the services they provide. The classic example of a shared service is where a parent has a centrally managed functional group. For example, a centrally managed IT department that provides all of the IT support for a parent's portfolio of businesses. Or, an accounting department, a treasury department, HR, legal, risk management, the list could go on. But it doesn't just have to be corporate functions, it could also be operational functions. Like when there's a centralized marketing group, or a customer service center, or a distribution center that serves the needs of more than just one business.

Shared services can relate to just about anything that people do in an organization which benefit more than one business. And by the way, it may not even be an entire department, it could just be one person, like a general manager, or a finance director. From oversight and management, to operations, and back-office functions, shared services are the things that people do in an organization that benefit more than one business, which can include the carve-out.

A lot like with shared costs, shared services will sometimes be identified by a parent and pushed down or allocated to the different businesses they serve, but sometimes they won't. And just like where there are shared costs in a carve-out, if there are shared services that a carve-out business needs, and that carve-out business is sold, then its needs for those services don't just go away. The question becomes, who's going to do it, and what's it going to cost?

You see, just like how a buyer needs to identify the shared costs that a carve-out business has, a buyer also needs to identify the shared services it needs. This way, a buyer can plan for how those services will continue in the future and the cost of providing them.

Stand-Alone and Replacement Costs

Once a buyer has done their due diligence and identified a carve-out's shared costs and services, that buyer needs to model the business on either a stand-alone or a replacement cost basis. A stand-alone basis means that the carve-out will become an independent, self-supporting entity going forward. And, it will need a cost structure that's capable of supporting it as a stand-alone entity.

A replacement cost basis means that instead of a carve-out becoming a stand-alone entity, it will become part of a new buyer's portfolio of businesses. Here, the buyer may already have an existing cost structure that can be leveraged to some degree. And what used to be provided by the old parent, will be replaced, and provided by the new parent going forward.

Let's say for example, that a carve-out business in the past did not have its own accounting function because its parent provided all of its accounting needs. If a new buyer decided that they wanted to acquire that business and run it on a stand-alone basis, then it's more likely than not, that an accounting function would need to be built. This means that the new buyer would need to plan for how they intend to build-out that function. And, they'd need to reflect the timing and costs of doing that in their projections. If the buyer planned to run the entire business on a stand-alone basis, then they would need to do this type of analysis for every shared cost and service that the carve-out business had. Planning how to transition it, and what its costs will look like in the future.

On the other hand, let's say that a corporate buyer wanted to buy the business and that they already had an accounting department. Here, it's possible that the corporate buyer may be able to leverage what they already have to some degree. If they can, then it's likely that any additional work they would take on in order to do the accounting for the carve-out, would come at a much lower cost than if they had to build it from scratch. This is a situation where the services that used to be provided by the old parent are going to be replaced by the new parent. Of course, the buyer would still need to understand what additional work they were taking on, because there could still be some level of incremental costs involved. And again, the buyer would have to do this type of analysis for every shared cost and service that the carve-out business had. Planning the transition, and what its costs will look like in the future.

At the end of the day, it comes down to a buyer doing their due diligence, doing their best to identify all of a carve-out's shared costs and services, developing a plan for how to transition those costs and services, and estimating the future cost structure of that business in their model.

Chapter 27: Cross-Border Deals

A cross-border deal is where a buyer from one country invests in or acquires a business that's located in another country. Which is also referred to as an international deal. Up until this point in the book, we've been fairly silent on doing international deals. But that's because, for the most part, the deal process, the way deals are structured, and the way businesses are valued, are all very similar whether you're doing a domestic deal or an international one.

There are some differences though, that buyers should be aware of when doing an international deal. Especially if they're entering into a new country for the first time. That's because, legal, regulatory, tax, accounting, employment, and other rules, can all be different when doing an international deal. And, these technical areas may not be the only differences, because different cultures can also have different ways of doing business.

These differences may not be that big when a buyer from one developed country is acquiring a business in another developed country. But when a buyer from a developed country is entering an emerging market, where there may not be the same level of rules, regulations, or oversight that a buyer is used to, there can be some pretty big differences.

In this chapter, we'll explain some of the different challenges that buyers can sometimes face when doing international deals. Because, while there are a lot of similarities in how domestic and international deals are done, there can be logistical challenges, technical issues, and cultural ways of doing business that a buyer would need to be aware of before doing an international deal. Because if they're not, or if they're overlooked, they can cause some pretty big issues down the road.

The (Cross-Border) M&A Playbook

For the most part, a buyer will follow the same playbook when doing a cross-border deal as they would when doing a domestic one. In other words, they would still have a deal team leader, a project manager, a business team that's involved, and functional teams all supporting the transaction. But once a buyer crosses borders and there's more than one country involved, it adds a whole new level of complexity that needs to be worked through. That's because, cross-border deals usually involve different languages, different time zones, different holidays, different legal and regulatory rules, different tax, and accounting rules. The list can go on. And all of these differences can create real challenges when doing a deal. Logistically, technically, operationally, and culturally.

Logistically, it means that a buyer is going to have to coordinate multiple teams, in multiple languages, across multiple time zones. Sometimes it's not an issue, for example when a buyer from the U.S. is acquiring a business in Canada where the languages and time zones are basically the same. But sometimes, it can be quite difficult. Like when a buyer from the U.S. is acquiring a business in Europe, Asia, or Latin America. Here, a buyer and seller could be operating in different languages and in different time zones. Which means, for the most part, the documents that need to be read, and the conversations that need to be had, probably won't be in the buyer's language or on the buyer's schedule.

From a technical perspective, there could be a whole host of issues. That's because, different countries have different legal and regulatory environments, different tax rules, and different employment rules. And probably one of the most challenging aspects of doing an international deal, can be the cultural differences in how people operate and conduct business in different countries.

You see, when a buyer from a developed country like the U.S. is entering another developed country, like Canada, or something in Northern or Western Europe, then there are probably going to be more similarities than differences in how those businesses operate. But when a buyer from a developed country is entering an emerging market like China or Brazil, or one where the culture is to hide your business from the government to avoid paying taxes, the differences can be quite large and pose real risks for buyers if they don't know what they're getting into.

When buyers cross borders, they need to overcome all of these challenges. Logistically, they need to manage the deal. Technically, they need to identify and understand all of the potential issues. And culturally, they need to understand how the target actually conducts its business.

The question becomes, how does a foreign buyer do all of this? The answer is that they need local teams to do the work. It can't be done remotely from an outside country looking in. A buyer needs teams with the language skills, technical skills, and the cultural knowledge that's needed to not only do a deal in that country, but to also manage the business after it's been acquired.

The Importance of Local Teams

When a buyer is acquiring a business in another country, they need to understand all of the same things that they would if they were doing a deal in their own country. Including the things that they would sometimes take for granted because of how familiar they already are with the environment they operate in. This is why, having a local team who understands the target's country and how business is done in that country is so important when investing abroad.

A buyer needs to know the market, the competitors, the suppliers, the political and regulatory environment, tax regimes, employment laws, and all of the cultural ways that business is actually done in the target's country. The same as they would if it were in their own country.

This means that a buyer needs a solid local business team. A team that understands both the local market and the buyer's strategy. A team that can screen potential acquisitions, and once a target has been identified, say whether or not there's a good strategic fit, or if culturally it even makes sense to bring the two businesses together. Questions like these are important to answer before a buyer even considers doing a deal. When a buyer has a solid local business team, with feet on the ground, who know the market and can screen potential acquisitions, it becomes less about whether or not the buyer knows the business, and more about how to support that local team, so that once a target has been identified they'll have the technical skills to execute.

On the other hand, if a buyer doesn't have a local business team, then it's a whole different conversation. And it's why sometimes when a buyer is entering a new market for the first time, they might not want to go all-in on an acquisition. Instead, they might be more inclined to invest with someone who's already operating in that market by doing a joint venture. For example, they might buy 50% of a business that's already operating in the country and keep the seller in as an equal partner.

Of course, joint ventures have their own challenges, like deciding how they should be governed and how the partners will exit at some point. But they can often be used as a way of hedging a buyer's risk when entering into a new market for the first time. Because the seller, who knows the market, is still just as equally invested as the buyer.

Selecting Cross-Border Advisors

In the same way that a buyer would have a business team and functional experts working together on a domestic deal, they'll do the same on an international one. The difference though, is that when it comes to international deals, the buyer's functional teams needs to have a local presence. This way, they can read the documents they need to read and have conversations they need to have in the seller's language. Also, by being local, they're more likely to have an appreciation for how business is conducted in that country and some of the cultural differences that a foreign buyer who's not from that country may not be aware of. This means, that a buyer will usually need to hire outside advisors who have cross-border experience to help support the transaction.

Depending on the circumstances, this could include legal, regulatory, tax, accounting, HR, IT, commercial, environmental, and possibly other advisors to not only help navigate the deal, but also perform the due diligence and negotiate contracts. But as foreign buyer, when it comes to selecting outside advisors to perform these roles, there's as added twist, because not all advisors have the same level of experience working on cross-border deals. In other words, if an advisor only had experience working with buyers from their own country, then they may not appreciate the types of concerns that an international buyer might have.

Foreign investment laws, anti-corruption laws, employment regulations, tax rules, accounting practices, environmental exposures. There can be many issues to deal with and differences in the way things are done between two countries when a buyer crosses borders. Which is why international buyers need advisors who have relevant cross-border experience, not only in their fields, but also in working with the two countries that are involved in the transaction. Usually this means working with law firms, accounting firms, and other advisors, in each functional area who have their own international presence and cross-border capabilities in the two countries that are involved.

For example, in some countries where the economies are still developing, or where there are oppressive tax regimes, the actual ways that people do business doesn't always align with the laws that they're supposed to follow. In a situation like this, things like gifts to government officials or hiding income to avoid taxes can be common and typical. And to be frank, a local advisor, who doesn't have experience working with a foreign corporate buyer might think nothing of it. But, to a U.S. buyer, these things can be real problems. Violations of the Foreign Corrupt Practices Act, or tax laws, or customs laws don't only carry liabilities with them, but can also involve reputational risk and even jail time. These are not things that a corporate buyer wants to be dealing with.

The truth is, not all advisors have the same capabilities or level of experience to identify what's important in a cross-border deal. As an international buyer, you're dependent on your advisors. Not only for their language skills and technical knowledge, but also for their experience and judgement to call things out when there's an issue. Just like a buyer would take their time to make sure they're selecting the right advisor in a domestic deal. They should be doing the same when selecting an advisor for an international one. Keeping in mind though, the added twist of needing relevant cross-border experience in both the buyer and seller's countries.

Chapter 28: Earn-Outs

An earn-out is a pricing mechanism where a buyer agrees to pay an additional amount of purchase price to a seller if the business can achieve certain milestones within a certain period of time after a deal has closed. For example, a buyer might be willing to pay an earn-out to a seller if a business can obtain FDA approval to sell a product, or obtain a patent, or achieve a certain level of profitability after the deal. Earn-outs are technically referred to as contingent purchase price, because they're contingent on the outcome of one or more future events.

Earn-outs will usually happen in situations where buyers and sellers just can't seem to agree on the current value of a business. For example, when a seller has a very bullish view on their business, but the buyer isn't as confident, and thinks that the seller's projections might be a little too aggressive and their asking price a little too high. Here, it's possible that an earn-out could make sense, to help bridge the gap.

The way it works, is that a buyer agrees to pay an up-front purchase price today for the business, based on what they're comfortable with. But, if it turns out after the deal, that the business actually does perform better than the buyer expected, and it hits the sellers' projections, then that buyer would pay an additional amount of purchase price in the form of an earn-out. After the results have been achieved.

Earn-outs aren't only used to bridge valuation gaps. They're also used as a way to hedge a buyer's risk. For example, if a buyer actually did believe a seller's projections but they're concerned about the business' ability to obtain an FDA approval, or a patent, or transfer key customers, or successfully defend itself in an ongoing patent infringement lawsuit. Here, if a buyer sees risk, they might be concerned about overpaying. Because if a business can't obtain FDA approval or a patent, it may not hit its projections. If it can't retain its key customers, it could lose sales. Or, if it's been infringing on another company's patents, there could be other issues. In situations like these, earn-outs can be used where the buyer would basically hold some amount of the purchase price back, which wouldn't be owed until the business had either obtained its regulatory approvals, successfully transitioned its customers, or settled its legal issues without any damages to the company.

In this chapter, we'll explain some of the mechanics of how earn-outs work, including how targets are sometimes set. We'll also discuss some of the challenges that come with structuring earn-outs. Because, while it's true that some people see them as a way of bridging a price gap or hedging a risk, there are challenges to structuring them. Because if a buyer and seller don't have realistic expectations, or if there are any misunderstandings on how an earn-out will be calculated, then once results come in, someone might not be happy. And if someone's not happy, there could be a dispute.

Setting Expectations

An earn-out is usually based on a business achieving certain milestones. These milestones can be specific events that need to happen, or results that need to be achieved. But usually, whether they're events or results, they need to happen within a specific period of time called the earn-out period.

A specific event would be something like obtaining FDA approval to sell a product or getting a patent. These kinds of milestones are usually pretty straight forward and easy to define for purposes of an earn-out because they'll either happen or they won't. But when an earn-out is based on results that need to be achieved, like hitting a revenue target or a profitability target, these can be a little more complicated to define and more likely to end in dispute. Why? Because of who's in charge after a deal and how results are measured.

Let's say for example that a buyer acquired a business, and as part of the deal, there was an earn-out that would be paid if the business achieved a certain level of profitability at the end of its first year. But, without giving it a second thought, after the deal closed and the buyer took ownership, they started making changes to that business. They changed the reporting structure of its key managers, so that they would begin reporting to people at the buyer's corporate level. They integrated some of its activities and took over its back-office functions. They started charging shared costs to the business. A year later, once it was time to tally-up the results of the business, the earn-out wasn't met. And the seller, who was still a partner and an operator in that business, was not happy.

The seller argued that it was because of the buyer's changes to the business that they weren't able to hit their earn-out targets. By changing the reporting structure of its key managers, the seller didn't have any control in where they focused their time. And by changing its cost structure, the seller wasn't able to manage the profitability of the business the way they would have if it were just left alone. The seller was furious and said that they never would have agreed to having an earn-out if they only knew how the buyer was going to make changes to that business.

You see, earn-outs can lead to some pretty uncomfortable situations when fingers are pointed about why targets were or weren't met. Especially when a seller is still a partner in a business. It's why from both a buyer and seller's perspectives, the targets, timeframes, and expectations about how a business will be run after a deal, all need to be clearly defined right up-front, before agreements are signed, and in as much detail as possible.

This is also why, when earn-outs are involved, sellers will usually want to keep as much day-to-day control in a business as they can. So that they can have as much influence as possible in achieving their results. Which by the way, can also create challenges for buyers who might have been thinking of integrating a business right away. The reality is, that when earn-outs are involved, a buyer may either have to wait to integrate, or at least be very selective in terms of what changes they do make to a business during the earn-out period.

Defining Targets

When a buyer and seller agree to having an earn-out, the terms of that earn-out need to be documented as part of the deal. This includes defining the targets that need to be hit, the timeframes in which they need to be hit, and the amounts that will be paid.

When an earn-out is based on an event, like obtaining FDA approval or a patent, it can be pretty straight forward to define. Because again, the event will either happen within the earn-out period, or it won't. But, when an earn-out is going to be based on a business' performance, things get more complicated. Because for one, there are different metrics that can be used to measure performance. Like revenue, gross profit, EBITDA, or something else. And quite frankly, some metrics are better than others when it comes to measuring the performance of a business. But another reason, is that no matter what performance metric is used, there can also be a lot of subjectivity in how those results are calculated. It all makes choosing the right metric, and then clearly defining how that metric should be calculated a very important exercise.

Let's say for example, that a target business was going to be fully integrated into a buyer's portfolio. And that the entire cost structure of that target business was either going to change or be completely absorbed into the buyer's cost structure. In a situation like this, if a buyer and seller wanted to base an earn-out on performance, then it could be too difficult, if not impossible, to agree on anything but revenue as the metric. Why? Because everything else, meaning all of the expenses, will change. And while the buyer may have a pretty good idea of what those expenses will be going forward, the seller probably wouldn't want to risk an earn-out on it, because they wouldn't have control over it.

There are problems with only using revenue though, because exactly as you would think, revenue doesn't capture any of the costs that are associated with generating it. For example, let's say that a seller stayed on to operate a business after it was acquired. But then, they spent a lot of money promoting sales so that they could hit their revenue target. Here it could be possible that while they generated enough revenue to hit their target, it came at the cost of reducing the business' margins because of all the money that was spent on promotions. Something like that could actually have a negative impact on the business, and probably not what the buyer would have intended when they agreed to having an earn-out. Similar issues can happen when gross profit is used as the earn-out metric.

In a different scenario, let's say that a buyer did not plan on fully integrating a business. And that for the most part, they planned to leave it alone and let it operate the way it always did. In a situation like this, a buyer and seller might both be comfortable using an overall profitability measure like EBITDA to set an earn-out target.

But, if this wasn't the case, and the buyer actually did plan on making some changes to the business, like integrating its back-office functions, then the seller might not want to include everything that EBITDA would capture. Because they won't have control over it. In a situation like this, the buyer and seller could probably still use EBITDA, but they might need to define it so that certain items, like the back-office functions that will be integrated, get carved-out from that EBITDA for purposes of measuring performance.

The reality is, that with earn-outs, a lot of thought needs to be put into how a business will be run after a deal and the performance metrics that will be used. Because depending on how it will be run, some performance metrics could be better or worse than others. In some situations it may make sense to use revenue, while in others it may make more sense to use gross profit or EBITDA. And sometimes, it may not even be a financial metric. It could be something like the number of customers acquired.

It all depends on the circumstances that are involved as to what metric makes the most sense. And then, once the metric has been decided, defining how that metric should be calculated. If certain revenues or expenses are intended to be left in, or out of any final calculation, then it needs to be clearly defined in the agreements, so that expectations are aligned and there is as little subjectivity as possible in how performance will be measured.

Also, when earn-outs are involved, it's usually the case that both the buyer and seller will want to have audit rights, so that when all is said and done, they can both validate and be comfortable that the final earn-out calculations were done consistently with what was agreed.

Earn-Outs versus Equity Rollovers

Occasionally, you hear about earn-outs that go out as much as five-years. Practicality speaking though, for an earn-out this is a long time. That's because, if it takes five years or sometimes even longer to prove-out the value of a business, then the question becomes, who's really executing on the value that's being created? Did it really exist when the deal was done? Or, was it built in the years that followed? The reality is, that if something takes more than a few years to prove-out, then there's an argument to be made that the growth and additional value that was created in that business, years after the deal, didn't actually exist at the time of the deal. The potential was there, but not the value.

The truth is that earn-outs don't fit all situations. Sometimes they do, but sometimes they don't. For the most part, they're intended to bridge a price gap that exists at the time of a deal where a buyer is a little unsure about how the business is going to execute over the next one, two, or even three years. The key with them, is to identify where the price gap exists at the time of the deal. Once the root cause of the price gap is identified, and it's understood what the buyer and the seller are each trying to accomplish, then it's a question of what's the best deal structure to fit the situation.

If a seller actually wants to stay in a business to operate it and participate in the upside of that business over a five, ten, or even a fifteen-year period. Then an earn-out may not be the best idea. It could be that the buyer and seller would be better off if the seller rolled over equity and stayed in the business as partner. This is often done as a way of aligning a buyer and a seller's interest in a business and allowing a seller to stay on and participate in the future growth of it.

This isn't to say that an equity rollover doesn't have its own challenges, it does. Because, there would probably need to be a shareholders' agreement governing how the business will be run and puts and calls for when a partner is ready to exit. But, if there's a long-term view on the business where both parties want to participate in its up-side, then rollovers will often make much more sense than earn-outs. And as we'll discuss later, there can also be some accounting benefits to them.

Cliffs, Tiers, and Caps

Earn-outs can be structured as cliff payments or tiered payments and have caps. A cliff payment means that once a target is met, the earn-out is paid. But, if that target isn't met, there's no payment. In other words, the target is either hit or it isn't, resulting in a payment or no payment. Tiered payments are where there's a series of targets that could potentially be hit. As each level of target is achieved, the earn-out payment can go up. In a structure like this, as a business performs better the earn-out payments can get larger, so that rather than have an all or nothing target, the seller can still get some level of payment even if the full earn-out isn't achieved. A cap is where there's an overall limit on the amount of earn-out that will be paid, limiting the buyer's potential liability.

Earn-Out Accounting

Under GAAP, when a buyer acquires a business and there's an earn-out in the deal, that buyer needs to estimate the fair value of that earn-out and record it on the opening balance sheet for the acquisition as a liability. It's all part of the purchase accounting that needs to take place. This earn-out liability basically represents the buyer's best estimate of what will likely be owed to the seller once the earn-out period has ended. It remains on the balance sheet, until the earn-out is either paid or it's written off.

As long as an earn-out liability exists, a buyer needs to re-estimate its value whenever it prepares financial statements. For a publicly traded company, this basically means revaluing it every quarter. When it's revalued, it usually needs to be adjusted either up or down, from its initial estimate, to reflect the buyer's most recent estimate of what will likely be paid to the seller once the earn-out period ends. This liability will usually go up or down because of how the business is performing.

When a buyer increases or decreases the estimated value of an earnout liability, it's offset in the accounting by recording either a gain or a loss on that buyer's income statement. In other words, the initial estimate of what an earn-out was worth at the time of a deal gets recorded on the opening balance sheet. But then, any increase or decrease to that initial estimate, after the acquisition date, ends up hitting the buyer's income statement.

For example, let's say that a buyer and a seller agreed on having a one-year earn-out in a deal. By using a tiered structure, the seller could potentially earn an additional $10 million of purchase price if the business achieved a certain level of EBITDA. Here, the buyer would perform an analysis at the time of the deal to estimate the likelihood that the business would achieve the earn-out targets. Based on the probability of the business achieving those targets, the buyer would record an earn-out liability on the opening balance sheet at the time of the deal.

So, let's say that a buyer did this and based on the probability of achieving results, they estimated the value of the earn-out to be $5 million at the date of the acquisition. This is the initial liability they would record. Once the year was up, if the seller was entitled to a $5 million payout, exactly as the buyer had estimated, then there would simply be a payment made from the buyer to the seller and the liability would come off the books. But, if the seller was entitled to anything more or less because the business performed better or worse than was initially estimated, then any increase or decrease in the amount that was finally paid to the seller, versus the initial estimate, would be a gain or a loss on the buyer's income statement.

In a situation where a business performs better than a buyer initially expected, and the seller ends up getting a bigger payout than the buyer initially estimated. That buyer basically has to increase the earn-out liability on their balance sheet as the business performs better and record a loss on their income statement. The opposite is true if the business performs worse than was initially expected. For example, if an earn-out was missed, a buyer would write down the liability, because they don't have to pay it, and in the process, they would record a gain on their income statement. It's completely counterintuitive.

If the business does better than expected, the buyer records a loss. But if the business does worse than expected, the buyer records a gain. Crazy right? It's because of the accounting rules that a lot of corporate buyers don't like earn-outs. It makes the accounting much more complicated and it creates earnings risk which can sometimes be hard to predict. If a buyer is publicly traded and gets graded on their EPS estimates, then an earn-out just creates noise in the numbers and can create losses even when a business is actually performing better than expected.

For publicly traded buyers, the accounting rules make earn-outs very challenging because of the impact that they can have on earnings. It makes structuring them and thinking through the financial impact that they can have on EPS a very challenging exercise. If an earn-out is likely to have a very small impact on a buyer's EPS, then it may not be an issue. But if an earn-out is a little unpredictable, and can have a very big impact on a buyer's EPS because of a big price gap that needs to be bridged, then a buyer might be better off keeping a seller in a business with some equity and not having an earn-out. This way the seller can participate in some of the future growth and exit when they want.

The accounting rules are different for equity rollovers. With these, instead of a buyer having to realize a gain or a loss like they would with an earn-out, when a seller wants to exit their minority position, it's treated like an equity purchase for the buyer and it doesn't hit their income statement. So, with these, a seller can still participate in some of the upside with a business, and a buyer can avoid the earnings risks.

Compensation Vs. Earn-Outs

When structuring an earn-out, a buyer needs to be careful about what might be considered compensation for services, as opposed to an earn-out based on the performance of a business. For example, let's say that a seller was going to stay on to operate a business as its general manager after a deal. And as part of the deal, the seller could earn an additional $5 million earn-out at the end of three years if the business performs to a certain level.

If the payment of that earn-out was dependent on the seller still working in the business at the end of the three years, then it's not an earn-out. The accounting rules would treat a situation like this as compensation expense because it's tied to the seller's continued employment in the business. In other words, under GAAP it's seen as more of a stay incentive, or a performance bonus, than an earn-out and it all gets recorded as compensations expense on the buyer's income statement.

In order for an earn-out to be treated like an earn-out and not compensation expense under GAAP, it can't depend on the continued employment of the seller. And it also can't treat selling shareholders who stay in the business differently than selling shareholders who don't. In other words, where one selling shareholder who stays with the business has the potential to earn more of an earn-out than other selling shareholders who don't stay with the business. Under GAAP, something like this would seem more like compensation expense than an earn-out. So, when a buyer is in the process of structuring an earn-out, and they want to be sure that it will receive earn-out treatment, they should be consulting with their financial advisors.

Chapter 29: Intangible Assets

Under GAAP, when a buyer acquires control of a business, they need to identify and record all of the assets and liabilities that are being acquired at their fair market values. This includes both the physical and intangible assets. The way it works, is that the buyer takes the purchase price that's being paid for the business, and they allocate that price to all of the identifiable assets and liabilities that are being acquired to create a balance sheet for the newly acquired business. This is called the opening balance sheet.

The fair value of all the business' working capital, physical assets, intangible assets, and liabilities are all recorded on the opening balance sheet. Any purchase price that's left over after allocating it to these items is also recorded, as goodwill. Going forward, the physical and intangible assets are depreciated and amortized, while the goodwill basically just sits on the balance sheet unless there's a reason to write it down at some point. For all of this, it doesn't matter if the assets were previously recorded by the target or not. It's on the buyer to identify them, value them, and record them.

Identifying the physical and intangible assets, estimating their values, and recording them on an opening balance sheet is all part of the purchase accounting that a buyer is required to follow under GAAP. And because the depreciation and amortization from these assets directly affects the amount of accretion and dilution a buyer gets from a deal, it's in the buyer's best interest to try and estimate these things as best they can before the deal happens. Not after.

When it comes to identifying the physical assets, it's usually a pretty straight forward exercise. This is because, physical assets tend to include things like inventory, vehicles, and buildings. They're the things you can see and touch. And usually, a business already has these things on its books because it had to buy them. So, for the most part, they just need to be revalued at their current fair market values. But the intangible assets are different.

Intangible assets are not physical, so you can't see and touch them, and they may have never been recorded on a company's books before. In an acquisition they can include things like the value of tradenames, customer relationships, and developed technologies. It's possible that some of these things may have been acquired by the target, in which case they may be on its books. But they may not have been acquired, because they were developed over time through the company's own efforts. If something was developed by a company through its own efforts, then it might not be on the books. It's just how the accounting works. It's also possible that intangible assets will be created for the very first time in a deal. For example, when a seller enters into a non-compete as part of an agreement.

When it comes to estimating the value of assets, generally speaking, it's easier to do for the physical assets than it is for the intangible ones. Why? Because if you wanted to revalue something like inventory, or equipment, or real estate, there are market prices. You could look at those market prices and use them to estimate the values of the assets being acquired. But with the intangible assets, it's not the case. You see, companies don't usually sell their intangible assets. Which can make valuing them much more of a theoretical exercise. Not to mention, things like tradenames, customer lists, developed technologies, and non-competes, these are all very specific and unique to an individual business. Which can make valuing them very subjective.

In this chapter, we'll explain the basics of what intangible assets are and how buyers can think about identifying these assets when doing a deal. We'll also explain some of the more common ways that intangible assets are valued and why it's usually a good idea to include a valuation specialist for identifying and valuing these assets in a model.

Identifying Intangible Assets

Intangible assets are things that have economic benefits, which either have contractual or legal rights associated with them, or they can somehow be considered separable, at least in theory, in terms of having their own economic values to a business. Technically, these are non-monetary assets (meaning that they're not cash or financial instruments), and they're non-physical assets.

For the most part, when it comes to identifying intangible assets in an acquisition, there are some that are very common like patents, copyrights, tradenames, developed technologies, customer relationships, exclusive contracts, and non-compete agreements. The list could go on. But, depending on the industry and the specifics of a business, there could also be others which aren't as common or obvious. Especially to a buyer who may not be familiar with doing a deal in that particular space.

It's for these reasons that buyers should always consider including a valuation specialist as part of their due diligence team. This way, as they go through their due diligence, they can ask the right questions and analyze the business in a way that will help identify where the intangible assets are. Once the intangible assets have been identified, they can be valued and the amortization from them can be included in the buyer's model for purposes of estimating accretion and dilution. Next, we'll explain how intangible assets are valued.

The Highest and Best Use Premise

Under GAAP, when intangible assets are valued, they need to be valued at their highest and best use from the perspective of a market participant. This basically means that when a buyer is identifying and valuing the intangible assets that are being acquired, they need to take the perspective of what someone else would be willing to pay for those assets. In other words, it doesn't really matter what that specific buyer plans to do with the assets. They need to be recorded at their fair market values, according to what someone else would be willing to pay.

For example, let's say that a buyer was acquiring a software business and that they didn't plan on using the software platform the target company had developed. Instead, they planned to buy the company, shut it down, and transfer the target's customers over to their own software platform. Here, the buyer couldn't just ignore the value of the target's software and not record it. Instead, under GAAP, they would

262

still need to value it at its highest and best use based on what someone else would be willing to pay for it, and they would still need to record it on the opening balance sheet. Later, the buyer would either have to amortize the asset, or if they weren't using it anymore, write it off.

The market participant premise also affects how synergies are treated when valuing intangibles. For example, when there's a synergy that's unique to only one particular buyer, it may not be included in the valuation of the intangibles. But, when there's a synergy that someone else (in other words, a market participant) would also be likely to have, then it probably would be included.

How Intangible Assets are Valued

Once the intangible assets have been identified, there are different ways to value them. Technically, these are referred to as the cost approach, the income approach, and the market approach. These basically mean, the cost of recreating an asset, the value of cash flows that will be generated by an asset, and the value of an asset based on market information. But because intangible assets are theoretically economic benefits that come from things, and there's usually not a lot of market information on them, they tend to be valued similar to how other income generating type assets are valued, by using some form of a cash flow based model. Now this isn't always the case, such as when there's an internal use asset that might be valued using a cost approach, but when it is the case, and the intangible assets are going to be valued using cash flows, most of the information that a buyer would need to value them should already be included in their DCF.

Remember, when a buyer builds a model, they're basically building out projections for how they expect a business to perform over time. They're projecting income statements, balance sheets, and cash flows. And once they've taken the extra step of calculating the enterprise value of a business based on those cash flows, they've already developed most of the assumptions that are needed to also value the intangibles. Because they've already had to think through most of the things that drive those values like growth rates, margins, and discount rates.

So, what does this mean? It means, that for the most part, if a buyer has already prepared a DCF for a business, then building out the value of the intangibles that are part of that business should really just be a matter of adding the right additional calculations and assumptions. For buyers who use template-based models where this functionality may already be built-in, it simply means identifying the intangible assets and then applying the right assumptions to value them. Next, we'll explain from a high level some of the more common ways that intangible assets are often valued and the assumptions that drive them.

Tradenames

Tradenames represent brands. These could be the brands of a business, a product line, or even just individual products. They can take years to develop. But once established, can resonate with customers who've come to associate those brands with a certain level of quality, value, reliability, or some other meaning. The basic idea behind a tradename having value is that it could, in theory, carry enough clout that someone else would be willing to pay a royalty to use it. This is also what gives rise to the name of the method that's used to value them, which is called the relief from royalty method.

The idea behind the relief from royalty method, is that the target company already owns the name, so in theory it would be 'relieved' from having to pay someone else a royalty to use it. This same method is used to value trademarks and other assets where someone could theoretically charge a royalty.

It's calculated by projecting out the amount of sales that are expected to occur as a result of having the tradename. A royalty rate, based on a combination of market information and what would appear to be reasonable for the business, would then be applied to those sales in order to calculate the royalty fees that the company would have to pay if it didn't already own the name. Those royalty fees are then adjusted for taxes and discounted back to a present value using an appropriate discount rate. The end result is a present value of the cash flow savings from not having to pay royalties.

With this type of valuation, there are certain assumptions that tend to drive its values. For the most part, these are the life of the tradename that's being assumed, because that's what determines how far out the buyer should be projecting the sales that are associated with it, the royalty rate, and the discount rate. To see an example of a tradename valuation using the relief from royalty method, refer to Appendix Sixteen.

Customer Relationships

Customer relationships aren't just lists with names and numbers. They're actual relationships. On the company side of things, there's information that's learned over time from working with customers. Like points of contact, knowing who the decision makers are, and understanding their preferences. On the customer side of things, there's a sense of knowing who you're dealing with, what to expect, and who to call if there's a problem. The stronger these relationships are, the more likely it is that customers will be loyal with their business. Which means, better customer stickiness and less customer attrition. These relationships could be contractual, or they could be informal. All that really matters, is that the relationships are strong, and customers keep coming back with their business.

Customer relationships are usually valued using what's called the multiperiod excess earnings method. This method basically tries to value the future profits that are expected to be generated by a company's existing customer base over time. It does this by taking the amount of revenues that are attributable to a company's customer base at the time of an acquisition. Which is often, but not always, the total amount of revenue that the company has. To which it then applies an attrition rate into the future. This attrition rate is basically the rate at which customers are expected to leave, or fall off, every year which is usually based on the company's actual experience with its customers.

The sales to these customers are then modeled out over a long period of time, in other words, multiple periods, where the sales to those customers will trickle down each year due to the rate of attrition. The expected future profits that are associated with those declining sales are then estimated and discounted back to a present value. The result is a present value of the expected future cash flows from that company's existing customer base at the time of the acquisition.

The assumptions that tend to drive the value of customer relationships tend to include the amount of sales that are attributable to those customers, the attrition rates that are used, and levels of profitability that are expected to be generated from those sales over time. To see an example of what a customer relationship valuation looks like, refer to Appendix Seventeen.

Developed Technology

Developed technology represents proprietary technology or know-how that a company either developed or acquired. This could include patents, copyrights, software applications, databases, and even trade secrets like formulas, processes, and recipes.

Developed technologies will often be valued using either the relief from royalty method, similar to how tradenames are valued, or the multiperiod excess earnings method, similar to how customer relationships are valued. Although, in the middle market, it's probably more common to see developed technologies valued using the relief from royalty method because of how simple it is.

As an example, let's say that a buyer was acquiring a business that sold licenses to customers who wanted to use its software. And let's say, the buyer wanted to use the relief from royalty method to value that software. Here, the buyer would first project the amount of sales that would be attributable to that software's technology over time. These sales though, would need to be adjusted, in order to reflect the fact that new technologies are constantly evolving. This is usually done by applying some sort of an obsolescence factor over the expected life of the technology that's being valued.

These adjusted sales would then be charged a royalty rate based on a combination of market information and what would appear to be reasonable for the business. This would calculate the amount of royalty fees that the company, in theory, would have to pay to someone else if it didn't already own the existing technology. These fees would then be adjusted for taxes and discounted back to a present value using an appropriate discount rate. The end result would be a present value of cash flow savings from not having to pay a licensing for the technology it already owns. This represents the value of that developed technology.

If the buyer were to use the multiperiod excess earnings method, a similar sales projection would be made to reflect sales over time as the software becomes obsolete. But, instead of using a royalty rate to estimate the value of cash flow savings, the buyer would estimate the expected future cash flow profits that would be generated from those sales over time. This would be similar to the method that was applied when valuing customer relationships. These cash flows would then be discounted back to a present value. Again, representing the value of the developed technology.

The assumptions that tend to drive the value of developed technologies include the expected life of the technology being valued, how quickly it could become obsolete, the royalty rates that are used, or in the case of the multiperiod excess earnings method, the level of profitability assumed, and the discount rate. To see an example of a developed technology valuation using the relief from royalty method refer to Appendix Eighteen.

Non-Compete Agreements

Most M&A deals include non-compete agreements so that sellers don't just sell a business one day, and then the very next day, turn around and start competing with it again. Usually, these agreements will last anywhere from three to five years after a deal has closed.

Non-compete agreements will often be valued by estimating the financial impact or loss of profits, if any, that would occur to a business if non-compete agreements were not in place. In other words, how much sales and related profit would a company lose, if it wasn't protected by having non-compete agreements. Because these agreements will usually cover more than one person, it's common that each one individually would need to be valued.

The way this works, is that the potential loss of sales and related profit that would occur to a business, if the seller or sellers were competing, are projected over time, for as long as the non-competes are in-place. These projected losses are then adjusted for taxes and discounted back at to a present value using an appropriate discount rate. The end result is the estimated value of having protection from the non-compete agreements.

The assumptions that tend to drive the valuation of non-compete agreements include the likelihood that a seller or sellers would compete. If they did compete, the ability for them to actually have an impact on the business, and the life span of the non-compete agreements. To see an example valuation for a non-compete agreement, refer to Appendix Nineteen.

Involving a Valuation Specialist

As you can see, the process of identifying and valuing the intangible assets of a newly acquired business can be very theoretical and technical. It involves, not only identifying where the intangible assets of a business are, but also deciding on how their values should be calculated. There are different methods that can be used and a lot of assumptions, which can all be very technical and subjective. Not only that, but for a publicly traded buyer, it may also be under the scope of an audit after the fact when a buyer's auditors want to review the purchase accounting that was done.

This means, it can't just be a swag. There has to be real thought and analysis that goes behind it. Because if a buyer's auditors have a different view of what the intangible assets are, or what they're worth, it means that there could be audit adjustments after the fact. This could have an impact on the amount of accretion and dilution from a deal. Why? Because if the auditors change the value of the intangible assets after the deal has already been done, it could change the amount of amortization expense, and that could change the amount of accretion and dilution from the deal.

These are all reasons why corporate buyers should consider involving a valuation specialist as part of their due diligence team. This way, they can help identify the intangible assets, value them, and estimate the impact that the amortization from them will have on the buyer's EPS before the deal is signed. And hopefully, they can do their work in way that once the deal is done, their analysis can standup to an audit and there won't be any surprises in the amount of accretion and dilution that comes from the deal after it's done.

Part 5:
Final Thoughts

'Don't be afraid to ask questions, or ask for help'

Chapter 30: M&A is a Team Effort

Congratulations! You've made it through the book. Hopefully, you've learned something useful and feel more confident in your understanding of the M&A concepts that were discussed and how to apply them.

As a final thought, we mentioned several times throughout this book, that there's no one thing to getting an M&A deal right. No one person that does it all, and no magic formula. There's a mindset and a process to it. Buyers that have the right mindset to approaching their deals, and a good process that involves the right people with the right skills, are much more likely to have success in M&A.

As a buyer, it's important that this is both appreciated and practiced. This way, all of the different skillsets that are necessary to execute a deal and successfully operate a business after it's been acquired, are working together as a team. And when any member of that team isn't sure of something, they shouldn't be afraid to ask questions or ask for help. Because again, nobody has all the answers. It's a team effort.

If you would like to reach out to the author of this book with questions or if you would like to learn more about Rock Center Financial Partners and the services they provide, you can find Kevin Tomossonie on LinkedIn or visit rockcenterfinancial.com.

Appendices

For free downloadable word and excel versions of these appendices,
visit rockcenterfinancial.com/resources

Appendix One: Sample Letter of Intent [Template]

[Date]

[Addressed to representative of the Seller(s)]

Dear [Name]:

Thank you for allowing [Name of Buyer] ("ABC" or the "Buyer") the opportunity to pursue a transaction with [Name of Target Company] ("XYZ" or the "Company"). We are pleased to present to you, this Letter of Intent ("LOI"), setting forth the principal terms and conditions that we are contemplating for the proposed transaction.

This LOI, except as expressly set forth below, is considered non-binding. It is based solely on information that has been provided to-date and is intended to summarize the principal terms of the proposed transaction. It does not purport to include all the terms and conditions that will ultimately be necessary to complete the transaction. If you agree with the content of this letter, we will immediately begin our due diligence and instruct our lawyers to begin preparing the definitive transaction documents (collectively, the "Definitive Agreements"), according to which the transaction will be governed. We are very excited for this opportunity and are looking forward to working with you.

The Transaction

ABC, either directly or through a controlled subsidiary, will acquire [xx]% of the Company's outstanding equity from its selling [members or shareholders] (the "Seller(s)") as soon as practicable pursuant to the Definitive Agreements.

Purchase Price

Based on the information provided to date, we have valued the Company at $[xx] million, on a cash-free, debt-free basis (the "Enterprise Value"). The purchase price that will be paid for the equity of the Company pursuant to the Definitive Agreements will be determined on this basis and will include a mechanism to ensure that an adequate level of working capital is delivered with the business at closing. For an illustrative summary of the calculated equity value of the Company, and the amount of proceeds expected to be paid to the Seller(s) on this basis, refer to Schedule A, attached hereto.

The Enterprise Value is subject to, among other things, (a) confirming and validating that the Company's [insert time period] normalized earnings before interest tax and depreciation ("EBITDA") is at least $[xx] million; (b) the continued operation of the Company in the normal course of business; and (c) the satisfactory completion of our due diligence.

Employment Agreements

During our due diligence, we may identify certain managers and employees with whom we will expect the Company enter into mutually satisfactory employment agreements going forward. It is our expectation that these employment agreements will include customary terms, and reasonable compensation and benefit amounts.

Exclusivity

Commencing from the mutual execution of this LOI, and continuing until the earliest of (a) [60] days, unless otherwise extended by agreement of the parties, or (b) the Company and ABC's mutually agreement in writing that they are no longer pursuing a transaction, the Company and Seller(s) agree that they, their agents, and their representatives, will work exclusively with ABC regarding the proposed transaction (the "Exclusivity Period"). During the Exclusivity Period, neither the Company, the Seller(s), nor any of their affiliates, agents, representatives, or employees shall take any action to solicit, initiate, negotiate, or pursue in any way, the sale of any assets or interests in the Company, or any recapitalization of the Company, with any party other than the Buyer.

Non-Competition and Non-Solicitation Agreements

As part of the Definitive Agreements, the Seller(s) will agree to be bound by covenants not to compete with the Company, and to not solicit its customers or employees for the duration that the Seller(s) remain [members or shareholders] of the Company, and for a period of at least three years after selling their interests in the Company.

Representations, Warranties, Covenants, and Indemnification Provisions

The Definitive Agreements will contain representations and warranties, covenants, and indemnification provisions that will be mutually satisfactory, customary, and appropriate for a transaction of this size and type. The transaction will also include a mutually agreeable [holdback or escrow] for an amount and time period that will also be customary, and appropriate for a transaction of this size and type. For a summary of the proposed terms and conditions associated these items, refer to Schedule B, attached hereto.

[Operating or Shareholder] Agreement (If Applicable)

As part of the transaction, the parties will enter into [an operating agreement (if LLC) or a shareholder agreement (if a corporation)] that will contain customary terms and conditions setting forth the ongoing governance of the Company, including customary minority protections and pro-rata board representation. In addition, the [operating or shareholder] agreement will also provide the terms of a minority [member or shareholder] put (the "Put Option") and a majority [member or shareholder] call (the "Call Option"), both of which will be exercisable on or after the [fifth] anniversary of the proposed transaction's closing.

It is envisioned that the minority [member or shareholder]'s Put Option will entitle the minority [member or shareholder] to put (or sell) their interests in the Company to the majority [member or shareholder] for fair market value at the time of exercise. Similarly, it is envisioned that the majority owner's Call Option will entitle the majority owner to call (or buy) the minority [member or shareholder]'s interest in the Company, also for fair market value at the time of exercise.

Confidentiality

Each party agrees, that neither party, nor any of their affiliates, agents, representatives, employees, or otherwise, shall make any public announcement, or disclose to any person that is not directly involved with the proposed transaction, the existence of this LOI or the proposed transaction, without the prior written consent of the other party, except as such disclosure may be required by law, or with respect to each party's legal, financial, tax or other advisors as may be necessary on a confidential basis in order to execute the proposed transaction.

Transaction Costs and Expenses

Each party shall be responsible for, and pay their own, costs and expenses incurred in connection with this LOI and the proposed transaction.

Conditions and Approvals

Completion of the proposed transaction will be subject to, among other things, standard conditions and approvals including an appropriate level of access to management, satisfactory completion of our due diligence, confirmation that the Company has continued to operate in the normal course, the absence of any material adverse events in the business, the receipt of any third-party consents that may be required, the execution of employment, consulting and non-competition agreements with key individuals as may be identified in our due diligence, successful negotiation of the Definitive Agreements, ABC investment committee and board member approval(s), and approval by any regulatory, governmental or antitrust authorities that may be necessary.

Governing Law

This LOI shall be governed by the substantive laws of the [State of New York] without regard to its conflict of law rules. The parties hereto irrevocably agree that any claim, controversy or dispute arising hereunder shall be submitted to the exclusive jurisdiction of the United States Federal and State courts for the [Southern District of New York] in connection with all matters hereto, and waive any objection to venue with respect to these courts.

Non-Binding

The parties agree that this LOI is non-binding, with the exceptions of (1) the Exclusivity Period, (ii) Transaction Costs and Expenses, and (iii) Governing Law, (collectively, the "Binding Sections"). This LOI does not constitute a legally binding offer and can be withdrawn at any time, for any reason or no reason at all in the sole discretion of ABC.

Acknowledgement

If you are in agreement with the content of this letter, please counter sign where indicated below and return to [insert name here] at your earliest convenience. We look forward to hearing from you.

Sincerely,

_____

[Name and title of authorized/signing representative of the Buyer]

Accepted and agreed on behalf of [insert the actual name of the target Company]:

_____

Name:
Title:
Date:

Schedule A
Illustrative Equity Value and Proceeds to Seller(s)

[Insert table here.]

Schedule B
Key Deal Terms

[Insert table here.]

Appendix Two: Sample Definition of Indebtedness

"Indebtedness" shall mean... (I) indebtedness for borrowed money or indebtedness issued or incurred in substitution or exchange for borrowed money, (II) indebtedness evidenced by any note, bond, debenture or other debt instrument or debt security, (III) obligations under any letter of credit, (IV) any prepayment penalties, breakage amounts, or other fees or liabilities that occur as a result of the prepayment of any item defined herein as indebtedness, (V) the amount of obligations required to be recorded by GAAP in respect of all finance leases, (VI) obligations under any interest rate, foreign currency or hedging arrangement, (VII) amounts owing as deferred purchase price for property (but expressly excluding trade payables), (VIII) amounts owing as earnouts or seller notes in connection with the prior acquisition of any business, (IX) payables included in accounts payable aged greater than 120 days, (X) payables or other amounts owed to any affiliate or related party of the Seller(s), (XI) guarantees in connection with any of the foregoing, (XII) accrued interest related to any of the foregoing, (XIII) accrued management fees, (XIV) restructuring reserves, and (XV) unfunded pension obligations.

Appendix Three: Example Working Capital Analysis

	Mo.1	Mo.2	Mo. 3	Mo.4	Mo.5	Mo.6	Mo.7	Mo.8	Mo.9	Mo.10	Mo.11	Mo.12	Mo.13	Mo. 14	Target
	_____ Trailing Twelve Months ("TTM") _____												Projected		Est.
Accounts Receivalble	3,167	3,277	3,389	3,246	3,446	3,388	3,241	3,444	3,562	3,592	3,531	3,469	3,590	3,620	3,605
Inventory	3,000	3,059	3,118	3,076	3,032	3,127	3,118	3,215	3,206	3,197	3,260	3,323	3,314	3,342	3,328
Prepaid and Other Assets	247	253	260	253	259	261	254	266	271	272	272	272	276	278	277
Current Assets	**6,413**	**6,589**	**6,767**	**6,575**	**6,737**	**6,775**	**6,613**	**6,926**	**7,039**	**7,060**	**7,062**	**7,064**	**7,181**	**7,240**	**7,211**
Accounts Payable	1,464	1,502	1,539	1,507	1,475	1,511	1,478	1,478	1,445	1,447	1,449	1,461	1,473	1,485	1,479
Accrued Expenses	625	677	728	643	676	732	638	687	725	634	687	745	646	709	678
Current Liabilities	**2,090**	**2,180**	**2,266**	**2,151**	**2,151**	**2,243**	**2,116**	**2,165**	**2,170**	**2,082**	**2,136**	**2,206**	**2,119**	**2,195**	**2,157**
Working Capital, As Reported	**4,324**	**4,409**	**4,501**	**4,424**	**4,586**	**4,532**	**4,497**	**4,760**	**4,869**	**4,978**	**4,927**	**4,889**	**5,061**	**5,046**	**5,054**
Adjustments:															
Accounts Payable > 120 Days	98	91	82	72	62	52	42	30	20	11	-	-	-	-	-
Accrued Management Fees	25	25	25	25	25	25	25	25	25	25	25	25	25	25	25
Accrued Income Taxes	40	80	120	44	88	132	48	97	145	53	106	160	59	117	88
Accrued Interest	121	122	121	122	121	122	121	122	121	122	121	122	121	122	122
Pro Forma Working Capital	**4,607**	**4,727**	**4,848**	**4,687**	**4,882**	**4,863**	**4,733**	**5,034**	**5,180**	**5,189**	**5,179**	**5,165**	**5,266**	**5,310**	**5,288**
Days Sales Outstanding ("DSO")	38	39	40	38	40	39	37	39	40	40	39	38	39	39	39
Days Inventory On-Hand ("DIO")	90	91	92	90	88	90	89	91	90	89	90	91	90	90	90
Days Payables Outstanding ("DPO")	44	45	45	44	43	43	42	42	41	40	40	40	40	40	40

Appendix Four: Sample Definition of Working Capital

"Working Capital" shall mean... as of the time immediately prior to closing, on the closing date, without giving effect to any of the transactions contemplated by the agreement, the remainder of Current Assets minus Current Liabilities as defined herein.

"Current Assets" shall mean... current assets, determined in accordance with GAAP, consistently applied in accordance with the Company's past practices; excluding: (I) cash, (II) shareholder loans receivable, (III) interest receivable, (IV) prepaid management fees, and (V) prepaid and deferred income taxes.

"Current Liabilities" shall mean... current liabilities, determined in accordance with GAAP, consistently applied in accordance with the Company's past practices; excluding; (I) payables included in accounts payable aged greater than 120 days, (II) accrued interest, (III) accrued management fees, (IV) accrued and deferred income taxes, and (V) any item included within the definition of Indebtedness.

Appendix Five: Example Comparable Transactions Analysis

Target	Buyer	Date Announced	Target Company Description	Enterprise Value	TTM Revenue	Revenue Growth Rate	TTM EBITDA	EBITDA Margin	Purchase Price Multiple Revenue	EBITDA
Target 1	Buyer A	MM-YYYY	[Description of target.]	300,000	135,000	9.5%	27,000	20.0%	2.22x	11.1x
Target 2	Buyer B	MM-YYYY	[Description of target.]	158,000	110,000	7.0%	17,600	16.0%	1.44x	9.0x
Target 3	Buyer C	MM-YYYY	[Description of target.]	156,000	85,000	8.0%	15,300	18.0%	1.84x	10.2x
Target 4	Buyer D	MM-YYYY	[Description of target.]	118,000	75,000	7.7%	12,375	16.5%	1.57x	9.5x
Target 5	Buyer E	MM-YYYY	[Description of target.]	71,000	55,000	8.3%	7,975	14.5%	1.29x	8.9x
High				300,000	135,000	9.5%	27,000	20.0%	2.22x	11.1x
Average				160,600	92,000	8.1%	16,050	17.0%	1.67x	9.7x
Low				71,000	55,000	7.0%	7,975	14.5%	1.29x	8.9x

Appendix Six: Example Model and Valuation Summary

Income Statement Summary	Pro Forma		TTM	Proj. TTM	Projected				
(Thousands $U.S.)	Dec-18	Dec-19	Oct-20	Dec-20	Year 1	Year 2	Year 3	Year 4	Year 5
Sales	104,000	110,500	117,792	119,250	130,450	144,000	158,110	169,060	177,940
Cost of Sales	52,000	55,361	59,131	59,864	65,781	72,606	79,883	85,574	90,238
Gross Profit	52,000	55,140	58,660	59,387	64,669	71,394	78,227	83,486	87,702
Annualized Sales Growth	6.7%	6.3%	7.9%	7.4%	9.4%	10.4%	9.8%	6.9%	5.3%
Gross Margin	50.0%	49.9%	49.8%	49.8%	49.6%	49.6%	49.5%	49.4%	49.3%
Operating Expenses	17,680	18,785	20,025	20,273	23,178	25,480	27,929	29,840	31,400
EBITDA	34,320	36,355	38,636	39,114	41,491	45,914	50,298	53,645	56,302
EBITDA Margin	33.0%	32.9%	32.8%	32.8%	31.8%	31.9%	31.8%	31.7%	31.6%
Depreciation & Amortization	-	-	-	325	17,709	17,852	17,995	18,138	18,281
Interest Expense/(Income)	-	-	-	-	-	-	-	-	-
Income Tax Expense/(Benefit)	-	-	-	-	6,421	7,577	8,722	9,587	10,266
Minority Interest	-	-	-	-	1,736	2,049	2,358	2,592	2,776
Net Income	34,320	36,355	38,636	38,789	15,625	18,437	21,223	23,328	24,980
	-	-	-	-	-	-	-	-	-
Accretion/(Dilution) (a)					$ 0.156	$ 0.184	$ 0.212	$ 0.233	$ 0.250
Pro Forma Fully Diluted Accretion/(Dilution) (b)					$ 0.112	$ 0.145	$ 0.177	$ 0.204	$ 0.226

Notes to table:
(a) Accretion/(dilution) based on projected net income.
(b) Accretion/(dilution) on a fully diluted basis as if all the funds used to make the acquisition were borrowed.

Purchase Price Multiples		TTM	Proj. TTM	Projected	Avg. Multiple
(Thousands $U.S.)		Oct-20	Dec-20	Year 1	Shown
Purchase Price		**Sales Multiples**			
Up Front Purchase Price on an EV Basis	355,500	Total Purchase Price (TEV) / Sales	3.0x	3.0x	2.7x	2.9x
Estimated Value of Earn-Out	n/a	DCF Implied EV (Before TAB) / Sales	3.0x	3.0x	2.7x	2.9x
Total Purchase Price (TEV)	355,500	DCF Implied EV (With 50% of TAB) / Sales	3.2x	3.1x	2.9x	3.1x
		DCF Implied EV (With Full Est. Val. of TAB) / Sales	3.4x	3.3x	3.0x	3.2x
DCF Implied Valuation		**EBITDA Multiples**			
DCF Implied EV Bef. Tax Amort. Benefit	354,721	Total Purchase Price (TEV) / EBITDA	9.2x	9.1x	8.6x	9.0x
Est. Val. of Tax Amort. Benefit (If Asset Deal)	41,393	DCF Implied EV (Before TAB) / EBITDA	9.2x	9.1x	8.5x	8.9x
Est. Val. of Tax Amort. Benefit (If Stock Deal)	-	DCF Implied EV (With 50% of TAB) / Sales	9.7x	9.6x	9.0x	9.5x
DCF Implied EV After Tax. Amort. Ben.	396,114	DCF Implied EV (With Full Est. Val. of TAB) / Sales	10.3x	10.1x	9.5x	10.0x
	-				

Balance Sheet & Cash Flow Summary	Pro Forma		TTM	Opening B/S	Projected				
(Thousands $U.S.)	Dec-18	Dec-19	Oct-20	Dec-20	Year 1	Year 2	Year 3	Year 4	Year 5
Working Capital (a)	15,430	16,350	17,400	17,895	19,338	21,416	23,598	25,286	26,650
Working Capital as a % of Sales	14.8%	14.8%	14.8%	15.0%	14.8%	14.9%	14.9%	15.0%	15.0%
Debt	-	-	-	-	-	-	-	-	-
Debt Leverage Ratio (Debt/EBITDA)	-	-	-	-	-	-	-	-	-
Free Cash Flow (b)					33,972	36,606	39,740	42,716	45,017
Increase/(Decrease) in Debt					-	-	-	-	-
Earn-Out Payment					-	-	-	-	-
Free Cash Flow to Equity (c)					33,972	36,606	39,740	42,716	45,017
	-	-	-	-	-	-	-	-	-

Notes to table:
(a) Working capital excludes cash.
(b) Cash flow after interest and taxes, before any debt paydowns, earn-out payments or dividends.
(c) Free cash flow to equity after debt paydowns and earn-out payments.

Return on Investment		Return on	Initial	FCFE + Residual Value of Equity at End of Year 5				
(Thousands $U.S.)		Investment	Investment	Year 1	Year 2	Year 3	Year 4	Year 5
Return on Buyer's Equity Investment	(a)	14.3%	(319,950)	30,575	32,945	35,766	38,445	431,396
Return on Minority Interest	(a)	14.3%	(35,550)	3,397	3,661	3,974	4,272	47,933
Return on Buyer Funded Loan (After Tax)		n/a	-	-	-	-	-	-
After Tax Returns on Buyer's Total Amount of Invested Capital		14.3%	(319,950)	30,575	32,945	35,766	38,445	431,396
		-	-	-	-	-	-	-
Return on Equity (During Projection Period)								
Free Cash Flow At Operating Entity Level	(b)			9.6%	10.3%	11.2%	12.0%	12.7%
Free Cash Flow to Equity at Operating Entity Level	(c)			9.6%	10.3%	11.2%	12.0%	12.7%

Notes to table:
(a) Year 5 includes both the FCFE generated during that year as well as the estimated value of equity based at the end of Year 5 on a buy and hold scenario.
(b) Free cash flow after interest expense, but before paying down any debt. This represents the ability to pay debt or make dividends to equity.
(c) Free cash flow to equity after paying down debt.

Appendix Seven: Example Model Projections

Income Statement

(Thousands $USD)	Pro Forma Dec-17	Dec-18	Dec-19	TTM Oct-20	Proj. TTM Dec-20	Projected Year 1	Year 2	Year 3	Year 4	Year 5
Total Sales	97,500	104,000	110,500	117,792	119,250	130,450	144,000	158,110	169,060	177,940
Annualized Growth	n/a	6.7%	6.3%	7.9%	7.4%	9.4%	10.4%	9.8%	6.9%	5.3%
Gross Profit	48,848	52,000	55,140	58,660	59,387	64,669	71,394	78,227	83,486	87,702
Gross Margin	50.1%	50.0%	49.9%	49.8%	49.8%	49.6%	49.6%	49.5%	49.4%	49.3%
Total Operating Expenses	16,575	17,680	18,785	20,025	20,273	23,178	25,480	27,929	29,840	31,400
As a Percent of Sales	17.0%	17.0%	17.0%	17.0%	17.0%	17.8%	17.7%	17.7%	17.7%	17.6%
EBITDA	32,273	34,320	36,355	38,636	39,114	41,491	45,914	50,298	53,645	56,302
EBITDA Margin	33.1%	33.0%	32.9%	32.8%	32.8%	31.8%	31.9%	31.8%	31.7%	31.6%
Depreciation Expense	-	-	-	-	325	377	520	663	805	948
Amortization Expense						17,332	17,332	17,332	17,332	17,332
EBIT	32,273	34,320	36,355	38,636	38,789	23,782	28,062	32,303	35,508	38,021
EBIT Margin	33.1%	33.0%	32.9%	32.8%	32.5%	18.2%	19.5%	20.4%	21.0%	21.4%
Operating Income	32,273	34,320	36,355	38,636	38,789	23,782	28,062	32,303	35,508	38,021
Interest Expense/(Income)	-	-	-	-	-	-	-	-	-	-
Earnings Before Tax	32,273	34,320	36,355	38,636	38,789	23,782	28,062	32,303	35,508	38,021
Income Tax Expense/(Benefit)	-	-	-	-	-	6,421	7,577	8,722	9,587	10,266
Minority Interest Expense/(Benefit)	-	-	-	-	-	1,736	2,049	2,358	2,592	2,776
Net Income/(Loss)	32,273	34,320	36,355	38,636	38,789	15,625	18,437	21,223	23,328	24,980
Pro Forma Capital Charges, Net of Tax						4,448	3,984	3,483	2,941	2,365
Pro Forma Fully Diluted Earnings	32,273	34,320	36,355	38,636	38,789	11,177	14,452	17,740	20,387	22,615

Balance Sheet

(Thousands $USD)	Pro Forma Dec-17	Dec-18	Dec-19	TTM Oct-20	Opening B/S Dec-20	Projected Year 1	Year 2	Year 3	Year 4	Year 5
Cash and Cash Equivalents	-	-	-	-	-	33,972	70,578	110,318	153,035	198,052
Accounts Receivable, Net	9,750	10,400	11,050	11,780	11,926	13,046	14,401	15,812	16,907	17,795
Inventories, Net	9,460	10,110	10,760	11,500	11,642	12,793	14,121	15,536	16,643	17,550
Inv. Purchase Accounting Mark-Up	-	-	-	-	-	-	-	-	-	-
Prepaid Expenses and Other	300	300	300	300	300	300	300	300	300	300
Total Current Assets	19,510	20,810	22,110	23,580	23,868	60,112	99,400	141,966	186,884	233,697
Property & Equipment, Net	2,700	2,750	2,800	2,850	2,850	3,473	3,954	4,291	4,486	4,538
Intangible Assets, Net	-	-	-	-	153,012	135,680	118,347	101,015	83,682	66,350
Goodwill	-	-	-	-	181,743	181,743	181,743	181,743	181,743	181,743
Other Assets	-	-	-	-	-	-	-	-	-	-
Total Assets	22,210	23,560	24,910	26,430	361,474	381,008	403,444	429,015	456,795	486,327
Accounts Payable	4,050	4,330	4,610	4,930	4,991	5,484	6,053	6,660	7,135	7,523
Accrued Liabilities	500	550	600	650	683	717	752	790	830	871
Deferred Revenue	450	500	550	600	600	600	600	600	600	600
Deferred Revenue Adjustment	-	-	-	-	(300)	-	-	-	-	-
Other Accrued Expenses	-	-	-	-	-	-	-	-	-	-
Total Current Liabilities	5,000	5,380	5,760	6,180	5,974	6,801	7,406	8,050	8,564	8,995
Deferred Tax Liability	-	-	-	-	-	1,346	2,692	4,037	5,383	6,729
Total Liabilities	5,000	5,380	5,760	6,180	5,974	8,147	10,098	12,088	13,948	15,724
Minority Interest	-	-	-	-	35,550	37,286	39,335	41,693	44,285	47,060
Stockholders' Equity	17,210	18,180	19,150	20,250	319,950	335,575	354,011	375,235	398,563	423,543
Total Liabilities & Stockholders' Equity	22,210	23,560	24,910	26,430	361,474	381,008	403,444	429,015	456,795	486,327

Purchase Price Allocation/Goodwill Calculation

(Thousands $USD)	
Purchase Price on an EV Basis (Excl. Earn-Out)	355,500
Current Assets Acquired	23,868
Fixed Assets Acquired	2,850
Other Long-Term Assets	-
Current Liabilities Assumed	(5,974)
Earn-Out Obligations	-
Other Long-Term Liabilities Assumed	-
Deferred Tax Liability	-
Net Tangible Assets Acquired	20,745
Intangible Assets Acquired	153,012
Goodwill	181,743
	-

Cash Flow Projections

(Thousands $USD)	Projected Year 1	Year 2	Year 3	Year 4	Year 5
Operating Activities					
Net Income	15,625	18,437	21,223	23,328	24,980
Minority Interest	1,736	2,049	2,358	2,592	2,776
Depreciation & Amortization	17,709	17,852	17,995	18,138	18,281
Change in Accounts Receivable	(1,120)	(1,355)	(1,411)	(1,095)	(888)
Change in Inventory	(1,151)	(1,327)	(1,415)	(1,107)	(907)
Inv. Purchase Accounting Mark-Up	-	-	-	-	-
Change in Prepaid & Other	-	-	-	-	-
Change in Accounts Payable	493	569	607	475	389
Change in Accrued Liabilities	34	36	38	40	41
Change in Deferred Revenue	300	-	-	-	-
Other Accrued Expenses	-	-	-	-	-
Deferred Tax Assets/Liabilities	1,346	1,346	1,346	1,346	1,346
Net Cash from Operating Activities	34,972	37,606	40,740	43,716	46,017
Investing Activities					
Capital Expenditures	(1,000)	(1,000)	(1,000)	(1,000)	(1,000)
Net Cash from Investing Activities	(1,000)	(1,000)	(1,000)	(1,000)	(1,000)
Financing Activities					
Increase/(Decrease) in Debt	-	-	-	-	-
Earn-Out Payment	-	-	-	-	-
Dividends	-	-	-	-	-
Net Cash from Financing Activities	-	-	-	-	-
Net Cash Flows	33,972	36,606	39,740	42,716	45,017
Cash in Beginning of Period	-	33,972	70,578	110,318	153,035
Net Cash Flows	33,972	36,606	39,740	42,716	45,017
Cash at End of Period	33,972	70,578	110,318	153,035	198,052

Appendix Eight: Example Discounted Cash Flow Analysis

Discounted Cash Flow Summary
(Thousands $USD)

EV Before Synergies & Tax Amortization Benefit	339,164
Value of Synergies	15,556
Enterprise Value Before Tax Amortization Benefit	354,721
PV of Tax Amortization Benefit (If Asset Deal)	41,393
PV of Tax Amortization Benefit (If Stock Deal)	-
Total Enterprise Value Based on Future Cash Flows	396,114
	-
Implied Multiple of EV/TTM Sales (Before Tax Benefit)	3.0x
Implied Multiple of TEV/TTM Sales (After Tax Benefit)	3.4x
Implied Multiple of EV/TTM EBITDA (Before Tax Benefit)	9.2x
Implied Multiple of TEV/TTM EBITDA (After Tax Benefit)	10.3x

Discounted Cash Flow Valuation
(Thousands $USD)

		Projected			
	Year 1	Year 2	Year 3	Year 4	Year 5
EBITDA	41,491	45,914	50,298	53,645	56,302
Minus Depreciation	(377)	(520)	(663)	(805)	(948)
EBITA	41,114	45,394	49,636	52,840	55,354
Minus Taxes	(11,101)	(12,256)	(13,402)	(14,267)	(14,946)
Net Operating Profit After Tax (NOPAT)	30,014	33,138	36,234	38,573	40,408
Add-back Depreciation	377	520	663	805	948
Changes in NWC	(1,443)	(2,078)	(2,182)	(1,688)	(1,365)
CAPEX	(1,000)	(1,000)	(1,000)	(1,000)	(1,000)
Unlevered FCF (Before Tax Amort. Benefit)	27,947	30,580	33,715	36,691	38,992
Residual Value at End of Yr. 5 (w/o Tax. Ben)					401,616
Discount Period — Mid-Year Conv.	0.5	1.5	2.5	3.5	4.5
Discount Factor — 13.0%	0.9407	0.8325	0.7367	0.6520	0.5770
Discounted Future Cash Flows	26,290	25,458	24,838	23,921	22,497

PV of Discounted Cash Flows From Above	123,004		
Discounted Residual Value	231,717	Residual Value Sales Multiple	2.4x
PV of Tax Amortization Benefit (If Asset Deal)	41,393	Res. Value EBITDA Multiple	7.7x
PV of Tax Amortization Benefit (If Stock Deal)	-	Res. Value as % of Total EV	58%
Total Enterprise Value of Future Cash Flows	396,114		

Appendix Nine: Example Valuation of Synergies

Value of Synergies				Projected		
Included in Projections		Year 1	Year 2	Year 3	Year 4	Year 5
Sales Synergies		2,000	5,000	7,500	7,500	7,500
COGS Synergies		(1,020)	(2,550)	(3,825)	(3,825)	(3,825)
OPEX Synergies		(950)	(1,000)	(1,050)	(1,100)	(1,150)
EBITDA Impact of Synergies		30	1,450	2,625	2,575	2,525
Tax Effect of Synergies		(8)	(392)	(709)	(695)	(682)
After Tax Effect of Synergies		22	1,059	1,916	1,880	1,843
Discount Period	Mid-Year Conv.	0.5	1.5	2.5	3.5	4.5
Discount Factor	13.0%	0.9407	0.8325	0.7367	0.6520	0.5770
Discounted Value of Expected Synergies		21	881	1,412	1,226	1,063

Residual Growth Rate Assumed for Synergies	3.0%
Residual Value of Synergies @ End of Yr.5	18,985

PV of Discounted Synergies from Above	4,603
Discounted Residual Value of Synergies	10,954
Total PV of Synergies	15,556

Appendix Ten: Valuing Tax Amortization Benefits

Tax Amortization Benefit If Step-up Applies	1	2	3	4	5	6	7	8	9	10	11	12	13	14	15
Value of Intangibles	153,012														
Value of Goodwill	181,743														
Value of Intangibles & Goodwill	334,755														
Annual Amortization	22,317	22,317	22,317	22,317	22,317	22,317	22,317	22,317	22,317	22,317	22,317	22,317	22,317	22,317	22,317
Annual Tax Benefit	6,026	6,026	6,026	6,026	6,026	6,026	6,026	6,026	6,026	6,026	6,026	6,026	6,026	6,026	6,026
Discount Period:	0.5	1.5	2.5	3.5	4.5	5.5	6.5	7.5	8.5	9.5	10.5	11.5	12.5	13.5	14.5
Present Value Factor	0.9407	0.8325	0.7367	0.6520	0.5770	0.5106	0.4518	0.3999	0.3539	0.3132	0.2771	0.2452	0.2170	0.1921	0.1700
PV of Annual Savings	5,668	5,016	4,439	3,928	3,477	3,077	2,723	2,409	2,132	1,887	1,670	1,478	1,308	1,157	1,024
PV of Tax Amort. Benefit in Total	41,393														

Appendix Eleven: Valuation Formulas

Weighted Average Cost of Capital = Cost of Equity x (Equity/Enterprise Value) + Cost of Debt x (Debt/Enterprise Value)

Cost of Equity	=	$Rf + B \times (Rm\text{-}Rf) + SRP + CRP + CSRP$
Rf	=	Risk free rate of return, typically using a 10-year or a 20-year U.S. Treasury
B	=	Beta
Rm-Rf	=	Represents the assumed forward looking market return in excess of the risk-free rate
SRP	=	Size risk premium
CRP	=	Country risk premium
CSRP	=	Company specific risk premium

Cost of Debt	=	Pre-tax cost of debt x (1 - tax rate)
Enterprise Value	=	The value of debt + the value of equity

Terminal, or Residual Value $= \dfrac{\text{Free Cash Flow x (1 + The Long-Term Growth Rate)}}{\text{Weighted Average Cost of Capital - The Long-Term Growth Rate}}$

Free Cash Flow = Free cash flow at end of projection period

288

Appendix Twelve: WACC Buildup Analysis

Comparable Benchmarks For Purposes of Finding an Unlevered (Asset) Beta	Ticker	TTM Revenue	Market Value of Debt (a)	Market Value of Equity (b)	Effective Tax Rate (c)	Levered (Equity) Beta	Include as Benchmark (Yes/No)	Total Enterprise Value	Debt to Enterprise Value Ratio	Equity to Enterprise Value Ratio	Debt to Equity Ratio	Unlevered (Asset) Beta
1 Example Benchmark Co. 1	[]	15,000	5,000	16,000	27%	0.99	Yes	21,000	23.8%	76.2%	31.3%	0.81
2 Example Benchmark Co. 2	[]	14,000	4,000	15,000	27%	0.99	Yes	19,000	21.1%	78.9%	26.7%	0.83
3 Example Benchmark Co. 3	[]	13,000	3,000	14,000	27%	0.99	Yes	17,000	17.6%	82.4%	21.4%	0.86
4 Example Benchmark Co. 4	[]	12,000	2,000	13,000	27%	0.99	Yes	15,000	13.3%	86.7%	15.4%	0.89
5 Example Benchmark Co. 5	[]	11,000	1,000	12,000	27%	0.99	Yes	13,000	7.7%	92.3%	8.3%	0.93

Assumed Beta and Capital Structure Based on Average of Comparable Benchmarks — 16.7% — 83.3% — 20.1% — 0.86

Risk-Free Interest & Corporate Borrowing Rates

Risk-Free Rates on U.S. Treasuries

Date That Rates Were Released/Published	4/1/2020
Risk Free Rate on 10-Year U.S. Treasures	0.62%
Risk Free Rate on 20-Year U.S. Treasures	1.04%

Moody's Baa Corporate Bond Yields

Date Last Updated	4/1/2020
Yield	4.59%

Weighted Average Cost of Capital Assumptions

Assumed Asset Beta From Above		0.86
Risk-Free Rate of Return	(d)	1.0%
Market Equity Risk Premium	(e)	6.0%
Size Risk Premium	(f)	3.0%
Company Specific Risk Premiu	(g)	5.3%
Country Risk Premium	(h)	0.0%
Debt Borrowing Rate	(i)	4.6%
Assumed Income Tax Rate		27.0%
Assumed Debt/EV Ratio		16.7%
Assumed Equity/EV Ratio		83.3%
Assumed Debt/Equity Ratio		20.1%

Weighted Average Cost of Capital

Risk-free Rate	1.04%
Relevered Equity Beta	0.99
Equity Risk Premium	6.00%
Size Risk Premium	3.00%
Company Specific Risk Premium	5.30%
Country Risk Premium	0.00%
Cost of Equity Capital	**15.28%**
Assumed Cost of Debt	4.59%
Assumed Tax Rate	27.0%
Assumed After-Tax Cost of Debt Capital	**3.35%**
Weighted Average Cost of Capital	**13.28%**

Notes to table:
(a) Book value of debt as of [xx] used as a proxy for market value.
(b) Market capitalization of equity as of [xx].
(c) Latest two-year average tax rate.
(d) Assumed to be the higher of risk free 20-year U.S. Treasuries or risk-free 10-year U.S. Treasuries as published by the Federal Reserve.
(e) Represents the assumed forward looking market return in excess of the risk-free rate. Searchable online, this assumption is based on the market equity risk premium calculated by subtracting the average return for long-term government bonds from the average return on the S&P 500 over time.
(f) Risk premium based on the size of the company and the historical returns of similarly-size companies compared to the overall market.
(g) Represents a risk premium based on qualitative factors such as competition, customer and supplier concentration and other company specific risk factors.
(h) Country risk premium when doing deals outside the U.S.
(i) Interest rate for Moody's 20-year Baa rated corporate bonds.

Appendix Thirteen: Company Specific Risks

Specific Risk Factors	(a)	Risk Level Percieved to be Above Benchmark Indicators	Assumed Company Specific Risk Premium
Private Company Liquidity Risk	(b)	20%	1.8%
Economic or Policital Risk			-
Risk from Competition			-
Lack of Product Diversification		10%	0.9%
Customer Concentration		10%	0.9%
Supplier Concentration			-
Dependence on Key Technology			-
Lack of Depth in Management		10%	0.9%
Lack of Proven Track Record		5%	0.4%
Financial Reporting Risk			-
Legal/Regulatory Risk		4%	0.4%
Company Specific Risk Premium			**5.3%**

Expectations About Rate of Return Irrespective of Technical Analysis	Weighting	Cost of Capital
Assumed Cost of Debt, Net of Tax Benefit	16.7%	3.35%
Rate of Return on Equity Before Company & Country Specific Risk	83.3%	9.98%
WACC Before Company Specific Risk Premium		8.87%
Company Specific Risk Premium		5.30%
Country Specific Risk Premium		0.00%
Rate of Return on Equity After Company & Country Risk Premiums		15.28%
WACC after Company & Country Specific Risk Premiums		13.28%
		-
Assumed Min. Level of Return for Business Like This (Regardless of Technical Analysis)		12.0%
Assumed Upper-End of Returns Range for Testing Reasonableness in Assumptions		18.0%
Within The Range of Expectations (Yes/No)		Yes

Notes to table:
(a) The benchmarks used for beta and size premiums in developing the WACC unter the CAPM are based on systematic market risks of publicly traded companies where investments are liquid and can be diversified by investing in an entire portfolio. When investing a substantial amount of money in a private company however, there are specific risks that cannot be diversified by allocating purchase price investment dollars. This analysis represents the specific company risks, with assigned risk premiums, that are believed to apply to the target company and should be reflected in its valuation.
(b) Represents higher level of risk due to the fact that the company is private. This premium tends to range from 20% - 30% based on the size and perceived marketablity of the business. This premium can be substantially higher if the target business is not very marketable, in which case it may not be likely to have many potential buyers in an exit.

Appendix Fourteen: Example Return on Investment Calculations

Return on Investment		Internal Rate of Return	Initial Investment	FCFE + Residual Value of Equity at End of Year 5				
				Year 1	Year 2	Year 3	Year 4	Year 5
Free Cash Flow to Buyer's Equity at Operating Entity Level	(a)			30,575	32,945	35,766	38,445	40,516
Residual Value of Buyer's Equity at End of Year 5	(b)			-	-	-	-	390,881
Return on Buyer's Equity Investment	(c)	14.3%	(319,950)	30,575	32,945	35,766	38,445	431,396
Free Cash Flow to Minority Interest at Operating Entity Level				3,397	3,661	3,974	4,272	4,502
Residual Value of Minority Interest Equity at End of Year 5	(d)			-	-	-	-	43,431
Return on Minority Interest		14.3%	(35,550)	3,397	3,661	3,974	4,272	47,933
Interest Income/(Loss) on I/C Loan, Before Tax				-	-	-	-	-
Return of Principal				-	-	-	-	-
Ending Balance on Loan at End of Year 5				-	-	-	-	-
Return on Buyer Funded Loan (Before Tax)		n/a	-	-	-	-	-	-
Return on Buyer Funded Loan (After Tax)		n/a	-	-	-	-	-	-
After Tax Returns on Buyer's Total Amount of Invested Capital		14.3%	(319,950)	30,575	32,945	35,766	38,445	431,396
Check				-	-	-	-	-
Return on Equity (During Projection Period)								
Free Cash Flow At Operating Entity Level	(e)			9.6%	10.3%	11.2%	12.0%	12.7%
Free Cash Flow to Equity at Operating Entity Level	(f)			9.6%	10.3%	11.2%	12.0%	12.7%

Notes to table:
(a) Includes the payment of any earn-outs that are included in the model during the 5 year projection period.
(b) This model assumes a buy and hold scenario and places a value on the equity of the business at the end of 5 years. If the plan were not to hold, but instead exit the business, a taxable gain would need to be factored in to the final proceeds from the sale of equity in order to estimate the after tax returns from the entire investment.
(c) Cash Flow to equity at the operating entity level does not include interest earned on any I/C loans at the holdco level.
(d) Applies a lack of control discount to the value of minority interest, if assumed in the intial transaction.
(e) Free cash flow after interest expense, but before paying down any debt. This represents the abilty to pay debt or make dividends to equity.
(f) Free cash flow to equity after paying down debt.

Appendix Fifteen: Example Quality of Earnings Schedule

Quality of Earnings	Yr.1	Yr.2	TTM
Net income	-	-	-
Addback interest expense	-	-	-
Addback income tax	-	-	-
Addback depreciation & amortization	-	-	-
EBITDA, as reported	-	-	-
Sell-side adjustments to EBITDA			
Sell-side adjustment #1	-	-	-
Sell-side adjustment #2	-	-	-
Sell-side adjustment #3	-	-	-
Sell-side adjustment #4	-	-	-
Sell-side adjusted EBITDA	-	-	-
Due diligence adjustments to EBITDA			
Due diligence adjustments #1	-	-	-
Due diligence adjustments #2	-	-	-
Due diligence adjustments #3	-	-	-
Due diligence adjustments #4	-	-	-
Normalized EBITDA	-	-	-

Appendix Sixteen: Example Tradename Valuation

Tradename Valuation	Year 1	Year 2	Year 3	Year 4	Year 5	Year 6	Year 7	Year 8	Year 9	Year 10
Sales Before Synergies	128,750	139,000	150,610	161,560	170,440	-	-	-	-	-
Sales From Synergies	2,000	5,000	7,500	7,500	7,500	-	-	-	-	-
Total Sales Tied to Tradename	130,750	144,000	158,110	169,060	177,940	-	-	-	-	-
Sales Growth Rate	n/a	10.1%	9.8%	6.9%	5.3%	n/a	n/a	n/a	n/a	n/a
Pre-Tax Releif From Royalty	2,615	2,880	3,162	3,381	3,559	-	-	-	-	-
After-Tax Royalty	1,909	2,102	2,308	2,468	2,598	-	-	-	-	-
Discount Factor	0.9366	0.8216	0.7207	0.6322	0.5545	0.4864	0.4267	0.3743	0.3283	0.2880
Present Value of Net Cash Flow	1,788	1,727	1,664	1,560	1,441	-	-	-	-	-

Total Present Value, Before Amortization Benefit	8,180
Tax Amortization Benefit	13.4%
Total Present Value, With Tax Benefit	9,275
Annual Amortization Expense	1,855

Assumptions	
Revenue Attributable to Tradename	100.0%
Include Sales From Synergies (Yes/No)	Yes
Assumed Royalty Rate	2.00%
Tax Rate	27.0%
Discount Rate	14%
Force a Value For Tradenames (Yes/No)	No
If Forced, Use This Amount as Value of Tradenames	20
Valuation Life	5
Amortization Life	5

293

Appendix Seventeen: Example Customer Relationship Valuation

Year	Roll-Over Customer Base	Cumulative Inflation Factor	Recurring Customer Revenue	EBITA Margin	Pre-tax Income	After Tax Income	Net Working Capital Charge	Fixed Asset Charge	Assembled Workforce Charge	Trade Name Charge	Non-Compete Charge	Developed Technology	After Tax Net Cash Flow	Months Between Close & Cash Flow	Assumed Mid-Point Discounting	Monthly Discount Rate	Discount Factor	Percent of Year Remaining	Discounted Cash Flow
0	100.0%	1.000	119,250																
1	95.0%	1.030	116,686	33.4%	38,938	28,424	350	117	350	1,704	584	2,044	23,276	12	6	0.0110	0.9366	100%	21,800
2	85.5%	1.061	108,168	33.4%	36,295	26,340	325	108	325	1,579	542	1,895	21,576	24	18	0.0110	0.8216	100%	17,726
3	77.0%	1.093	100,272	33.4%	33,460	24,426	301	100	301	1,464	502	1,757	20,001	36	30	0.0110	0.7207	100%	14,414
4	69.3%	1.126	92,952	33.4%	31,018	22,643	279	93	279	1,357	465	1,629	18,541	48	42	0.0110	0.6322	100%	11,721
5	62.3%	1.159	86,166	33.4%	28,753	20,990	258	86	258	1,258	431	1,510	17,188	60	54	0.0110	0.5545	100%	9,531
6	56.1%	1.194	79,876	33.4%	26,654	19,458	240	80	240	1,166	-	1,399	16,333	72	66	0.0110	0.4864	100%	7,945
7	50.5%	1.230	74,045	33.4%	24,709	18,037	222	74	222	1,081	-	1,297	15,141	84	78	0.0110	0.4267	100%	6,460
8	45.4%	1.267	68,640	33.4%	22,905	16,721	206	69	206	1,002	-	1,203	14,035	96	90	0.0110	0.3743	100%	5,253
9	40.9%	1.305	63,629	33.4%	21,235	15,500	191	64	191	929	-	1,115	13,011	108	102	0.0110	0.3283	100%	4,272
10	36.8%	1.344	58,984	33.4%	19,683	14,368	177	59	177	861	-	1,033	12,061	120	114	0.0110	0.2880	100%	3,474
11	33.1%	1.384	54,678	33.4%	18,246	13,320	164	55	164	798	-	958	11,181	132	126	0.0110	0.2526	100%	2,825
12	29.8%	1.426	50,687	33.4%	16,914	12,347	152	51	152	740	-	888	10,364	144	138	0.0110	0.2216	100%	2,297
13	26.8%	1.469	46,987	33.4%	15,679	11,446	141	47	141	686	-	823	9,608	156	150	0.0110	0.1944	100%	1,868
14	24.1%	1.513	43,557	33.4%	14,535	10,610	131	44	131	636	-	763	8,906	168	162	0.0110	0.1705	100%	1,519
15	21.7%	1.558	40,377	33.4%	13,474	9,836	121	40	121	590	-	707	8,256	180	174	0.0110	0.1496	100%	1,235
16	19.6%	1.605	37,430	33.4%	12,490	9,118	112	37	112	546	-	656	7,654	192	186	0.0110	0.1312	100%	1,004
17	17.6%	1.653	34,697	33.4%	11,578	8,452	104	35	104	507	-	608	7,095	204	198	0.0110	0.1151	100%	817
18	15.8%	1.702	32,164	33.4%	10,733	7,835	96	32	96	470	-	564	6,577	216	210	0.0110	0.1010	100%	664
19	14.3%	1.754	29,816	33.4%	9,950	7,263	89	30	89	435	-	522	6,097	228	222	0.0110	0.0886	100%	540
20	12.8%	1.806	27,640	33.4%	9,223	6,733	83	28	83	404	-	484	5,652	240	234	0.0110	0.0777	100%	439
21	11.5%	1.860	25,622	33.4%	8,550	6,241	77	26	77	374	-	448	5,239	252	246	0.0110	0.0681	100%	357
22	10.4%	1.916	23,752	33.4%	7,926	5,786	71	24	71	347	-	416	4,857	264	258	0.0110	0.0599	100%	290
23	9.4%	1.974	22,018	33.4%	7,347	5,363	66	22	66	321	-	386	4,502	276	270	0.0110	0.0524	100%	236
24	8.4%	2.033	20,410	33.4%	6,811	4,972	61	20	61	298	-	358	4,173	288	282	0.0110	0.0460	100%	192
25	7.6%	2.094	18,921	33.4%	6,314	4,609	57	19	57	276	-	331	3,869	300	294	0.0110	0.0403	100%	156

	Amount
Total Present Value, Before Amortization Benefit	$ 117,035
Tax Amortization Benefit	13.4%
Total Present Value, With Tax Benefit	$ 132,700

Annual Amortization Expense $ 13,270

Assumptions	Amount
Revenue Attributable to Customer Relationships	100.0%
Annual Customer Attrition Rate	10.0%
Annual Inflation Factor	3.0%
New Customer Marketing Spend as a % of Sales	2.0%
EBITA Margin for Purposes of Valuing Cust. Rel.	33.4%
Include Impact of Synergies in EBITA Margin (Yes/No)	Yes
Include Other (Income)/Expense in EBITA Margin (Yes/No)	No
Tax Rate	27.0%
Assembled Workforce Charge	0.3%
Net Working Capital Charge	0.3%
Fixed Asset Charge	0.1%
Trade Name Charge	1.5%
Non-Compete Charge	0.5%
Developed Technology Charge	1.8%
Discount Rate	14%
Valuation Life	25
Amortization Life	10

Pro Forma EBITA Margin Calculations	Year 1	Year 2	Year 3	Year 4	Year 5	Average
Sales Before Synergies	128,750	139,000	150,610	161,560	170,440	150,072
COGS Before Synergies & One-Time Costs	64,761	70,056	76,058	81,749	86,413	75,808
Operating Expenses Before Synergies and One-Time Costs	22,228	24,480	26,879	28,740	30,250	26,515
EBITDA Before Synergies and One-Time Costs	41,761	44,464	47,673	51,070	53,777	47,749
Sales From Synergies	2,000	5,000	7,500	7,500	7,500	5,900
COGS Impact From Synergies	1,020	2,550	3,825	3,825	3,825	3,009
OPEX Impact From Synergies	950	1,000	1,100	1,100	1,100	1,050
EBITDA From Synergies	30	1,450	2,625	2,575	2,525	1,841
EBITDA From Above, Excluding One-Time Items	41,791	45,914	50,298	53,645	56,302	49,590
Exclude New Cust. Mktg. Spend for Valuing Pre-Existing Customer Relationship	2,615	2,880	3,162	3,381	3,559	3,119
Include Other Income/(Expense), if Applicable						
Include Depreciation (Expense)	(377)	(320)	(663)	(803)	(948)	(663)
EBITA, Excluding One-Time Items	44,029	48,274	52,798	56,221	58,913	52,047
EBITA Margin for Purposes of Valuing Customer Relationships	33.7%	33.5%	33.4%	33.3%	33.1%	33.4%
EBITA Margin for Purposes of Valuing Non-Competes	31.7%	31.5%	31.4%	31.3%	31.1%	31.4%

Appendix Eighteen: Example Developed Technology Valuation

Developed Technology (External Use Software)	Year 1	Year 2	Year 3	Year 4	Year 5	Year 6	Year 7	Year 8	Year 9	Year 10
Sales Before Synergies	38,625	41,700	45,183	48,468	51,132	-	-	-	-	-
Sales Growth Rate	n/a	8.0%	8.4%	7.3%	5.5%	n/a	n/a	n/a	n/a	n/a
Obscolescence Factor	100.0%	100.0%	75.0%	50.0%	25.0%	0.0%	0.0%	0.0%	0.0%	0.0%
Pre-Tax Releif From Royalty	3,090	3,336	2,711	1,939	1,023	-	-	-	-	-
After-Tax Royalty	2,256	2,435	1,979	1,415	747	-	-	-	-	-
Discount Factor	0.9366	0.8216	0.7207	0.6322	0.5545	0.4864	0.4267	0.3743	0.3283	0.2880
Present Value of Net Cash Flow	2,113	2,001	1,426	895	414	-	-	-	-	-

Total Present Value, Before Amortization Benefit	6,848
Tax Amortization Benefit	13.4%
Total Present Value, With Tax Benefit	7,765
Annual Amortization Expense	1,553

Assumptions	
Royalty Rate	8.00%
Discount Rate	14%
Tax Rate	27%
Valuation Life	5
Amortization Life	5

Appendix Nineteen: Example Non-Compete Valuation

Non-Compete Valuation	Year 1	Year 2	Year 3	Year 4	Year 5	Year 6	Year 7	Year 8	Year 9	Year 10
Sales Before Synergies	128,750	139,000	150,610	161,560	170,440	-	-	-	-	-
Sales From Synergies	2,000	5,000	7,500	7,500	7,500	-	-	-	-	-
Sales From Exclusive Products/Agreements	-	-	-	-	-	-	-	-	-	-
Potential Sales Open to Competition	130,750	144,000	158,110	169,060	177,940	-	-	-	-	-
Probability to Compete	15.0%	15.0%	15.0%	15.0%	15.0%	0.0%	0.0%	0.0%	0.0%	0.0%
Ability to Compete	15.0%	15.0%	15.0%	15.0%	15.0%	0.0%	0.0%	0.0%	0.0%	0.0%
Potential Sales Loss to Competition	2,942	3,240	3,557	3,804	4,004	-	-	-	-	-
EBITA Margin for Purposes of Valuing Non-Competes	31.4%	31.4%	31.4%	31.4%	31.4%	0.0%	0.0%	0.0%	0.0%	0.0%
Potential Annual EBIT Loss to Competition	923	1,016	1,116	1,193	1,256	-	-	-	-	-
After Tax Income Loss to Competition	674	742	815	871	917	-	-	-	-	-
Discount Factor	0.9366	0.8216	0.7207	0.6322	0.5545	0.4864	0.4267	0.3743	0.3283	0.2880
Present Value of Net Cash Flow	631	610	587	551	508	-	-	-	-	-

Total Present Value, Before Amortization Benefit	2,887
Tax Amortization Benefit Factor	13.4%
Total Present Value, With Tax Benefit	3,273
Annual Amortization Expense	655

Assumptions	Year 1	Year 2	Year 3	Year 4	Year 5	Year 6	Year 7	Year 8	Year 9	Year 10
Exclusive Prods./Agrmts.	0.0%	0.0%	0.0%	0.0%	0.0%	0.0%	0.0%	0.0%	0.0%	0.0%
Probability to Compete	15.0%	15.0%	15.0%	15.0%	15.0%	0.0%	0.0%	0.0%	0.0%	0.0%
Ability to Compete	15.0%	15.0%	15.0%	15.0%	15.0%	0.0%	0.0%	0.0%	0.0%	0.0%
Include Sales From Synergies (Yes/No)	Yes									
Tax Rate	27.0%									
Discount Rate	14%									
Force a Value For Non-Competes (Yes/No)	No									
If Forced, Use This Amount as Value of Non-Competes	500									
Valuation Life	5									
Amortization Life	5									

Definition of Terms

Capital:	Source of funding or financial wherewithal
CEO:	Chief executive officer
CFO:	Chief financial officer
DCF:	Discounted cash flow
EBITDA:	Earnings before interest, tax, depreciation, and amortization
EPS:	Earnings per share
FTC:	Federal trade commission
GAAP:	Generally accepted accounting principles
HR:	Human resources
HSR:	Hart Scott Rodino Act
IPO:	Initial public offering
IRR:	Internal rate of return
IT:	Information technology
LLC:	Limited liability company
LOI:	Letter of intent
M&A:	Mergers & acquisitions
MAC:	Material adverse change
MAE:	Material adverse effect
NDA:	Non-disclosure agreement
NOL:	Net operating loss
ROI:	Return on investment
Target:	The target business that's about to be acquired
TSA:	Transition services agreement
TTM:	Trailing twelve months
VDD:	Vendor due diligence
WACC:	Weighted average cost of capital

Index

Made in the USA
Middletown, DE
05 May 2021